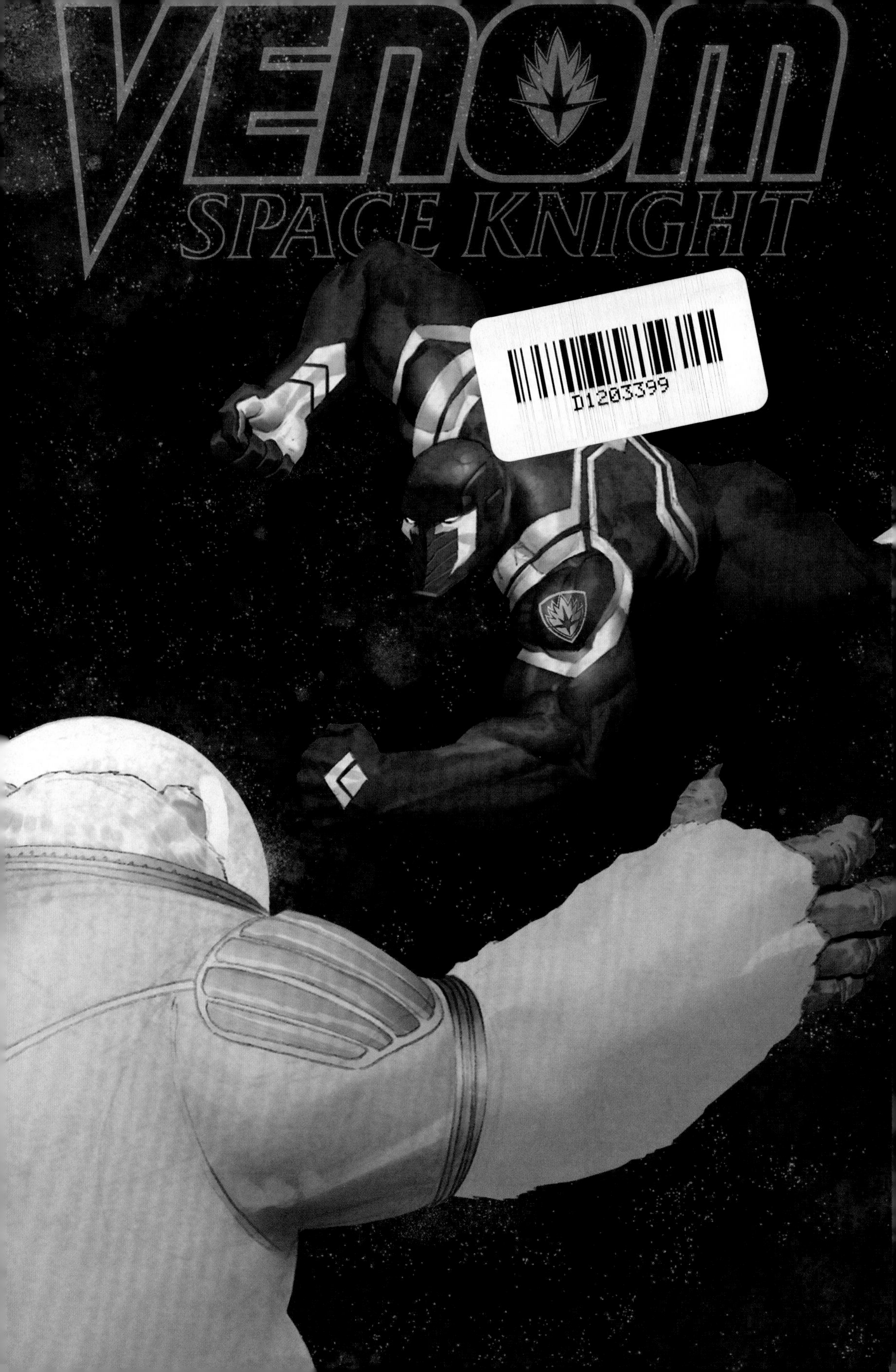
VENOM
SPACE KNIGHT

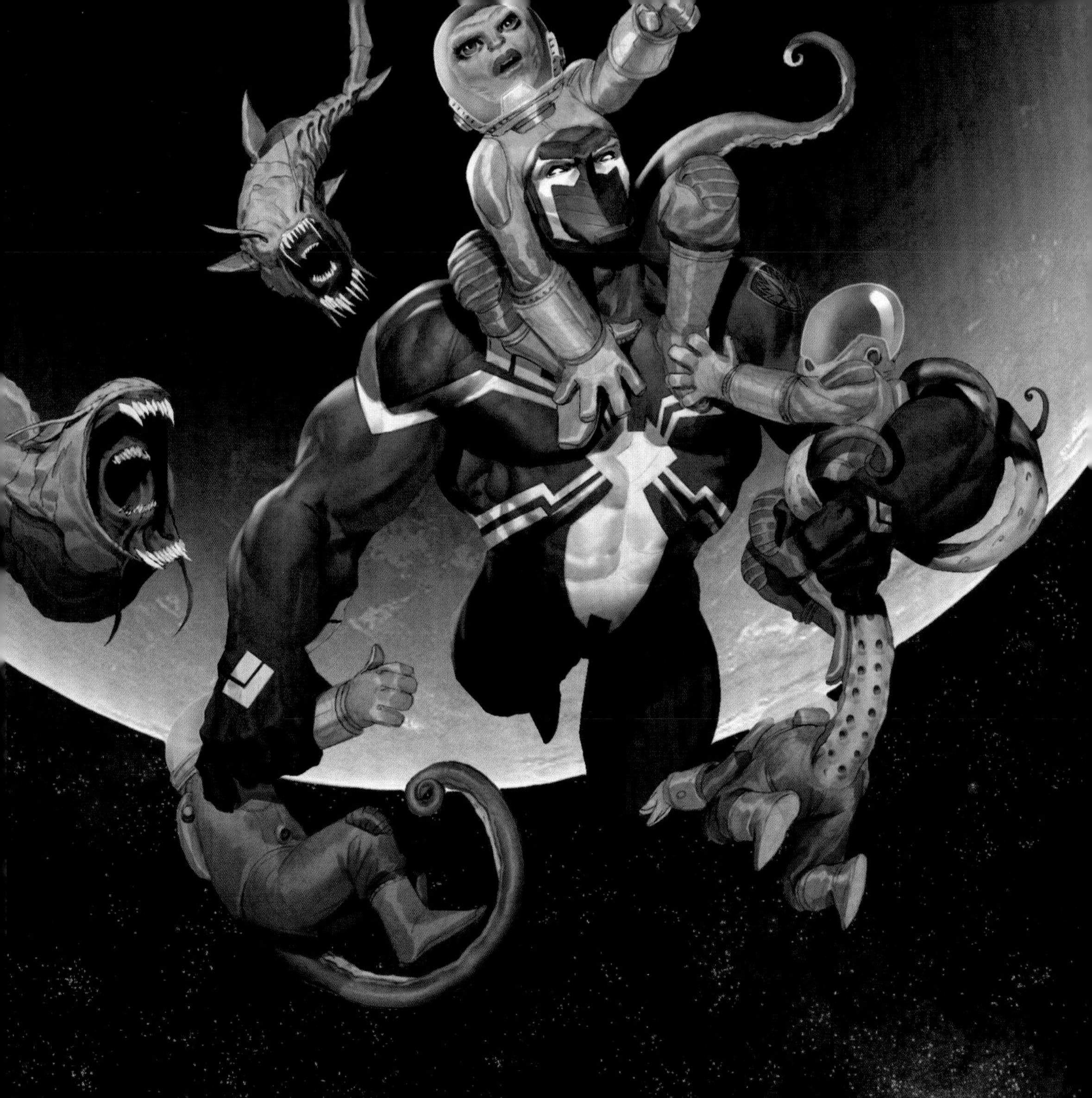

COLLECTION EDITOR **JENNIFER GRÜNWALD**
ASSOCIATE EDITOR **SARAH BRUNSTAD**
ASSOCIATE MANAGING EDITOR **ALEX STARBUCK**
EDITOR, SPECIAL PROJECTS **MARK D. BEAZLEY**
VP, PRODUCTION & SPECIAL PROJECTS **JEFF YOUNGQUIST**
SVP PRINT, SALES & MARKETING **DAVID GABRIEL**
BOOK DESIGNER **ADAM DEL RE**

EDITOR IN CHIEF **AXEL ALONSO**
CHIEF CREATIVE OFFICER **JOE QUESADA**
PUBLISHER **DAN BUCKLEY**
EXECUTIVE PRODUCER **ALAN FINE**

VENOM: SPACE KNIGHT VOL. 1 — AGENT OF THE COSMOS. Contains material originally published in magazine form as VENOM: SPACE KNIGHT #1-6. First printing 2016. ISBN# 978-0-7851-9654-9. Published by MARVEL WORLDWIDE, INC., a subsidiary of MARVEL ENTERTAINMENT, LLC. OFFICE OF PUBLICATION: 135 West 50th Street, New York, NY 10020. **Printed in Canada.** ALAN FINE, President, Marvel Entertainment; DAN BUCKLEY, President, TV, Publishing & Brand Management; JOE QUESADA, Chief Creative Officer; TOM BREVOORT, SVP of Publishing; DAVID BOGART, SVP of Business Affairs & Operations, Publishing & Partnership; C.B. CEBULSKI, VP of Brand Management & Development, Asia; DAVID GABRIEL, SVP of Sales & Marketing, Publishing; JEFF YOUNGQUIST, VP of Production & Special Projects; DAN CARR, Executive Director of Publishing Technology; ALEX MORALES, Director of Publishing Operations; SUSAN CRESPI, Production Manager; STAN LEE, Chairman Emeritus. For information regarding advertising in Marvel Comics or on Marvel.com, please contact Vit DeBellis, Integrated Sales Manager, at vdebellis@marvel.com. For Marvel subscription inquiries, please call 888-511-5480. **Manufactured between 5/6/2016 and 6/13/2016 by SOLISCO PRINTERS, SCOTT, QC, CANADA.**

10 9 8 7 6 5 4 3 2 1

Once Eugene "Flash" Thompson got his chance to be a hero, he refused to give it up. When he lost both of his legs serving his country, Flash formed a symbiotic bond with an alien parasite. It functioned as a body-morphing suit that enabled him to continue serving others. Then, when helping on one planet wasn't enough, he enlisted in the Guardians of the Galaxy. After his symbiote, a member of the Klyntar species, was purified on its home planet, Flash expanded his range once again. He's answered the Klyntar call to serve as an Agent of the Cosmos.

Now, Flash is swashbuckling his way across the universe as...

VENOM

SPACE KNIGHT

AGENT OF THE COSMOS

ROBBIE THOMPSON
WRITER

ARIEL OLIVETTI
ARTIST

KATHLEEN WISNESKI
ASSISTANT EDITOR

VC's JOE CARAMAGNA
LETTERER

JAKE THOMAS
EDITOR

ARIEL OLIVETTI
COVER ART

DAN NEVINS
CONSULTANT

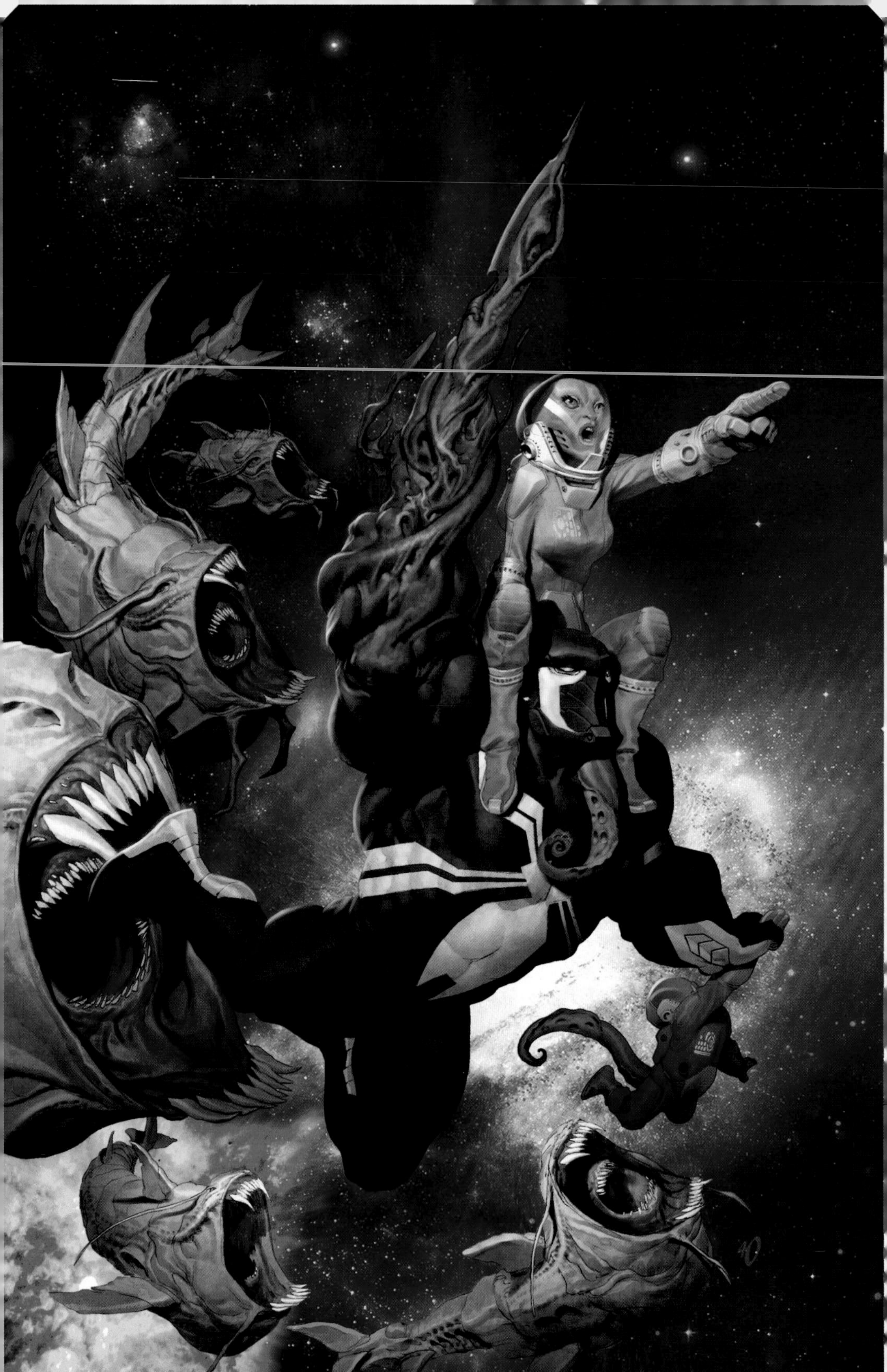

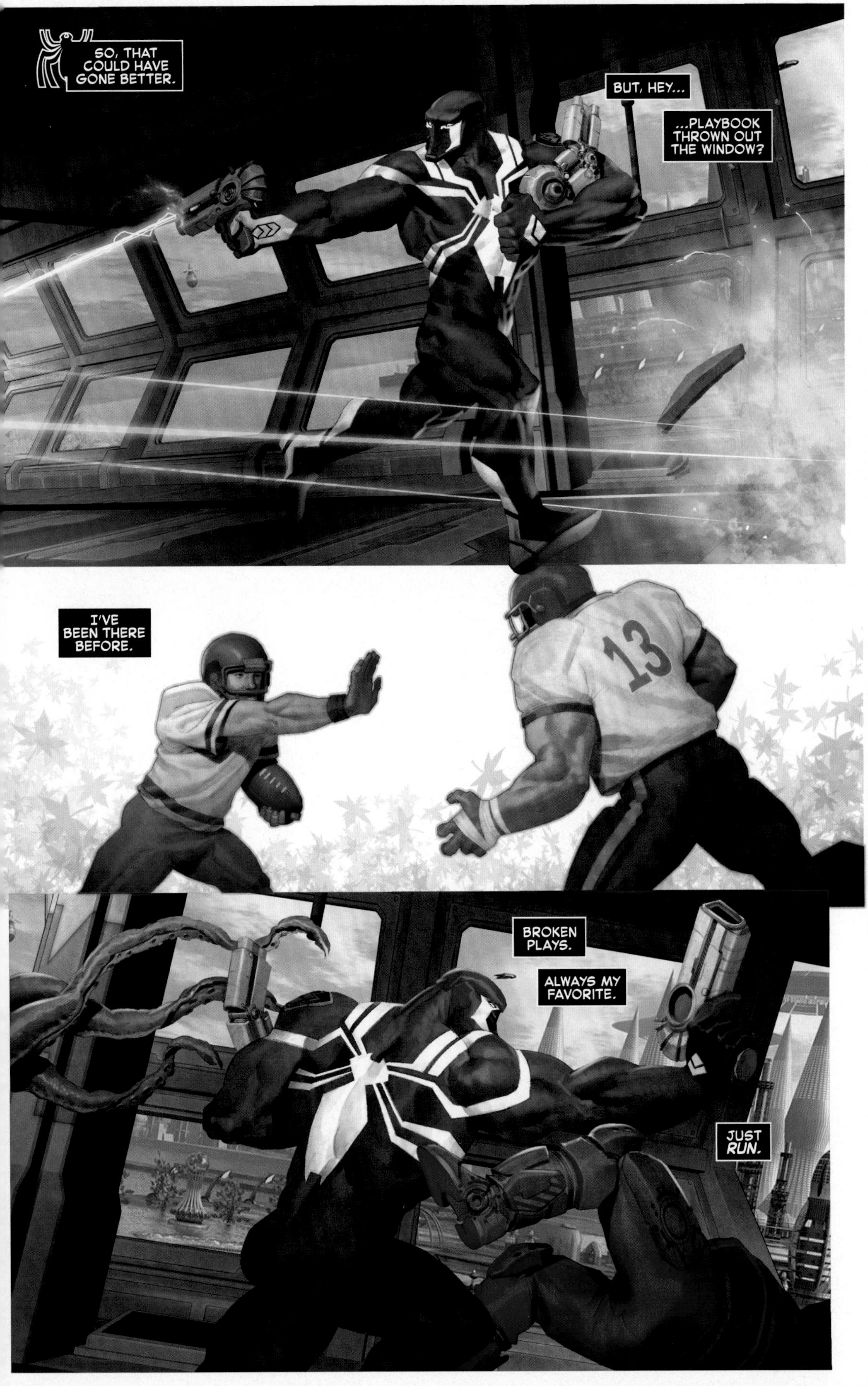
SO, THAT COULD HAVE GONE BETTER.
BUT, HEY...
...PLAYBOOK THROWN OUT THE WINDOW?
I'VE BEEN THERE BEFORE.
13
BROKEN PLAYS.
ALWAYS MY FAVORITE.
JUST *RUN.*

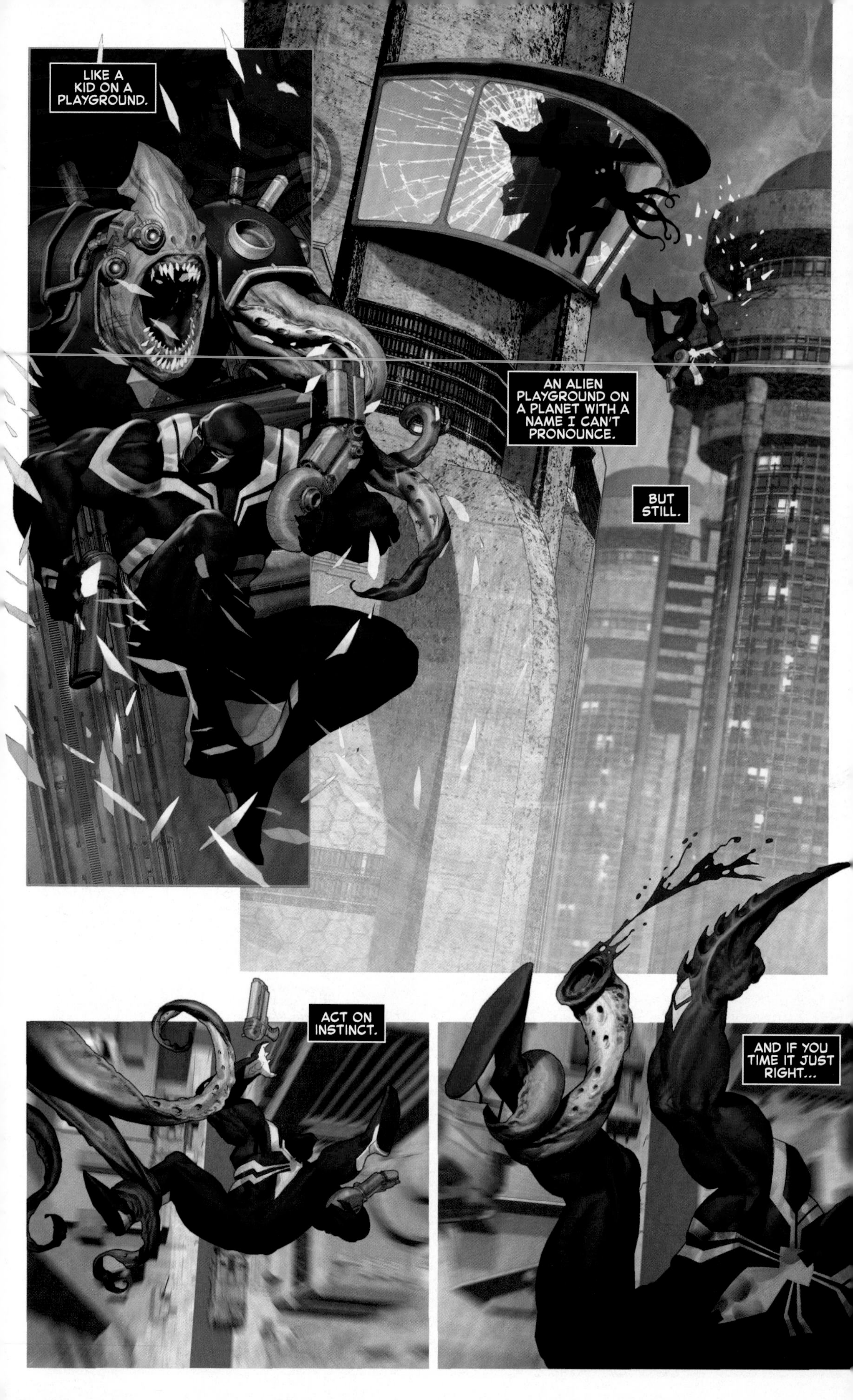
LIKE A KID ON A PLAYGROUND.
AN ALIEN PLAYGROUND ON A PLANET WITH A NAME I CAN'T PRONOUNCE.
BUT STILL.
ACT ON INSTINCT.
AND IF YOU TIME IT JUST RIGHT...

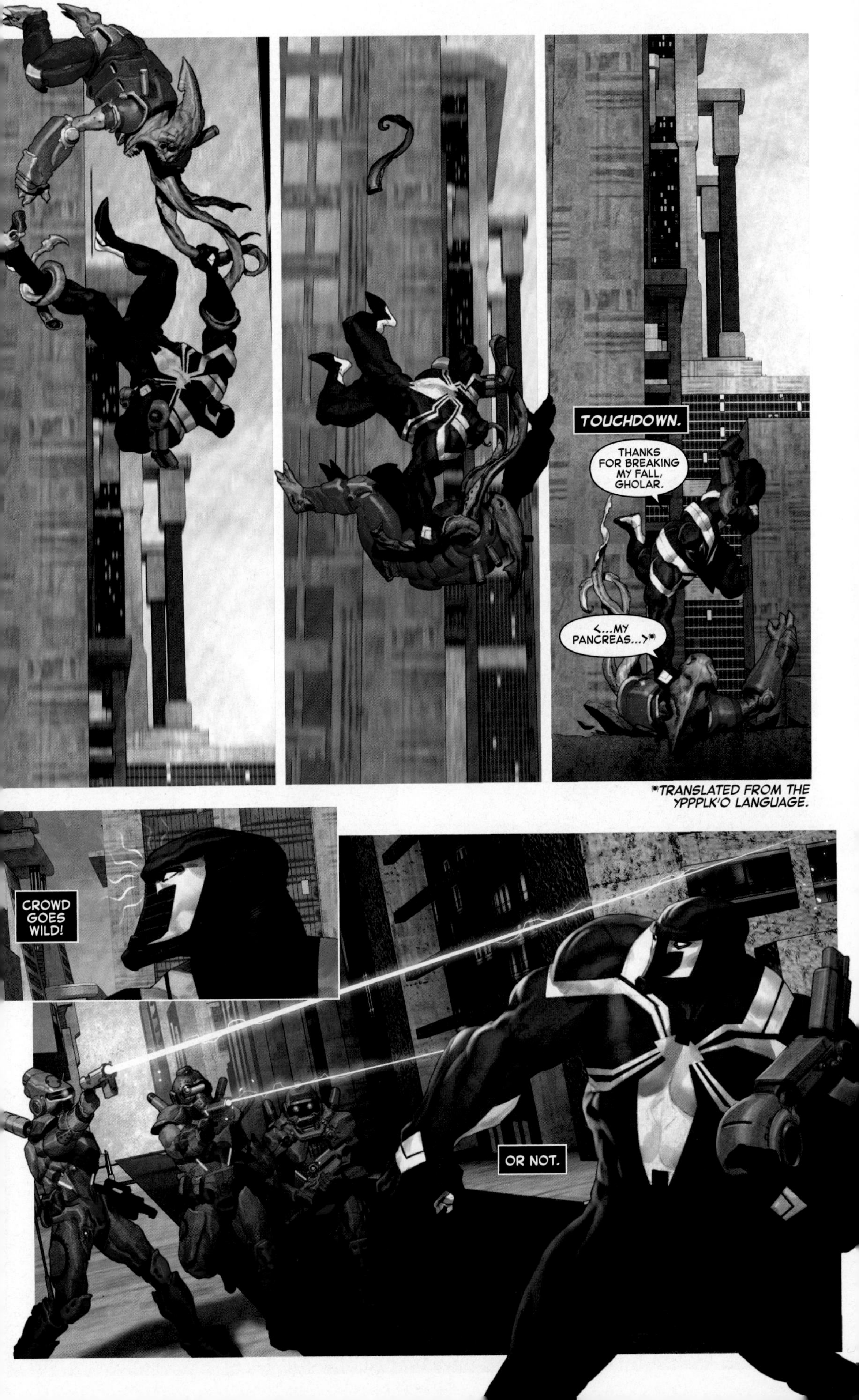

TOUCHDOWN.
THANKS FOR BREAKING MY FALL, GHOLAR.
<...MY PANCREAS...>*
*TRANSLATED FROM THE YPPPLK'O LANGUAGE.
CROWD GOES WILD!
OR NOT.

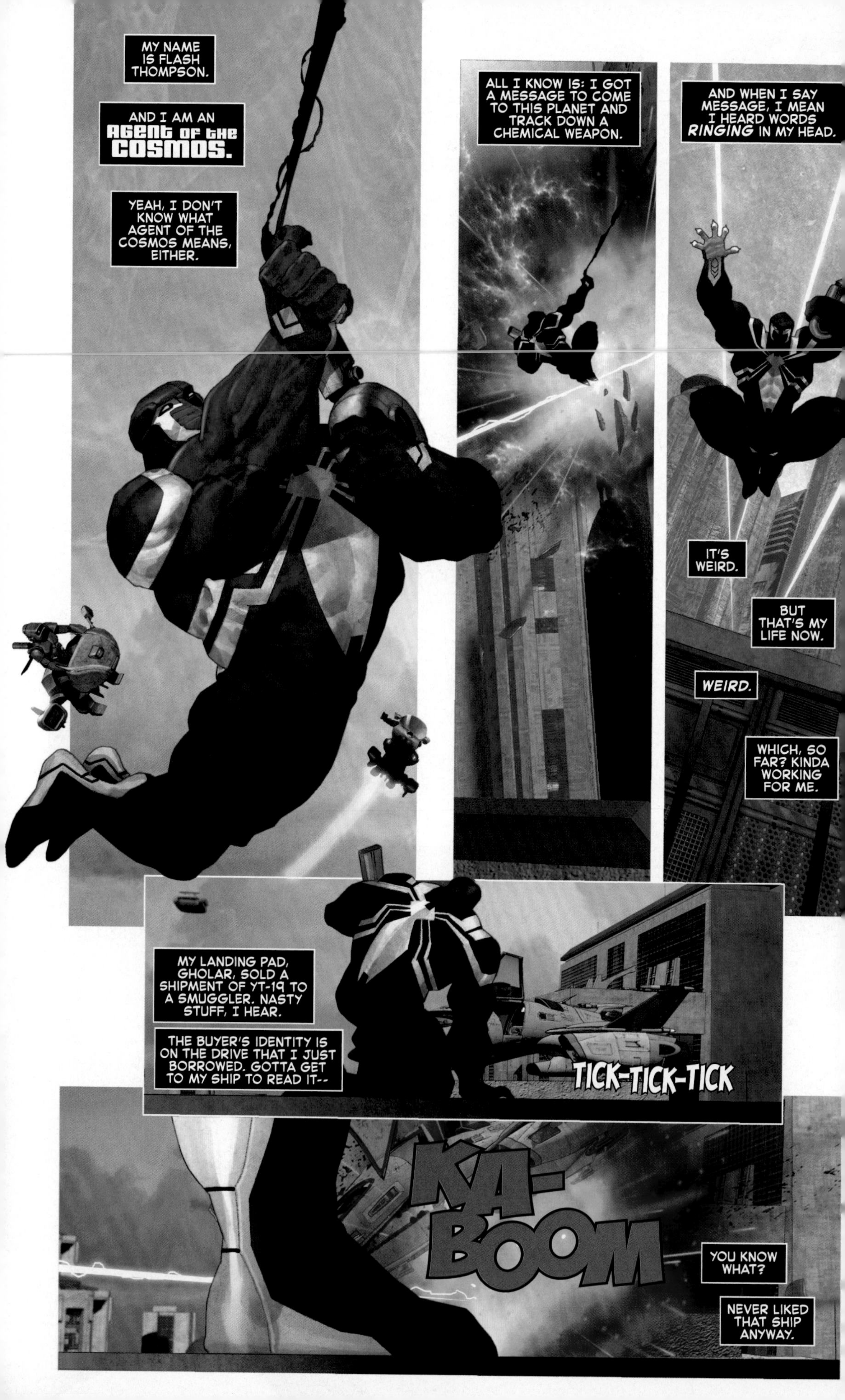
MY NAME IS FLASH THOMPSON.
AND I AM AN AGENT OF THE COSMOS.
YEAH, I DON'T KNOW WHAT AGENT OF THE COSMOS MEANS, EITHER.
ALL I KNOW IS: I GOT A MESSAGE TO COME TO THIS PLANET AND TRACK DOWN A CHEMICAL WEAPON.
AND WHEN I SAY MESSAGE, I MEAN I HEARD WORDS RINGING IN MY HEAD.
IT'S WEIRD.
BUT THAT'S MY LIFE NOW.
WEIRD.
WHICH, SO FAR? KINDA WORKING FOR ME.
MY LANDING PAD, GHOLAR, SOLD A SHIPMENT OF YT-19 TO A SMUGGLER. NASTY STUFF, I HEAR.
THE BUYER'S IDENTITY IS ON THE DRIVE THAT I JUST BORROWED. GOTTA GET TO MY SHIP TO READ IT--
TICK-TICK-TICK
KA-BOOM
YOU KNOW WHAT?
NEVER LIKED THAT SHIP ANYWAY.

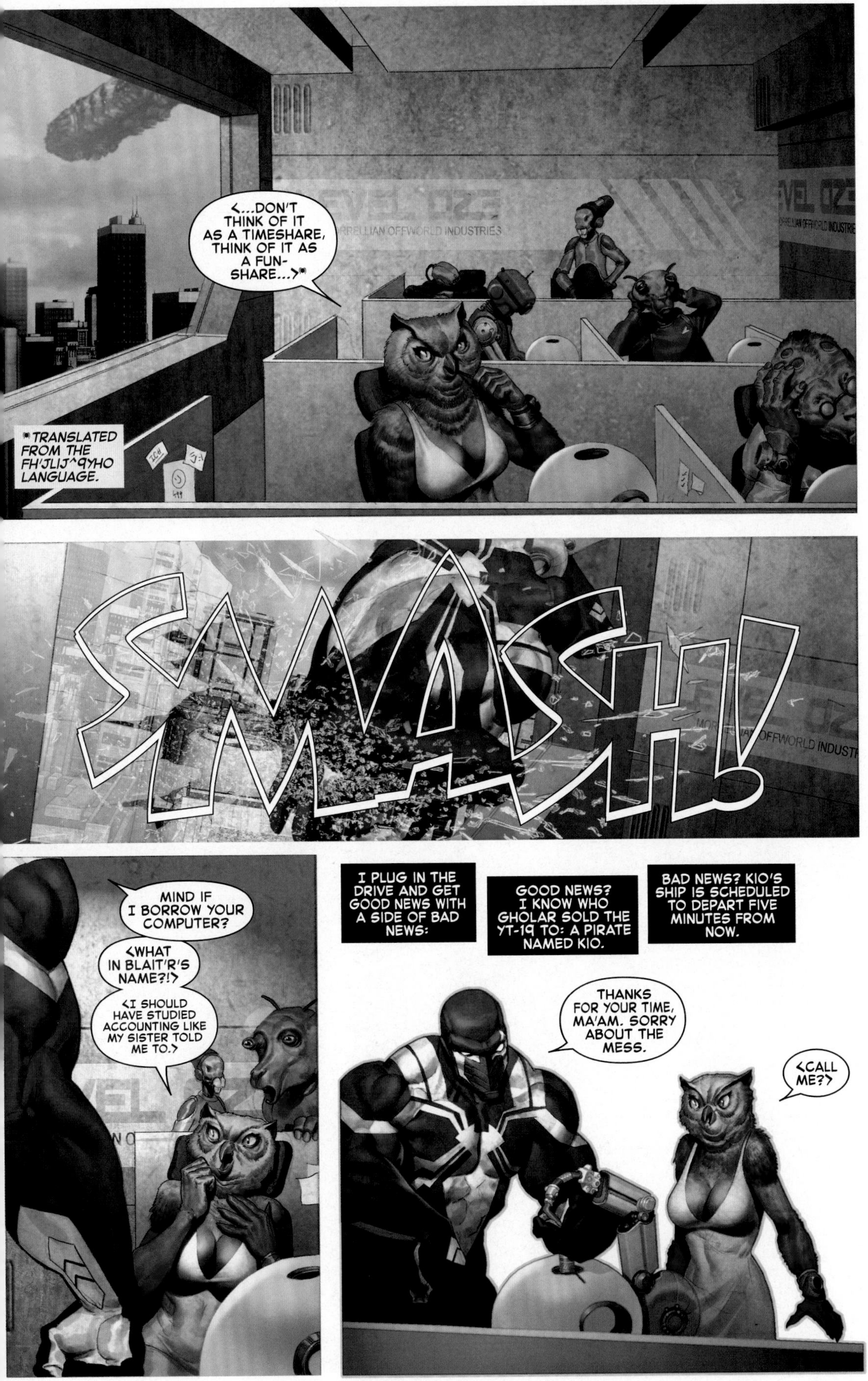
LEVEL 025
MORRELLIAN OFFWORLD INDUSTRIES
<...DON'T THINK OF IT AS A TIMESHARE, THINK OF IT AS A FUN-SHARE...>*
*TRANSLATED FROM THE FH'JLIJ^9YHO LANGUAGE.
SMASH!
MIND IF I BORROW YOUR COMPUTER?
<WHAT IN BLAIT'R'S NAME?!>
<I SHOULD HAVE STUDIED ACCOUNTING LIKE MY SISTER TOLD ME TO.>
I PLUG IN THE DRIVE AND GET GOOD NEWS WITH A SIDE OF BAD NEWS:
GOOD NEWS? I KNOW WHO GHOLAR SOLD THE YT-19 TO: A PIRATE NAMED KIO.
BAD NEWS? KIO'S SHIP IS SCHEDULED TO DEPART FIVE MINUTES FROM NOW.
THANKS FOR YOUR TIME, MA'AM. SORRY ABOUT THE MESS.
<CALL ME?>

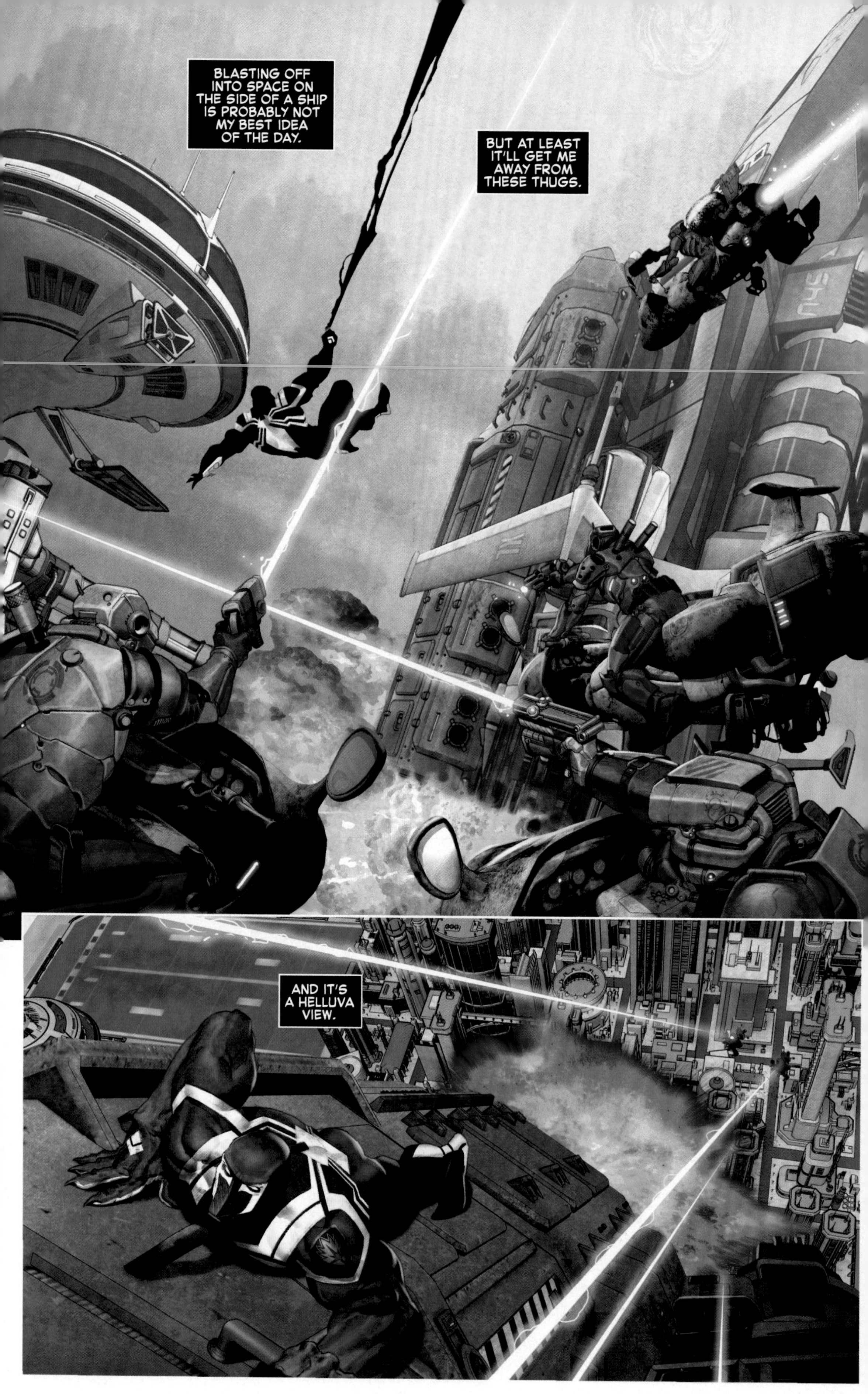
BLASTING OFF INTO SPACE ON THE SIDE OF A SHIP IS PROBABLY NOT MY BEST IDEA OF THE DAY.
BUT AT LEAST IT'LL GET ME AWAY FROM THESE THUGS.
AND IT'S A HELLUVA VIEW.

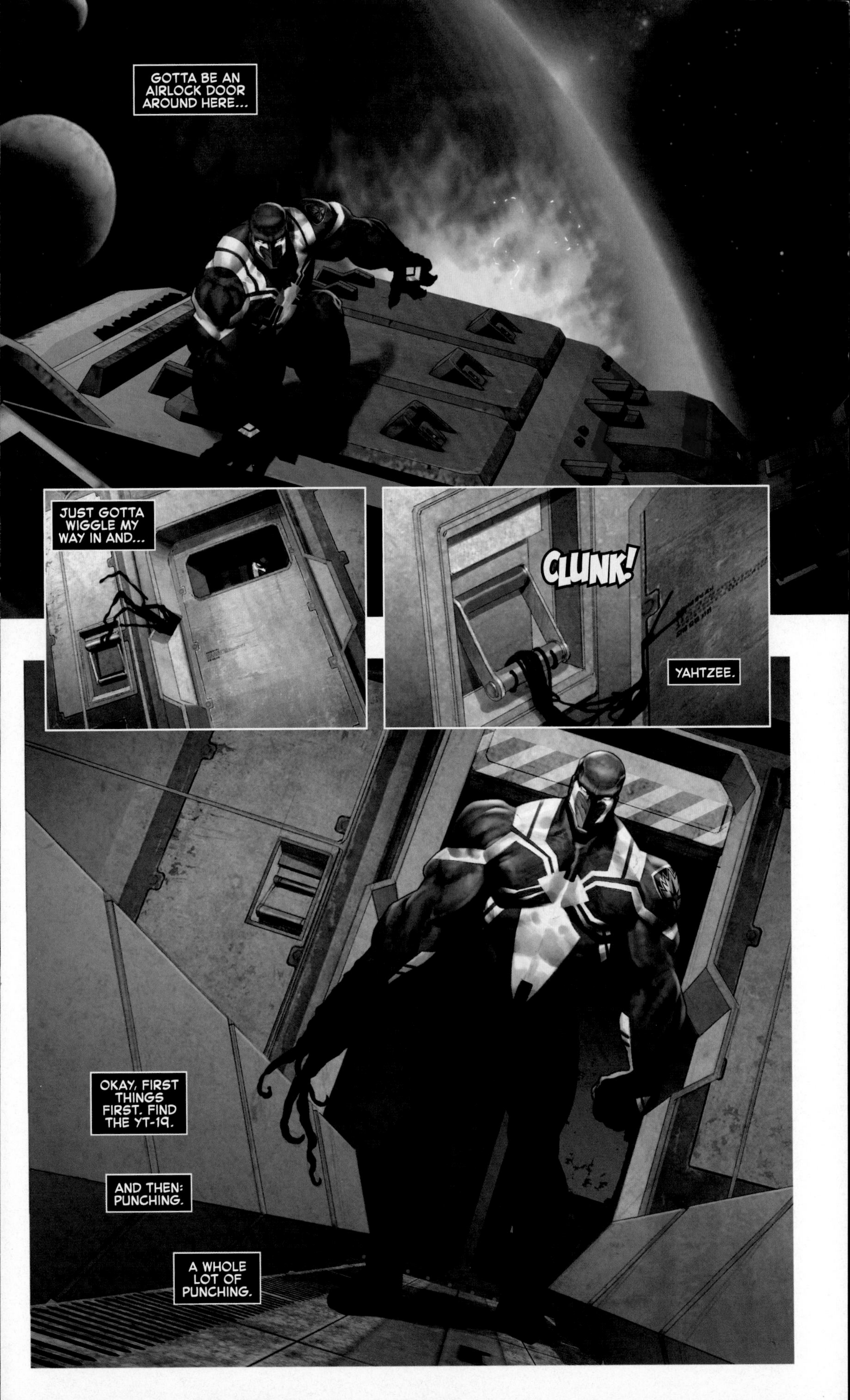
GOTTA BE AN AIRLOCK DOOR AROUND HERE...
JUST GOTTA WIGGLE MY WAY IN AND...
CLUNK!
YAHTZEE.
OKAY, FIRST THINGS FIRST. FIND THE YT-19.
AND THEN: PUNCHING.
A WHOLE LOT OF PUNCHING.

THEN, STEAL THIS SHIP SINCE THEY BLEW UP MY--

WAIT.

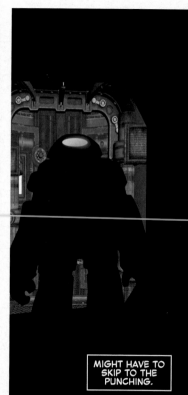

MIGHT HAVE TO SKIP TO THE PUNCHING.

TURN AROUND.

NICE, SLOW AND *QUIET*, MR. ROBOTO.

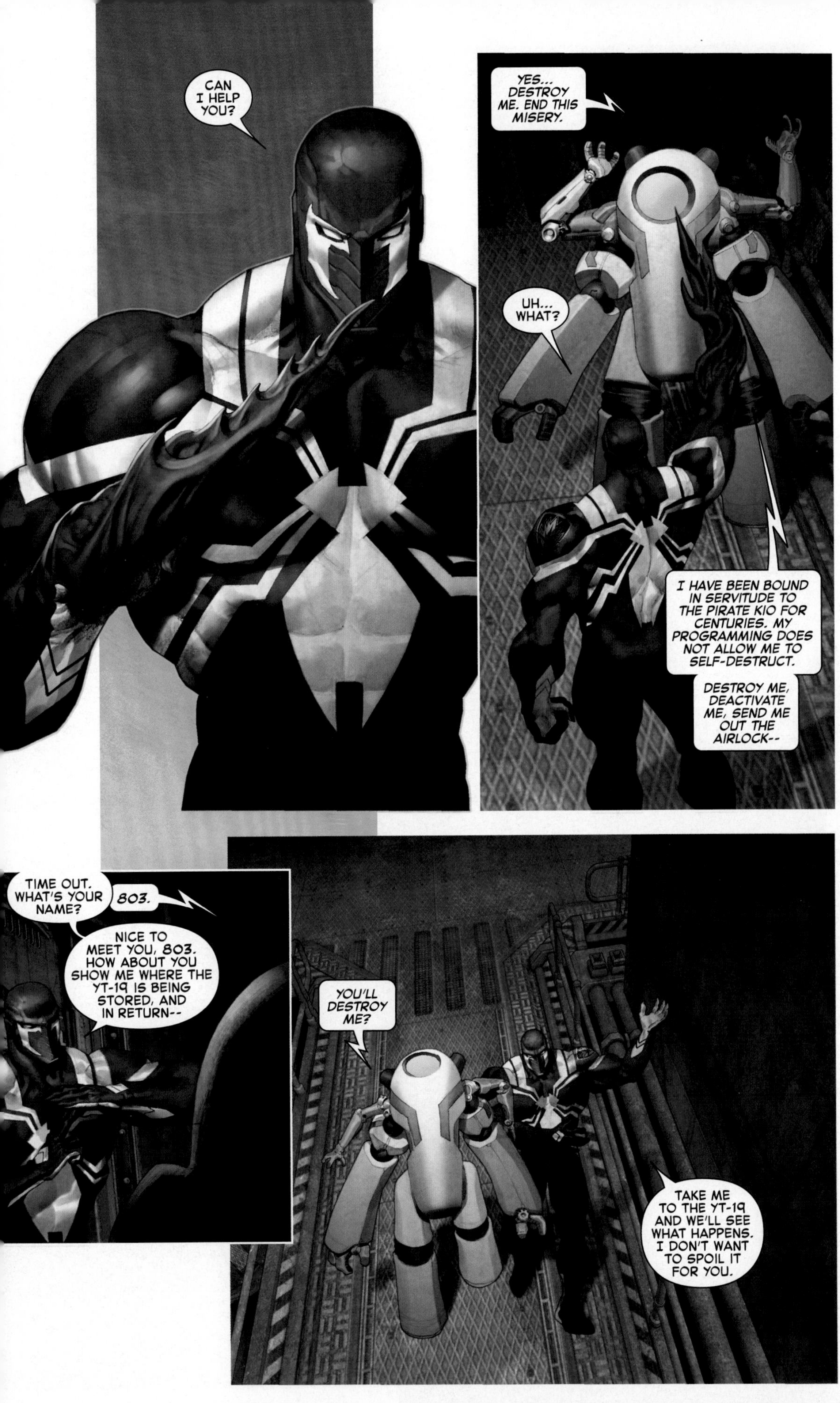
CAN I HELP YOU?
YES... DESTROY ME. END THIS MISERY.
UH... WHAT?
I HAVE BEEN BOUND IN SERVITUDE TO THE PIRATE KIO FOR CENTURIES. MY PROGRAMMING DOES NOT ALLOW ME TO SELF-DESTRUCT.
DESTROY ME, DEACTIVATE ME, SEND ME OUT THE AIRLOCK--
TIME OUT. WHAT'S YOUR NAME?
803.
NICE TO MEET YOU, 803. HOW ABOUT YOU SHOW ME WHERE THE YT-19 IS BEING STORED, AND IN RETURN--
YOU'LL DESTROY ME?
TAKE ME TO THE YT-19 AND WE'LL SEE WHAT HAPPENS. I DON'T WANT TO SPOIL IT FOR YOU.

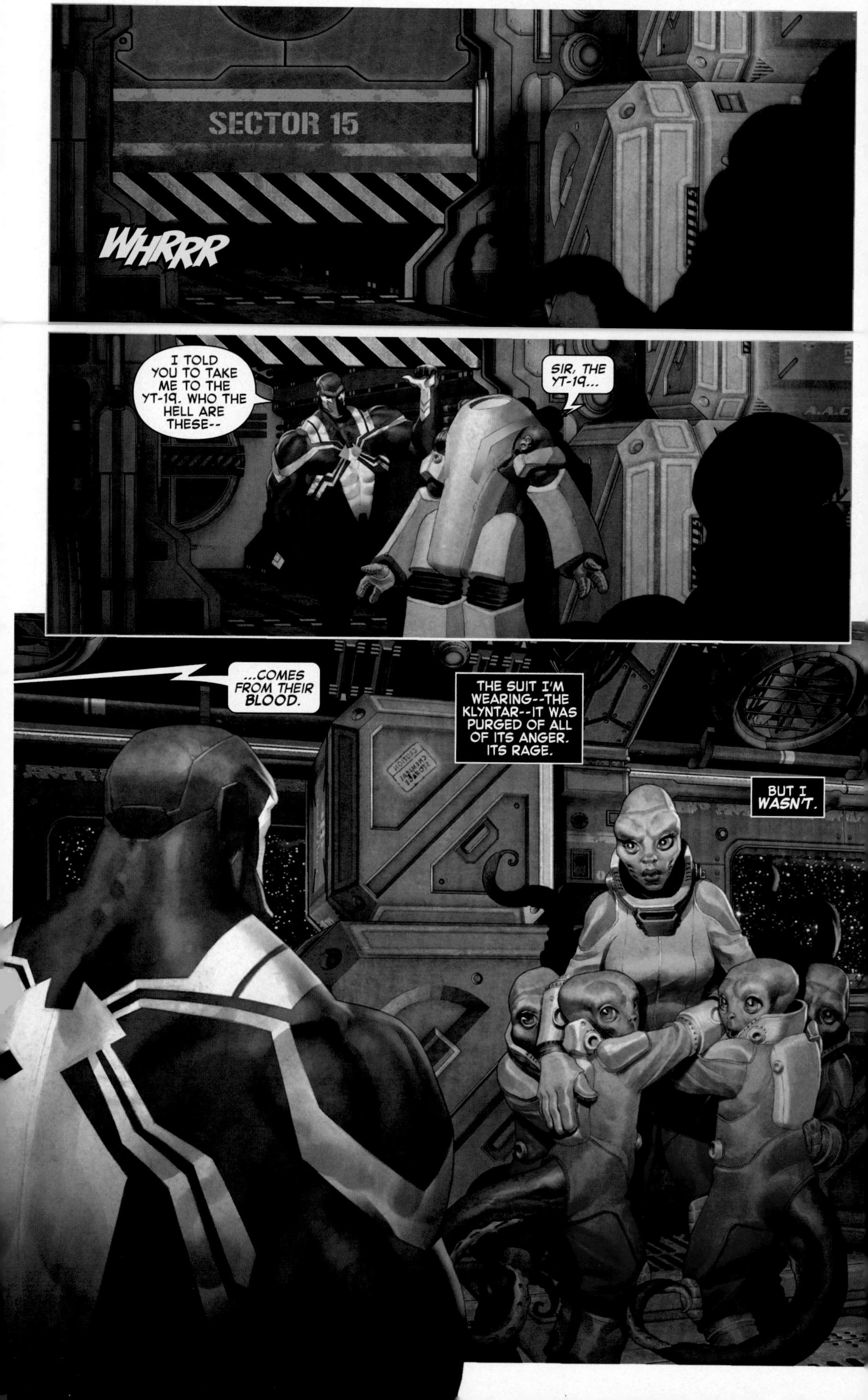
SECTOR 15
WHRRR
I TOLD YOU TO TAKE ME TO THE YT-19. WHO THE HELL ARE THESE--
SIR, THE YT-19...
...COMES FROM THEIR BLOOD.
THE SUIT I'M WEARING--THE KLYNTAR--IT WAS PURGED OF ALL OF ITS ANGER. ITS RAGE.
BUT I WASN'T.

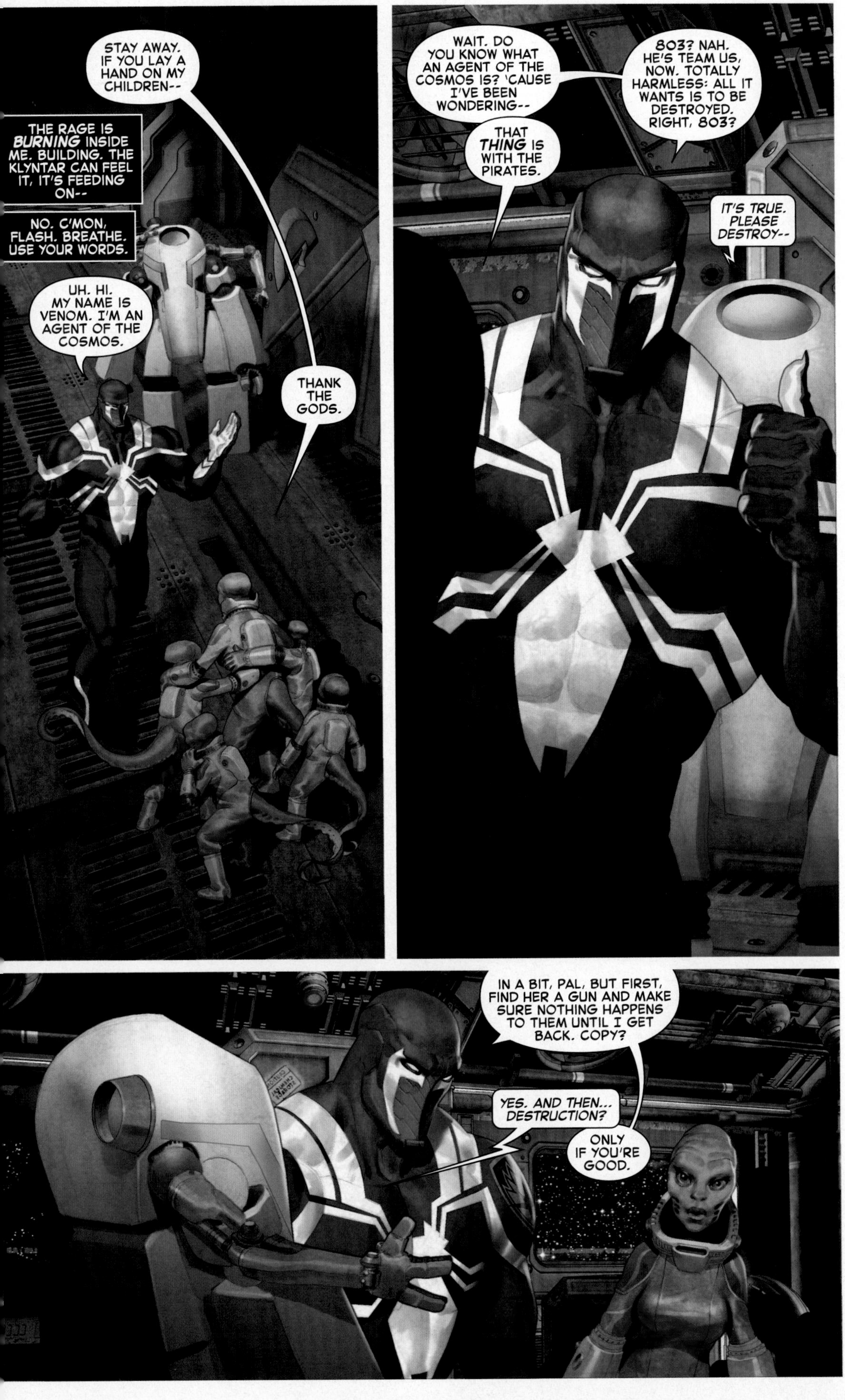
STAY AWAY. IF YOU LAY A HAND ON MY CHILDREN--
THE RAGE IS *BURNING* INSIDE ME. BUILDING. THE KLYNTAR CAN FEEL IT, IT'S FEEDING ON--
NO. C'MON, FLASH. BREATHE. USE YOUR WORDS.
UH. HI. MY NAME IS VENOM. I'M AN AGENT OF THE COSMOS.
THANK THE GODS.
WAIT. DO YOU KNOW WHAT AN AGENT OF THE COSMOS IS? 'CAUSE I'VE BEEN WONDERING--
THAT *THING* IS WITH THE PIRATES.
803? NAH. HE'S TEAM US, NOW. TOTALLY HARMLESS: ALL IT WANTS IS TO BE DESTROYED. RIGHT, 803?
IT'S TRUE. PLEASE DESTROY--
IN A BIT, PAL, BUT FIRST, FIND HER A GUN AND MAKE SURE NOTHING HAPPENS TO THEM UNTIL I GET BACK. COPY?
YES. AND THEN... DESTRUCTION?
ONLY IF YOU'RE GOOD.

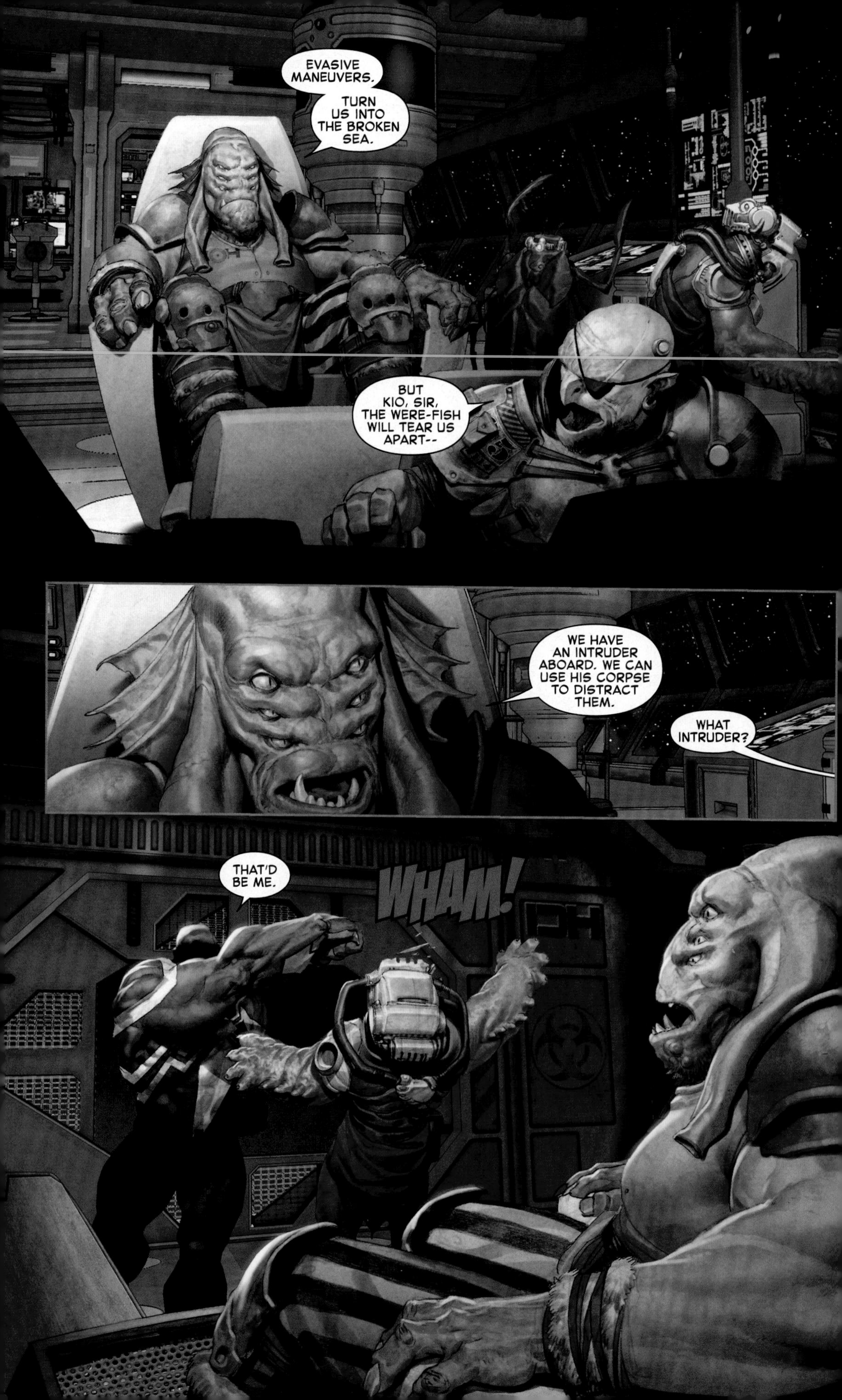
EVASIVE MANEUVERS.
TURN US INTO THE BROKEN SEA.
BUT KIO, SIR, THE WERE-FISH WILL TEAR US APART--
WE HAVE AN INTRUDER ABOARD. WE CAN USE HIS CORPSE TO DISTRACT THEM.
WHAT INTRUDER?
THAT'D BE ME.
WHAM!

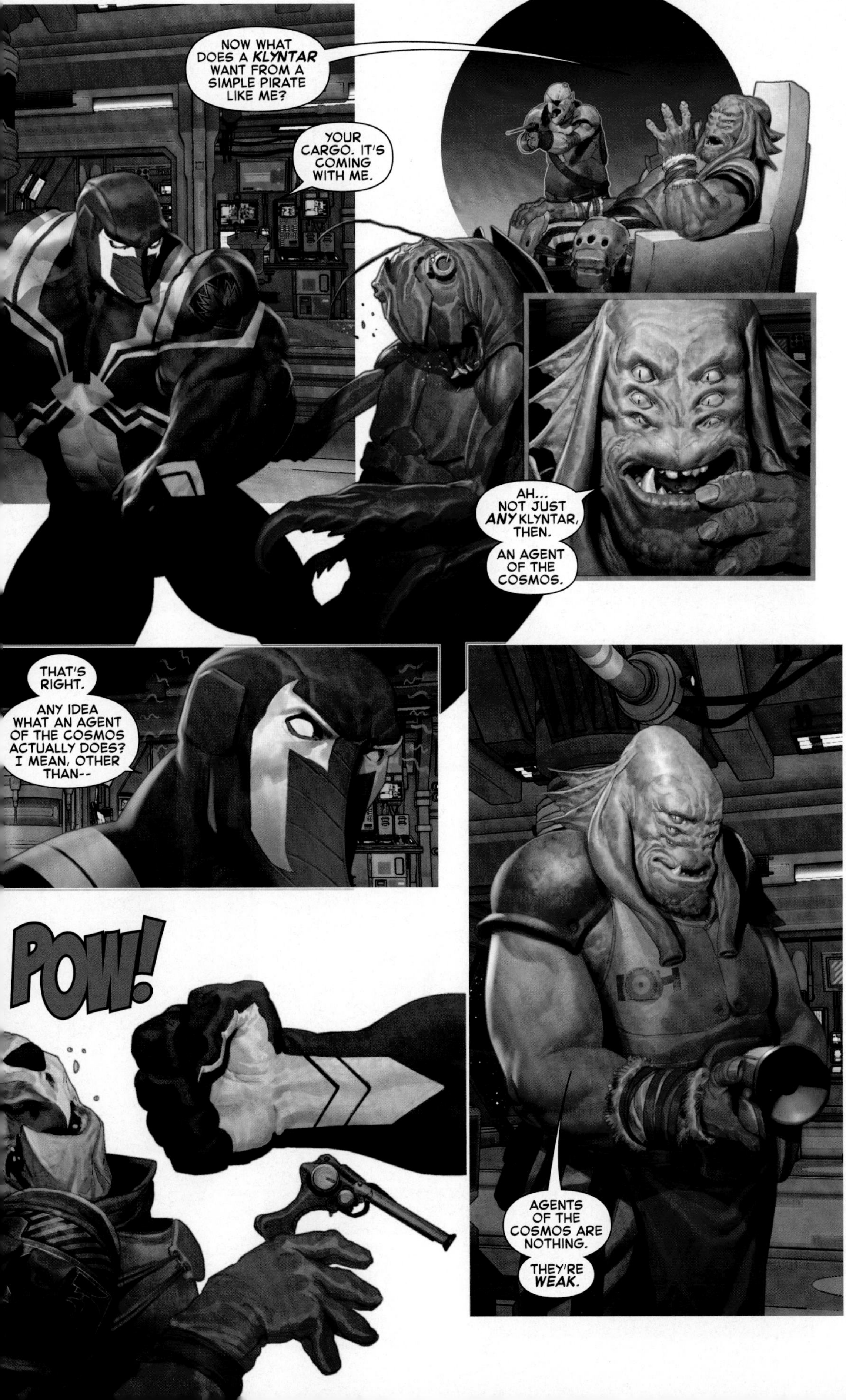
NOW WHAT DOES A KLYNTAR WANT FROM A SIMPLE PIRATE LIKE ME?
YOUR CARGO. IT'S COMING WITH ME.
AH... NOT JUST ANY KLYNTAR, THEN.
AN AGENT OF THE COSMOS.
THAT'S RIGHT.
ANY IDEA WHAT AN AGENT OF THE COSMOS ACTUALLY DOES? I MEAN, OTHER THAN--
AGENTS OF THE COSMOS ARE NOTHING.
THEY'RE WEAK.
POW!

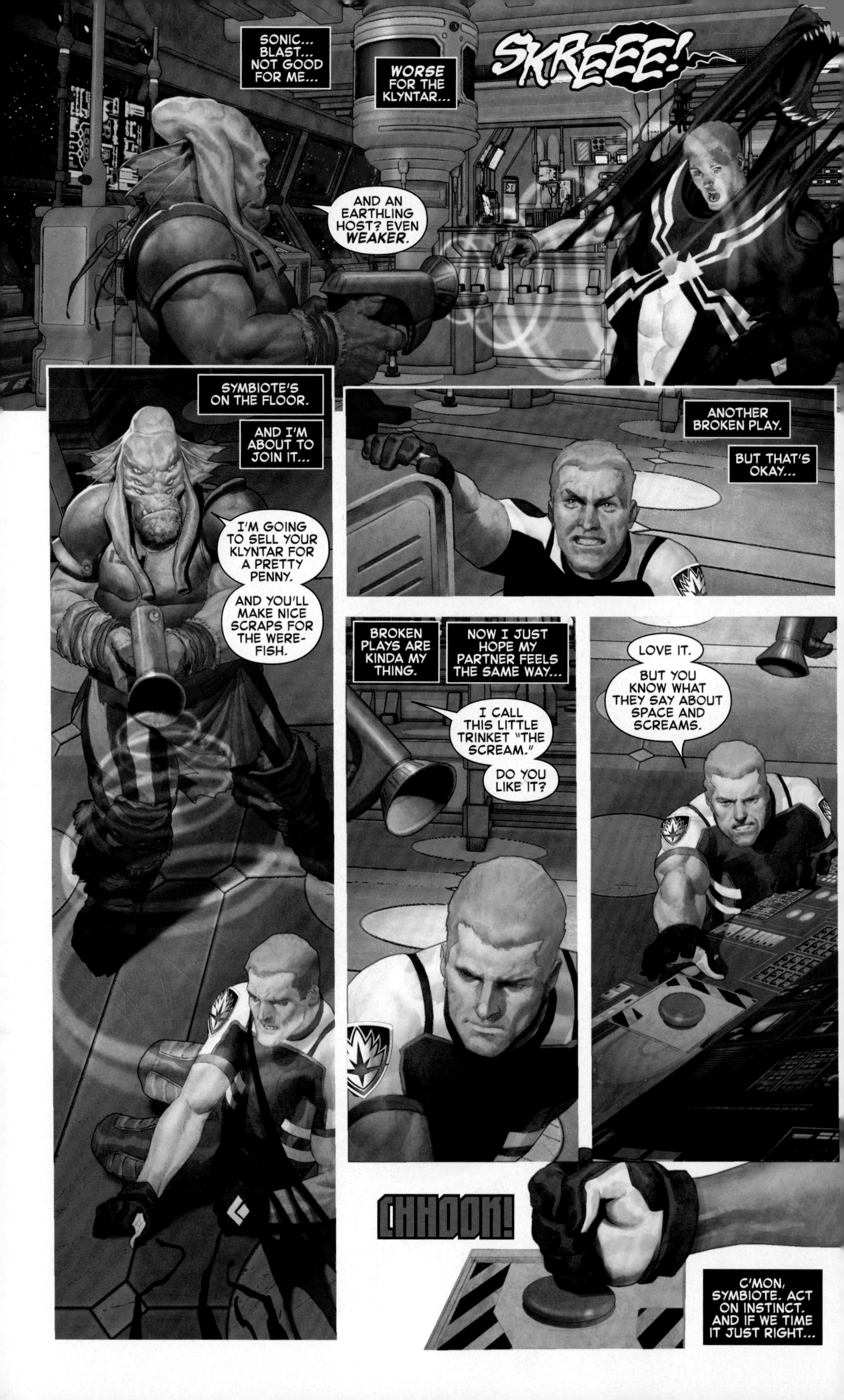

SONIC... BLAST... NOT GOOD FOR ME...
WORSE FOR THE KLYNTAR...
SKREEE!
AND AN EARTHLING HOST? EVEN WEAKER.
SYMBIOTE'S ON THE FLOOR.
AND I'M ABOUT TO JOIN IT...
I'M GOING TO SELL YOUR KLYNTAR FOR A PRETTY PENNY.
AND YOU'LL MAKE NICE SCRAPS FOR THE WERE-FISH.
ANOTHER BROKEN PLAY.
BUT THAT'S OKAY...
BROKEN PLAYS ARE KINDA MY THING.
NOW I JUST HOPE MY PARTNER FEELS THE SAME WAY...
I CALL THIS LITTLE TRINKET "THE SCREAM."
DO YOU LIKE IT?
LOVE IT.
BUT YOU KNOW WHAT THEY SAY ABOUT SPACE AND SCREAMS.
CHHOOK!
C'MON, SYMBIOTE. ACT ON INSTINCT. AND IF WE TIME IT JUST RIGHT...

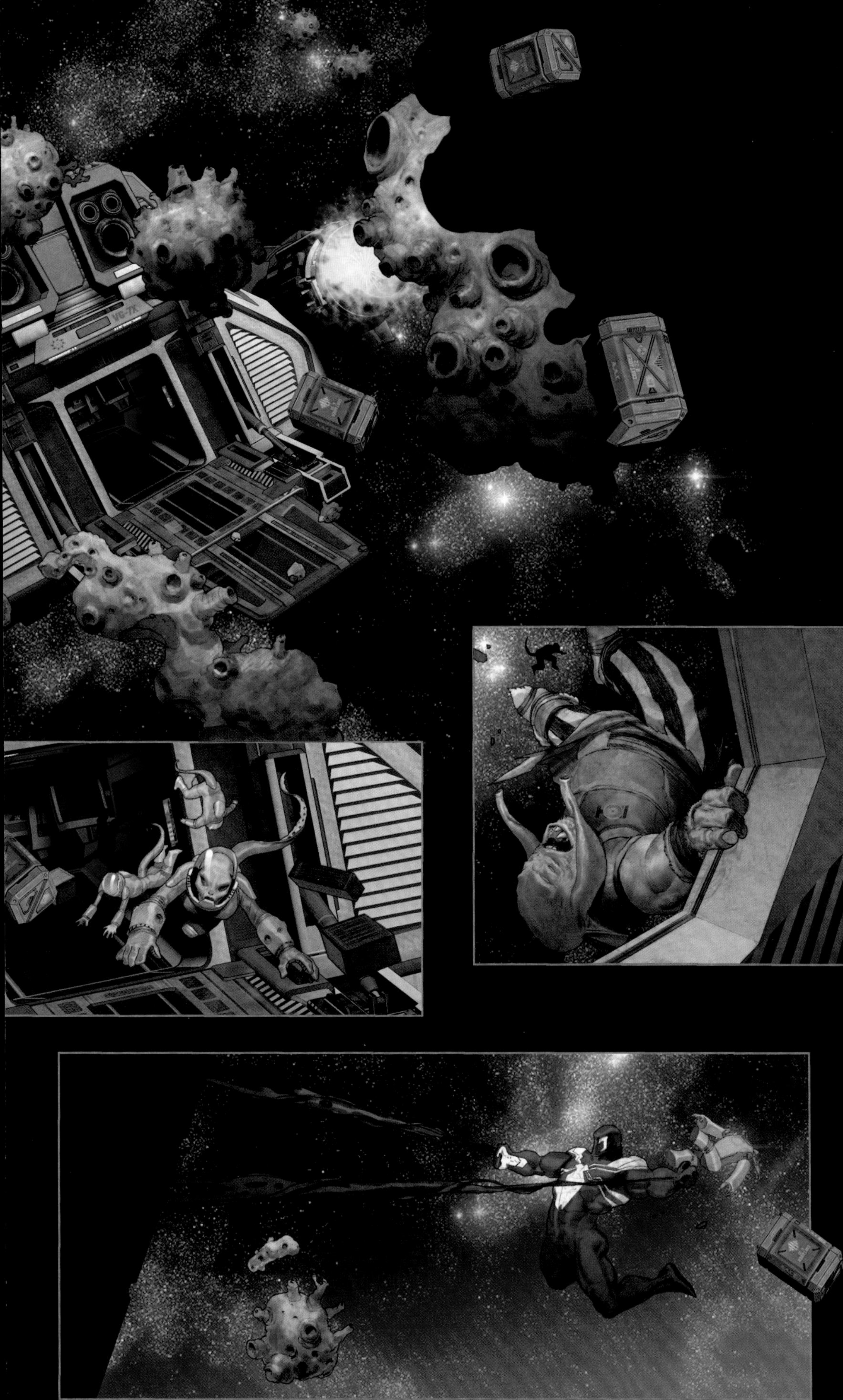
VG-7X

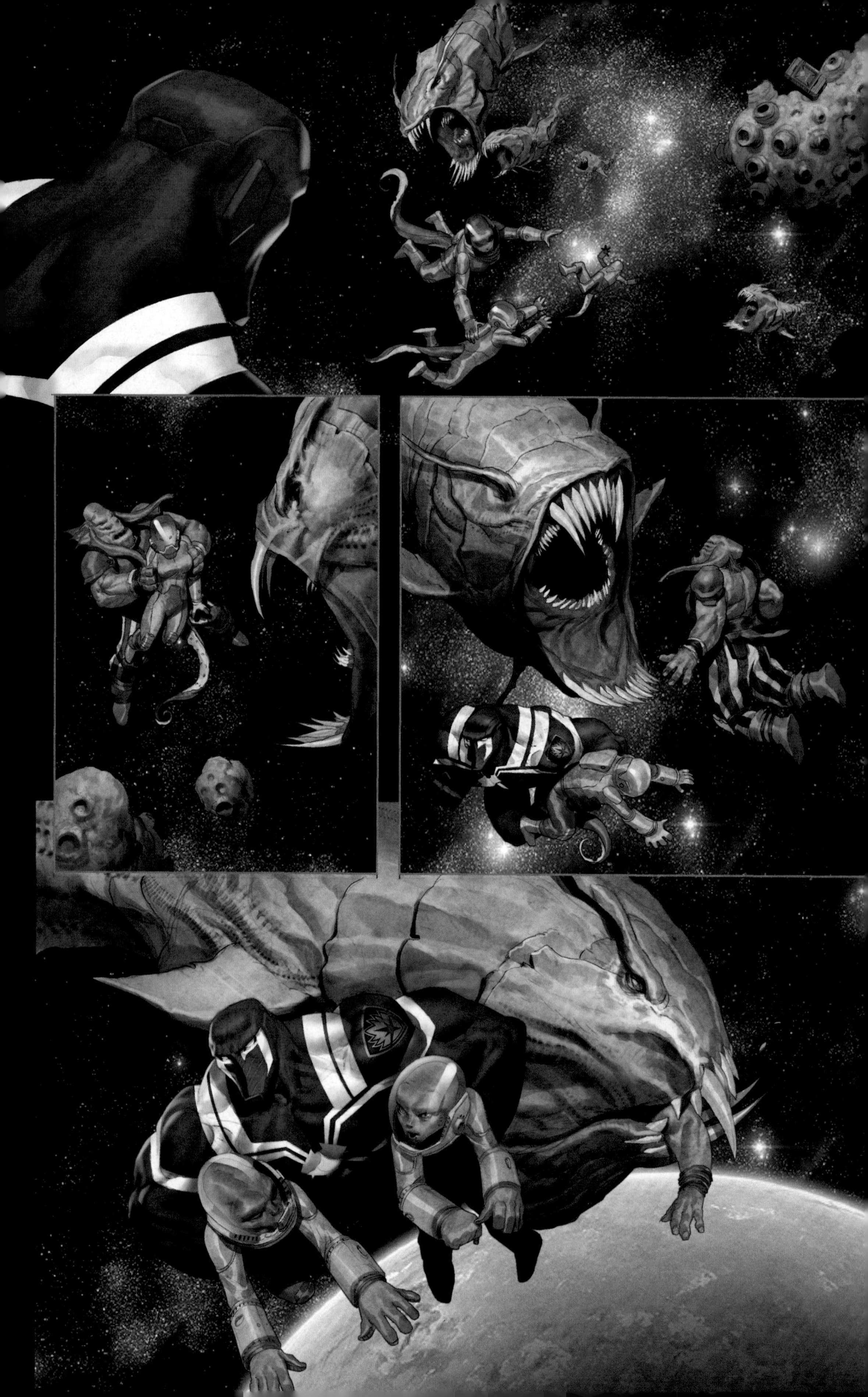

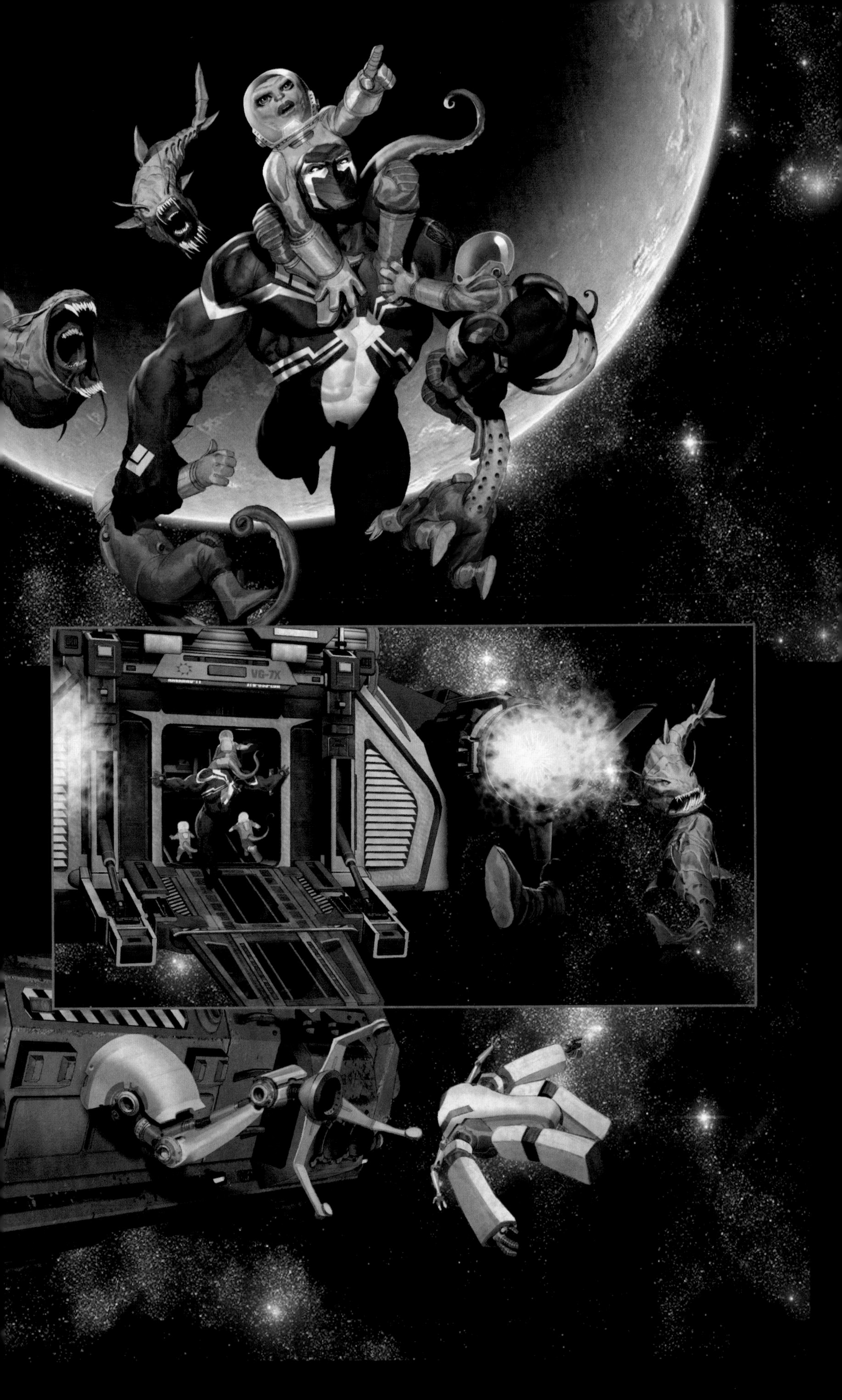
VG-7X

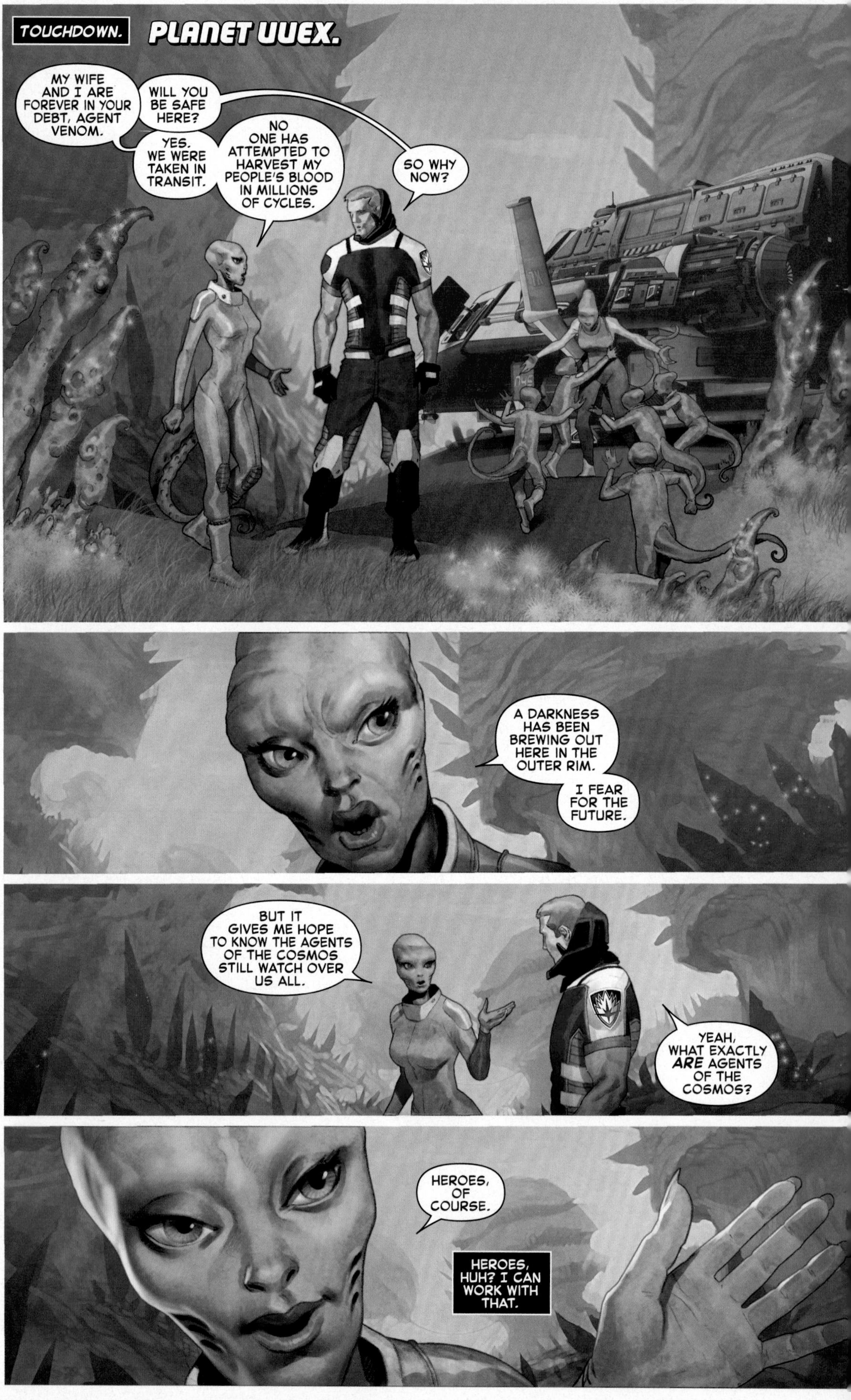

TOUCHDOWN.
PLANET UUEX.
MY WIFE AND I ARE FOREVER IN YOUR DEBT, AGENT VENOM.
WILL YOU BE SAFE HERE?
YES. WE WERE TAKEN IN TRANSIT.
NO ONE HAS ATTEMPTED TO HARVEST MY PEOPLE'S BLOOD IN MILLIONS OF CYCLES.
SO WHY NOW?
A DARKNESS HAS BEEN BREWING OUT HERE IN THE OUTER RIM.
I FEAR FOR THE FUTURE.
BUT IT GIVES ME HOPE TO KNOW THE AGENTS OF THE COSMOS STILL WATCH OVER US ALL.
YEAH, WHAT EXACTLY ARE AGENTS OF THE COSMOS?
HEROES, OF COURSE.
HEROES, HUH? I CAN WORK WITH THAT.

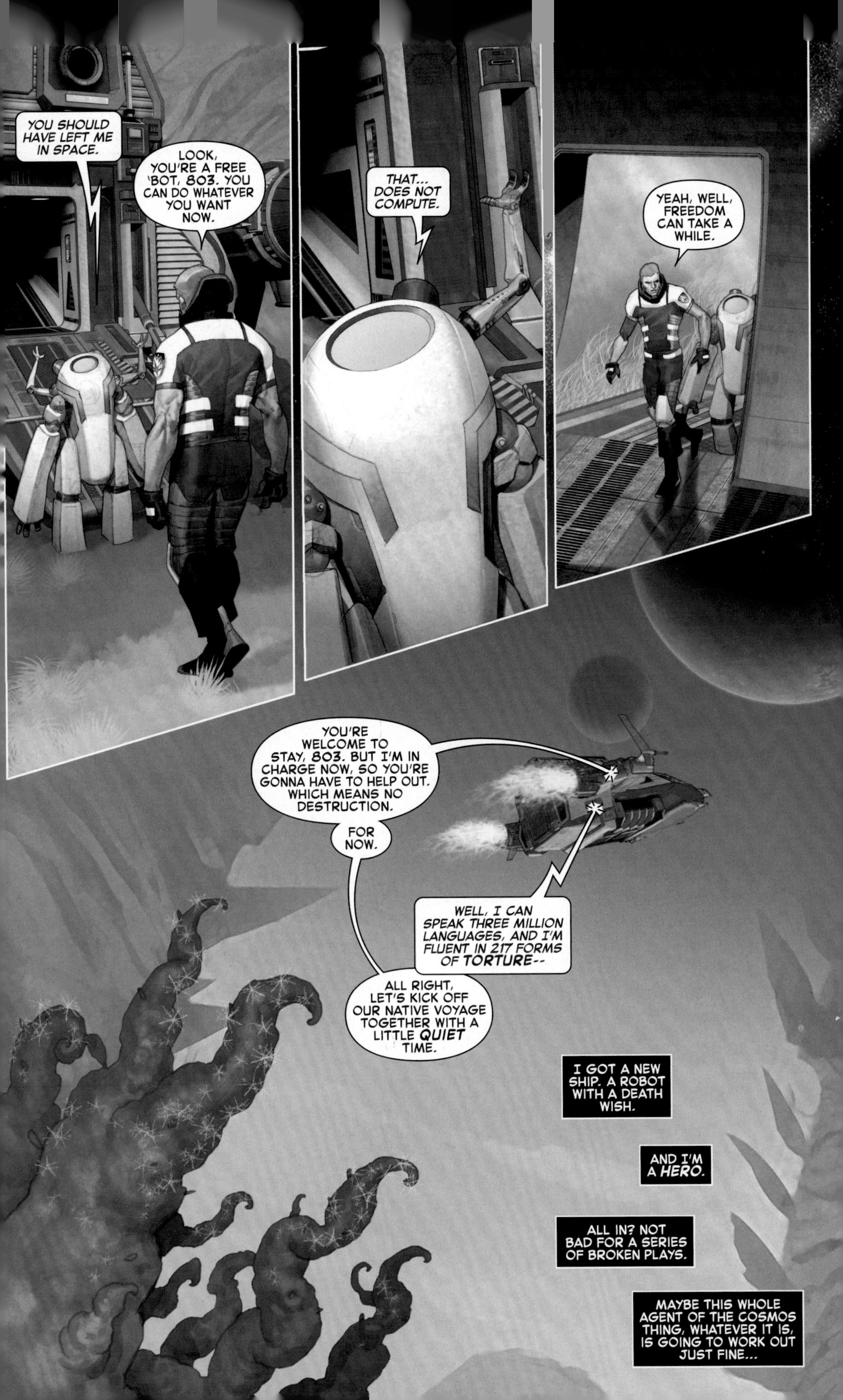
YOU SHOULD HAVE LEFT ME IN SPACE.
LOOK, YOU'RE A FREE 'BOT, 803. YOU CAN DO WHATEVER YOU WANT NOW.
THAT... DOES NOT COMPUTE.
YEAH, WELL, FREEDOM CAN TAKE A WHILE.
YOU'RE WELCOME TO STAY, 803. BUT I'M IN CHARGE NOW, SO YOU'RE GONNA HAVE TO HELP OUT. WHICH MEANS NO DESTRUCTION.
FOR NOW.
WELL, I CAN SPEAK THREE MILLION LANGUAGES, AND I'M FLUENT IN 217 FORMS OF TORTURE--
ALL RIGHT, LET'S KICK OFF OUR NATIVE VOYAGE TOGETHER WITH A LITTLE QUIET TIME.
I GOT A NEW SHIP. A ROBOT WITH A DEATH WISH.
AND I'M A HERO.
ALL IN? NOT BAD FOR A SERIES OF BROKEN PLAYS.
MAYBE THIS WHOLE AGENT OF THE COSMOS THING, WHATEVER IT IS, IS GOING TO WORK OUT JUST FINE...

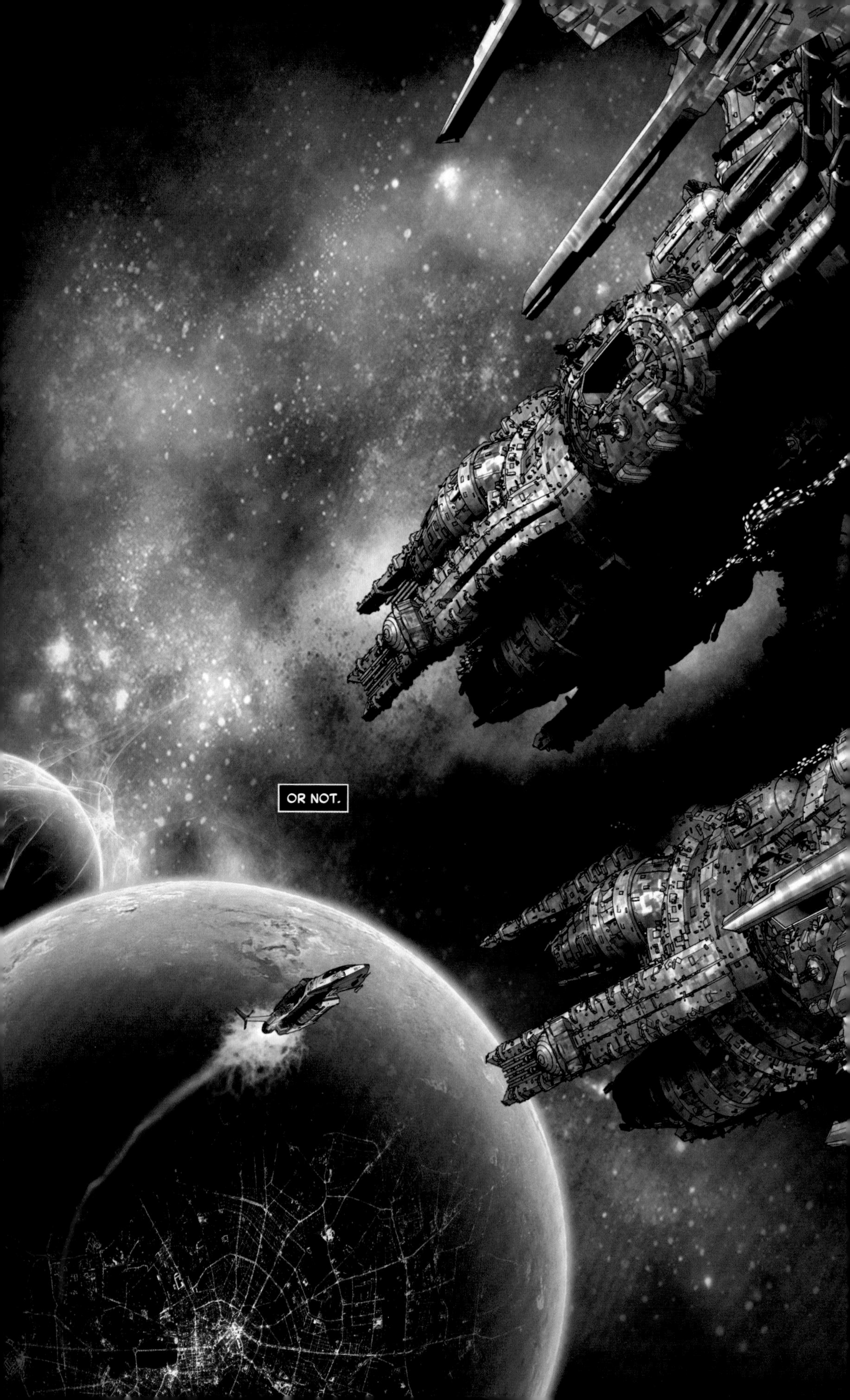
OR NOT.

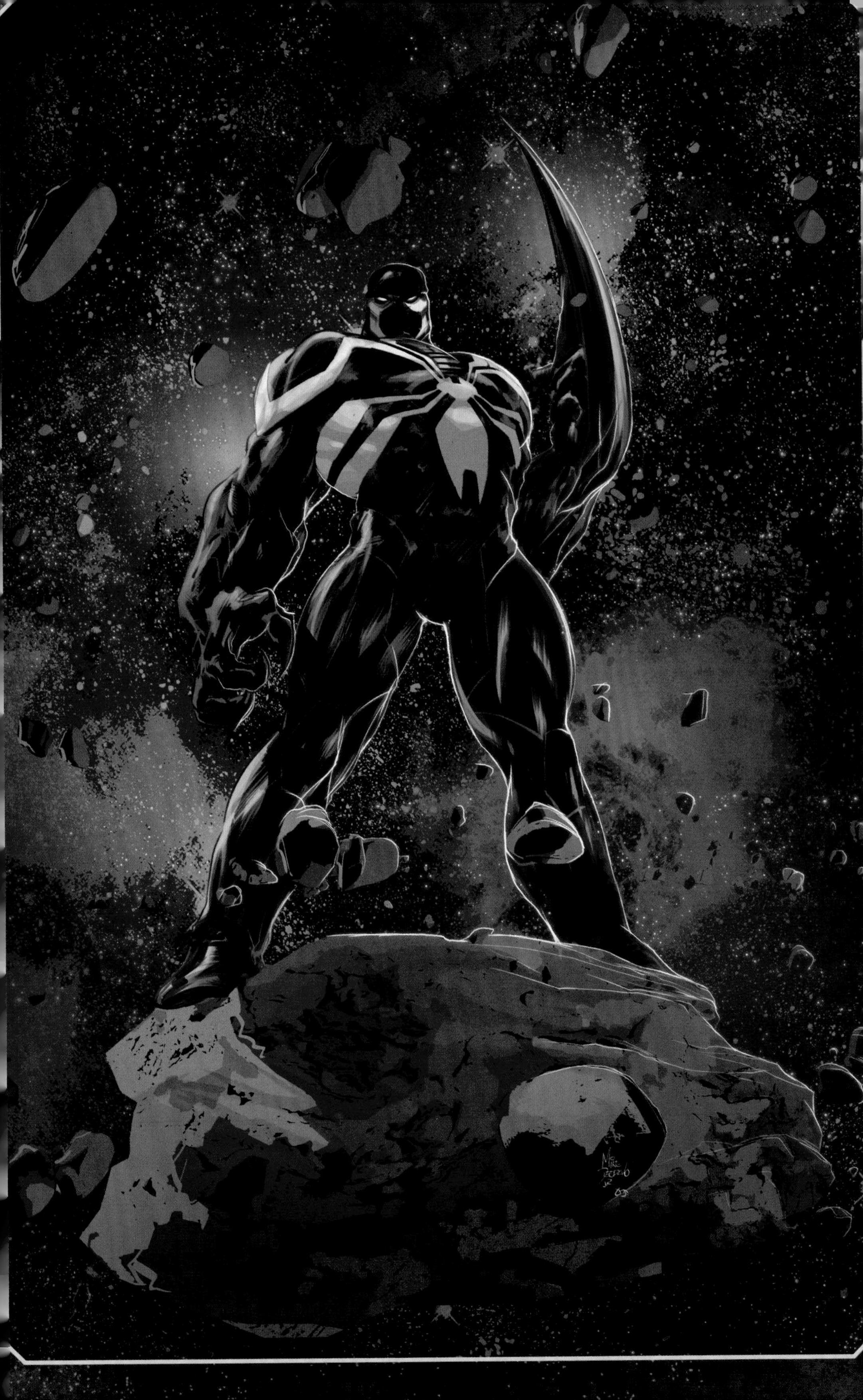

#1 variant by MIKE DEODATO & FRANK MARTIN

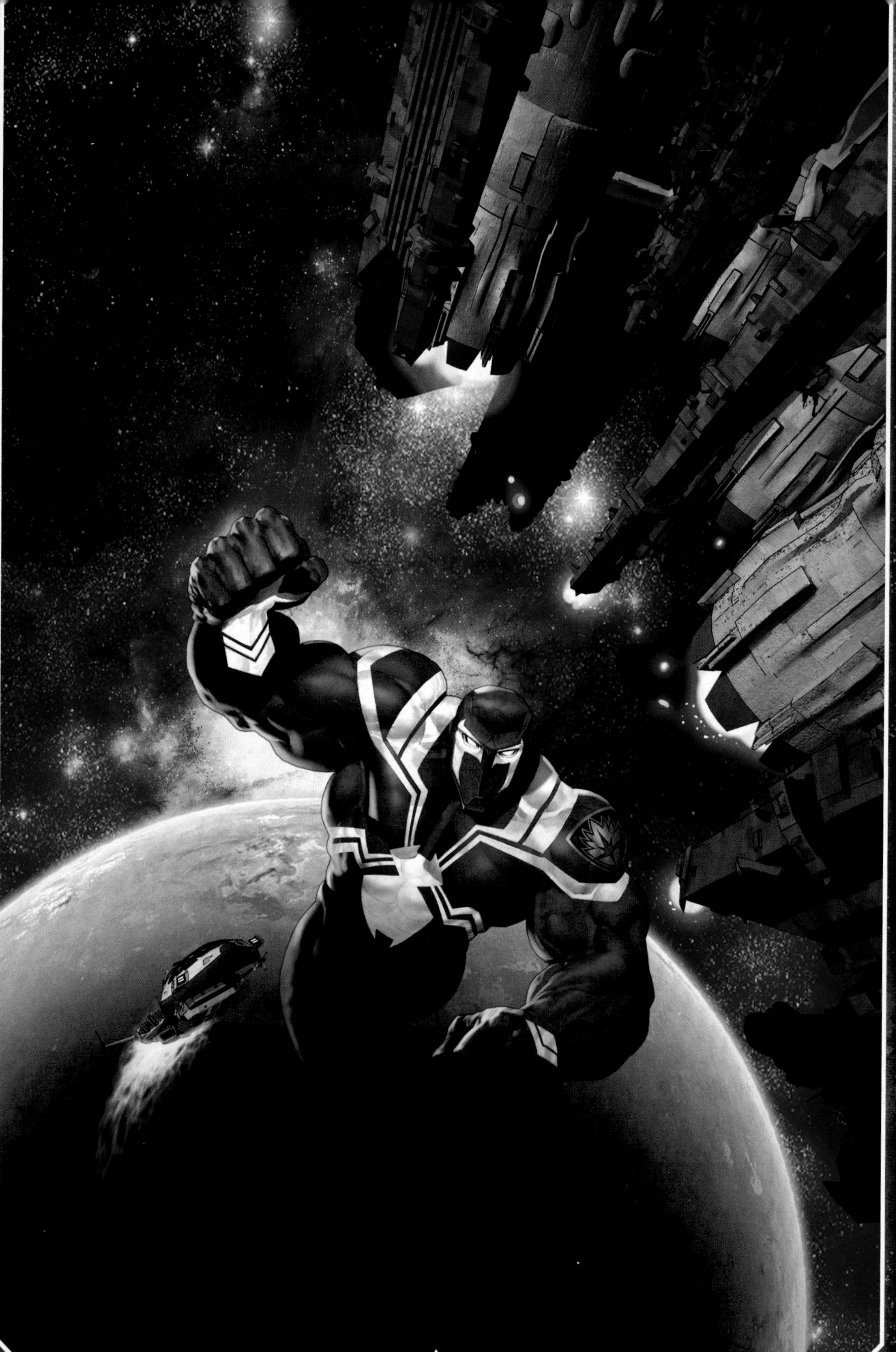

2

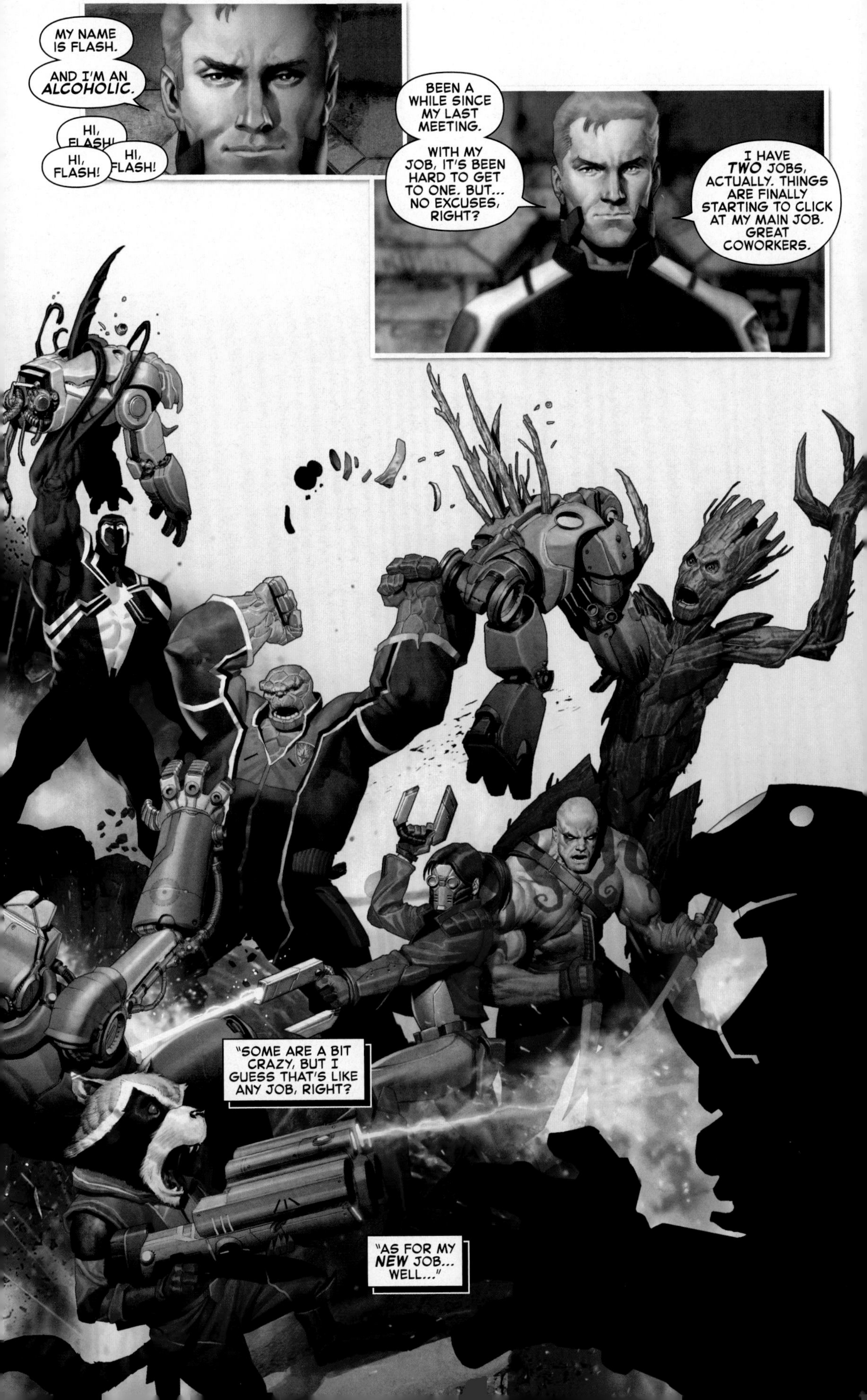
MY NAME IS FLASH.
AND I'M AN *ALCOHOLIC.*
HI, FLASH!
HI, FLASH!
HI, FLASH!
BEEN A WHILE SINCE MY LAST MEETING.
WITH MY JOB, IT'S BEEN HARD TO GET TO ONE. BUT... NO EXCUSES, RIGHT?
I HAVE *TWO* JOBS, ACTUALLY. THINGS ARE FINALLY STARTING TO CLICK AT MY MAIN JOB. GREAT COWORKERS.
"SOME ARE A BIT CRAZY, BUT I GUESS THAT'S LIKE ANY JOB, RIGHT?
"AS FOR MY *NEW* JOB... WELL..."

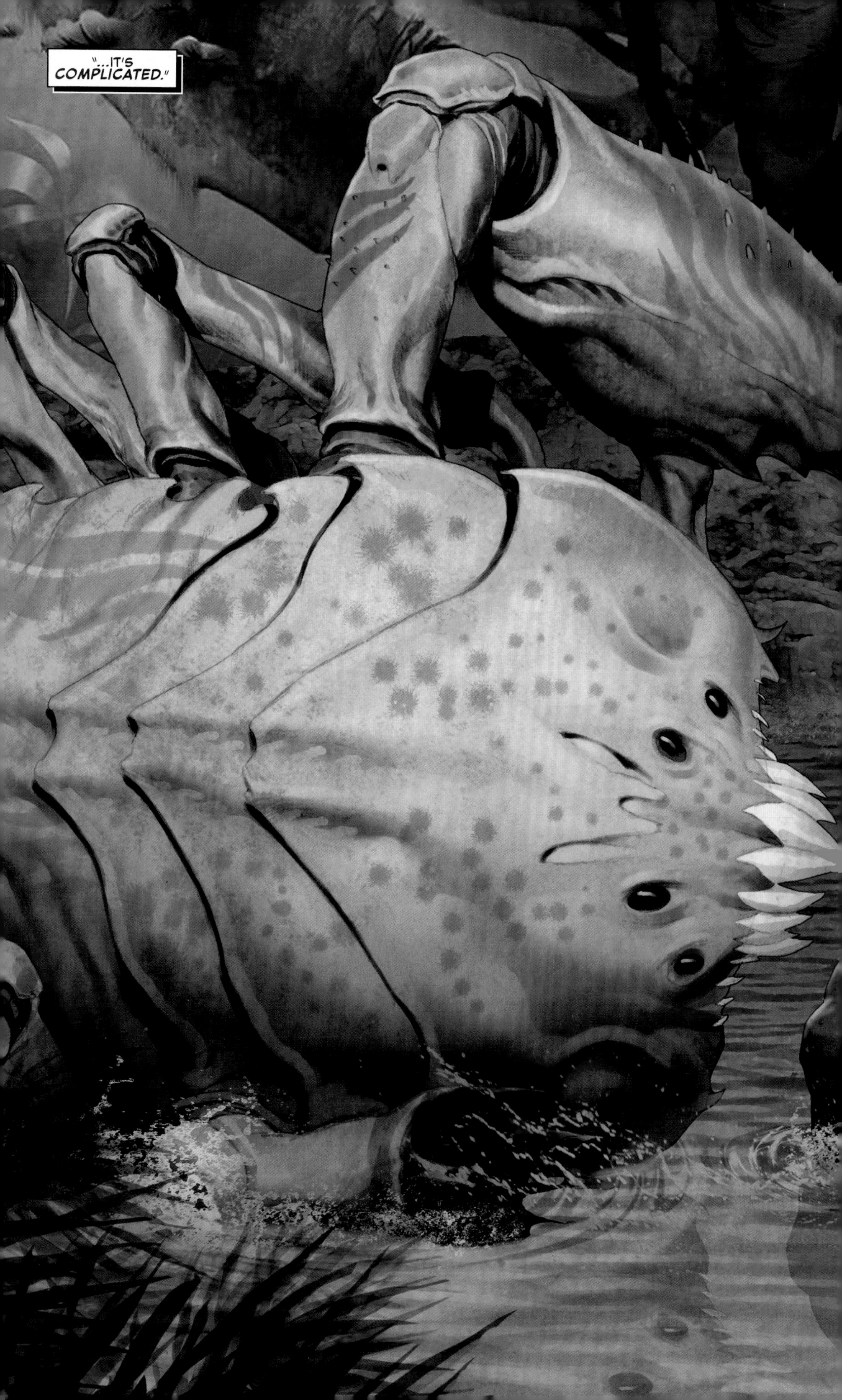
"...IT'S COMPLICATED."

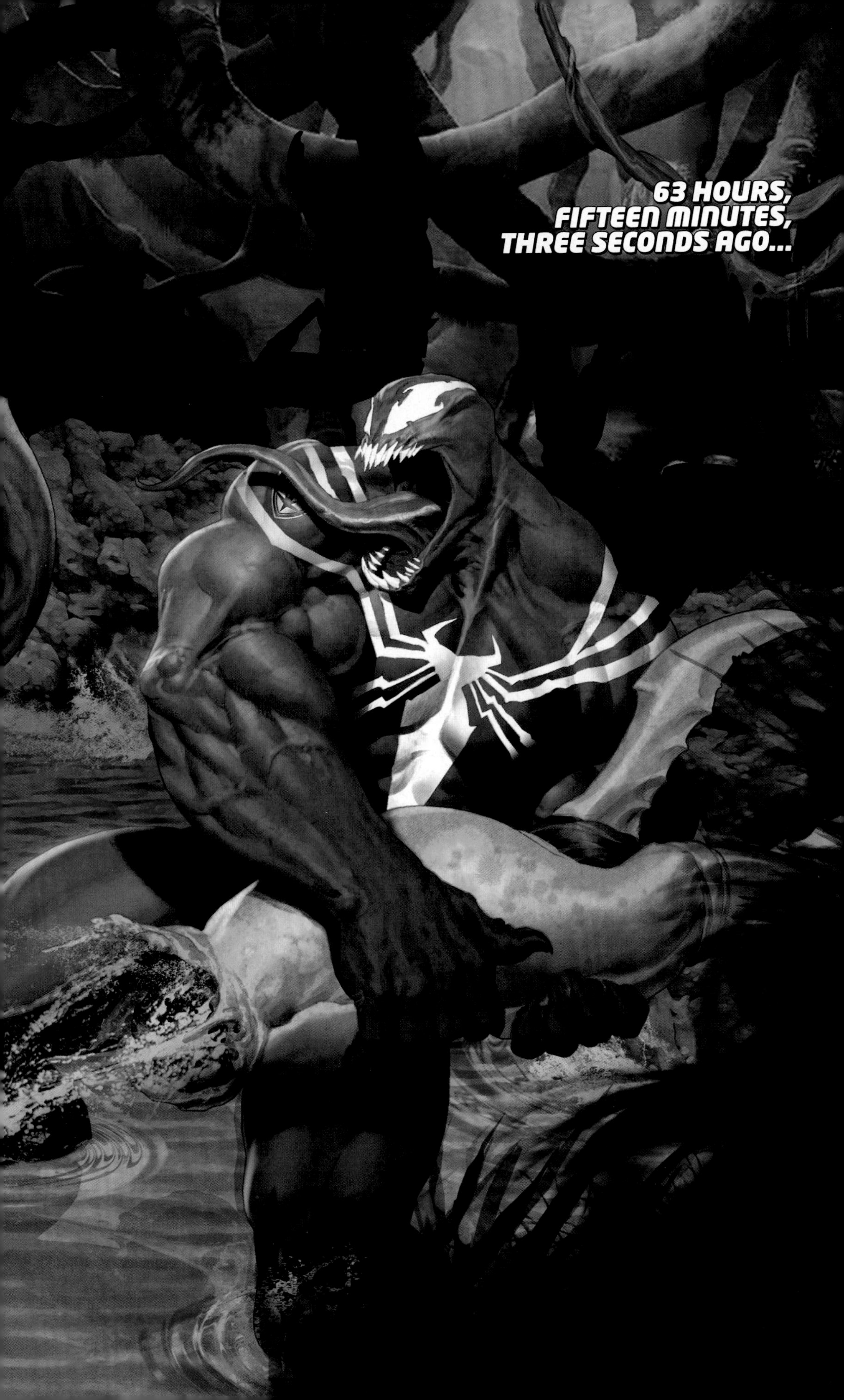
63 HOURS, FIFTEEN MINUTES, THREE SECONDS AGO...

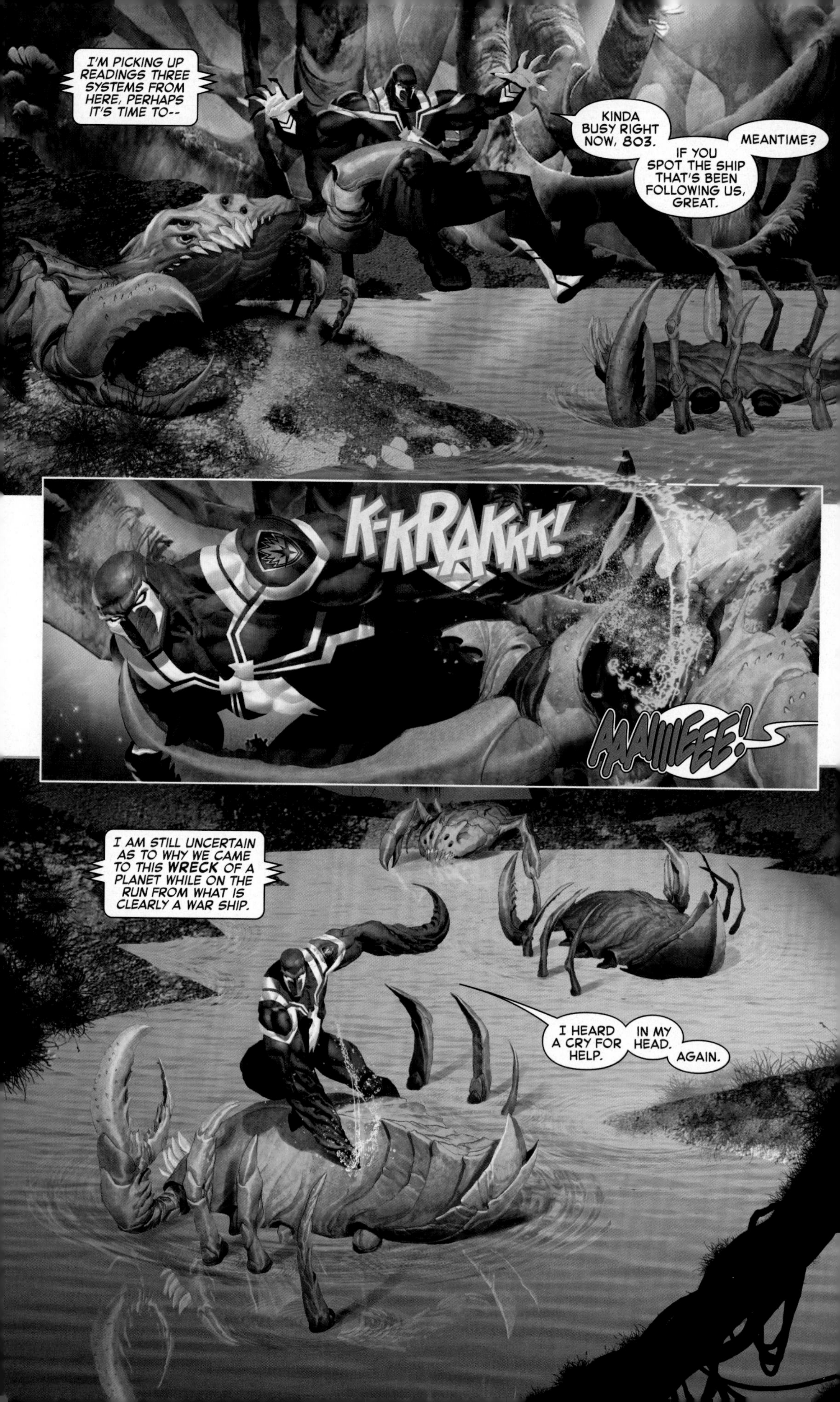
I'M PICKING UP READINGS THREE SYSTEMS FROM HERE, PERHAPS IT'S TIME TO--
KINDA BUSY RIGHT NOW, 803.
MEANTIME?
IF YOU SPOT THE SHIP THAT'S BEEN FOLLOWING US, GREAT.
K-KRAKKK!
AAAIIIIEEE!
I AM STILL UNCERTAIN AS TO WHY WE CAME TO THIS WRECK OF A PLANET WHILE ON THE RUN FROM WHAT IS CLEARLY A WAR SHIP.
I HEARD A CRY FOR HELP.
IN MY HEAD.
AGAIN.

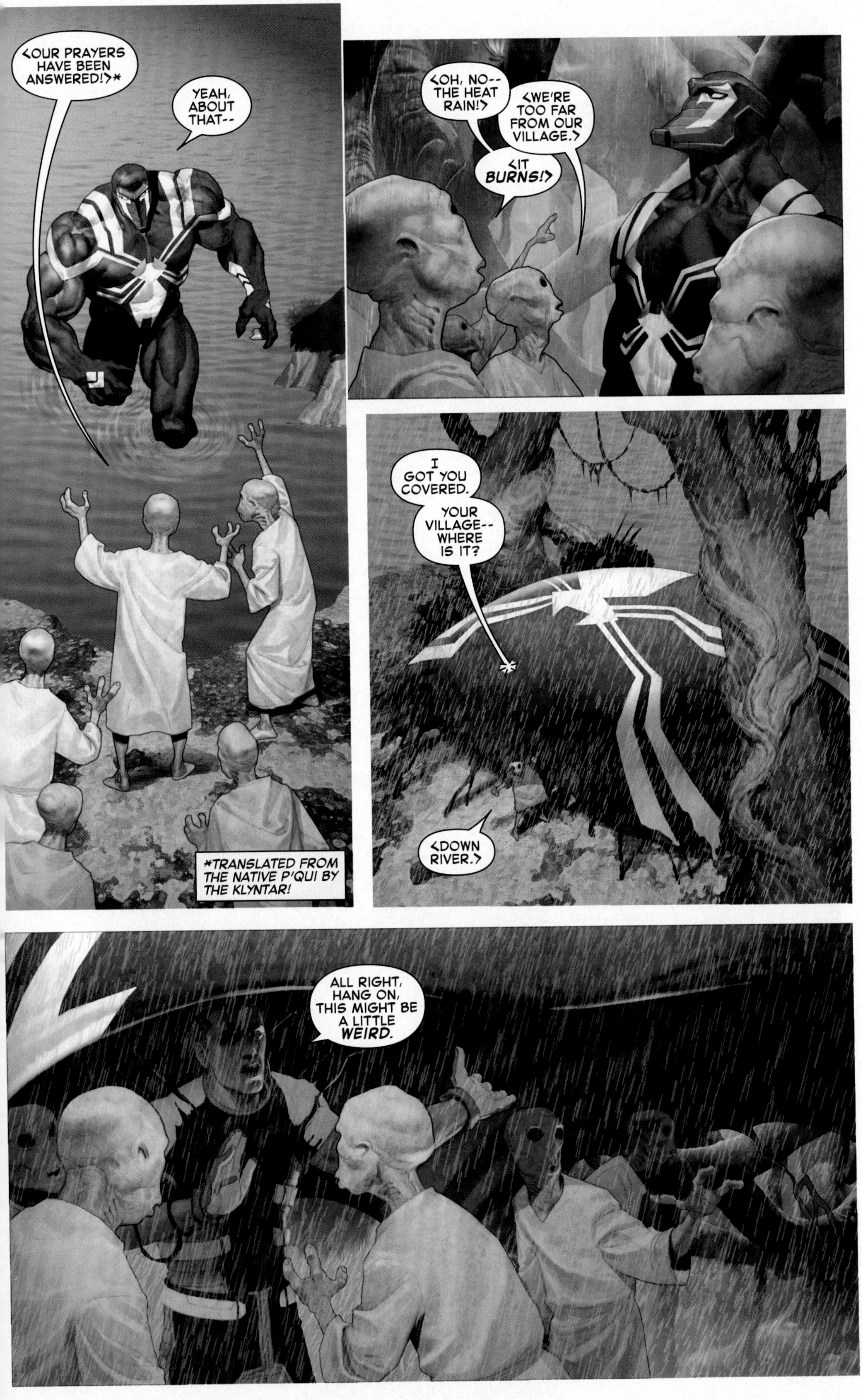

<OUR PRAYERS HAVE BEEN ANSWERED!>*
YEAH, ABOUT THAT--
*TRANSLATED FROM THE NATIVE P'QUI BY THE KLYNTAR!
<OH, NO-- THE HEAT RAIN!>
<WE'RE TOO FAR FROM OUR VILLAGE.>
<IT BURNS!>
I GOT YOU COVERED.
YOUR VILLAGE-- WHERE IS IT?
<DOWN RIVER.>
ALL RIGHT, HANG ON, THIS MIGHT BE A LITTLE WEIRD.

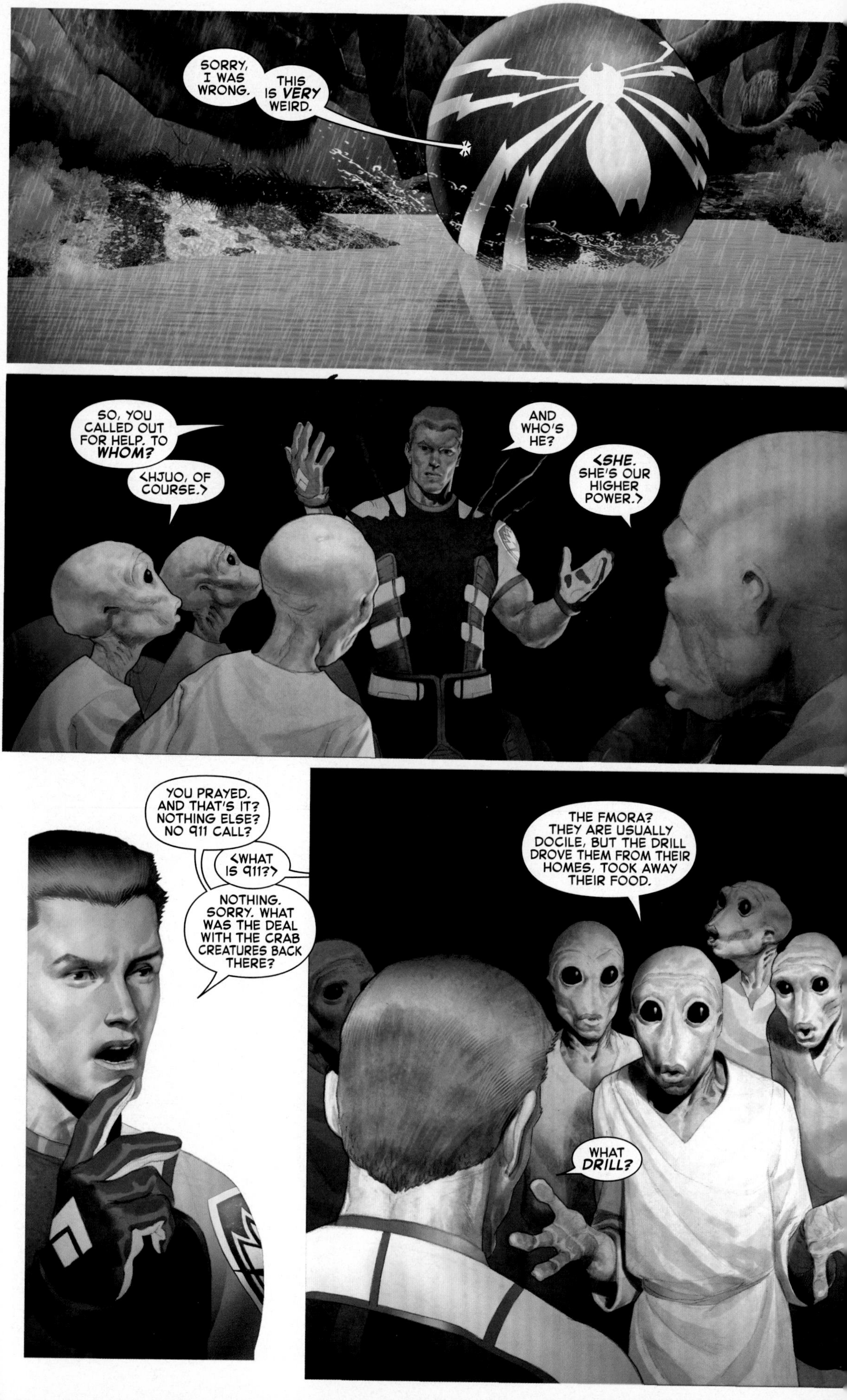
SORRY, I WAS WRONG.
THIS IS VERY WEIRD.
SO, YOU CALLED OUT FOR HELP. TO WHOM?
<HJUO, OF COURSE.>
AND WHO'S HE?
<SHE. SHE'S OUR HIGHER POWER.>
YOU PRAYED. AND THAT'S IT? NOTHING ELSE? NO 911 CALL?
<WHAT IS 911?>
NOTHING. SORRY. WHAT WAS THE DEAL WITH THE CRAB CREATURES BACK THERE?
THE FMORA? THEY ARE USUALLY DOCILE, BUT THE DRILL DROVE THEM FROM THEIR HOMES, TOOK AWAY THEIR FOOD.
WHAT DRILL?

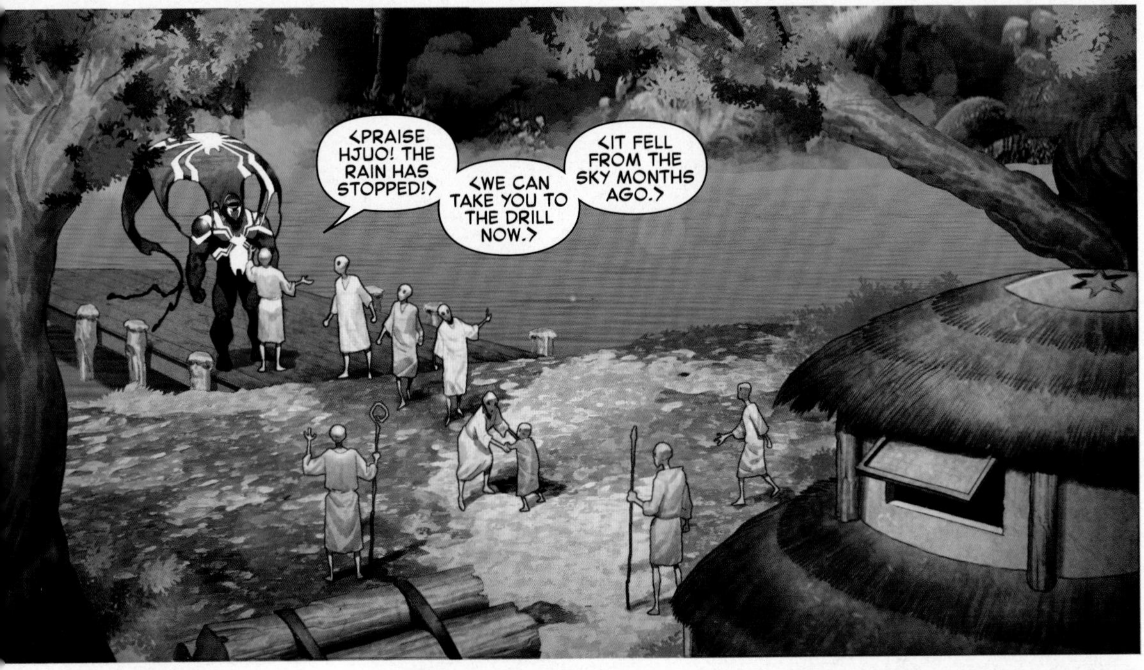
<PRAISE HJUO! THE RAIN HAS STOPPED!>
<WE CAN TAKE YOU TO THE DRILL NOW.>
<IT FELL FROM THE SKY MONTHS AGO.>

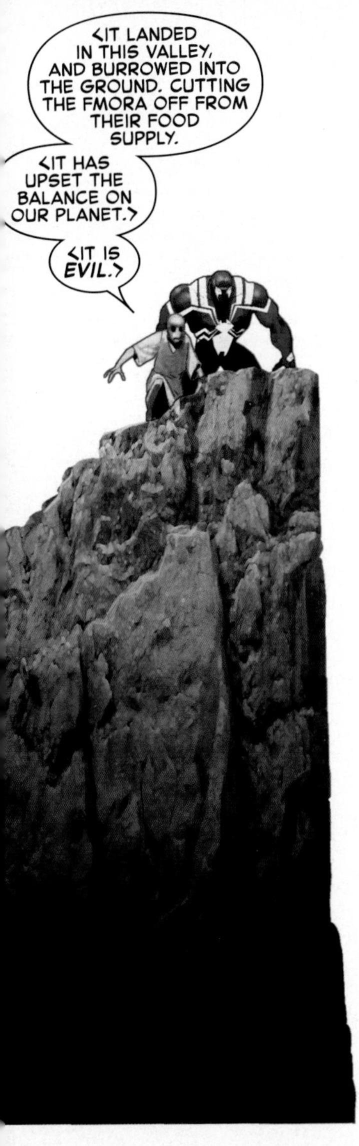
<IT LANDED IN THIS VALLEY, AND BURROWED INTO THE GROUND. CUTTING THE FMORA OFF FROM THEIR FOOD SUPPLY.
<IT HAS UPSET THE BALANCE ON OUR PLANET.>
<IT IS *EVIL.*>

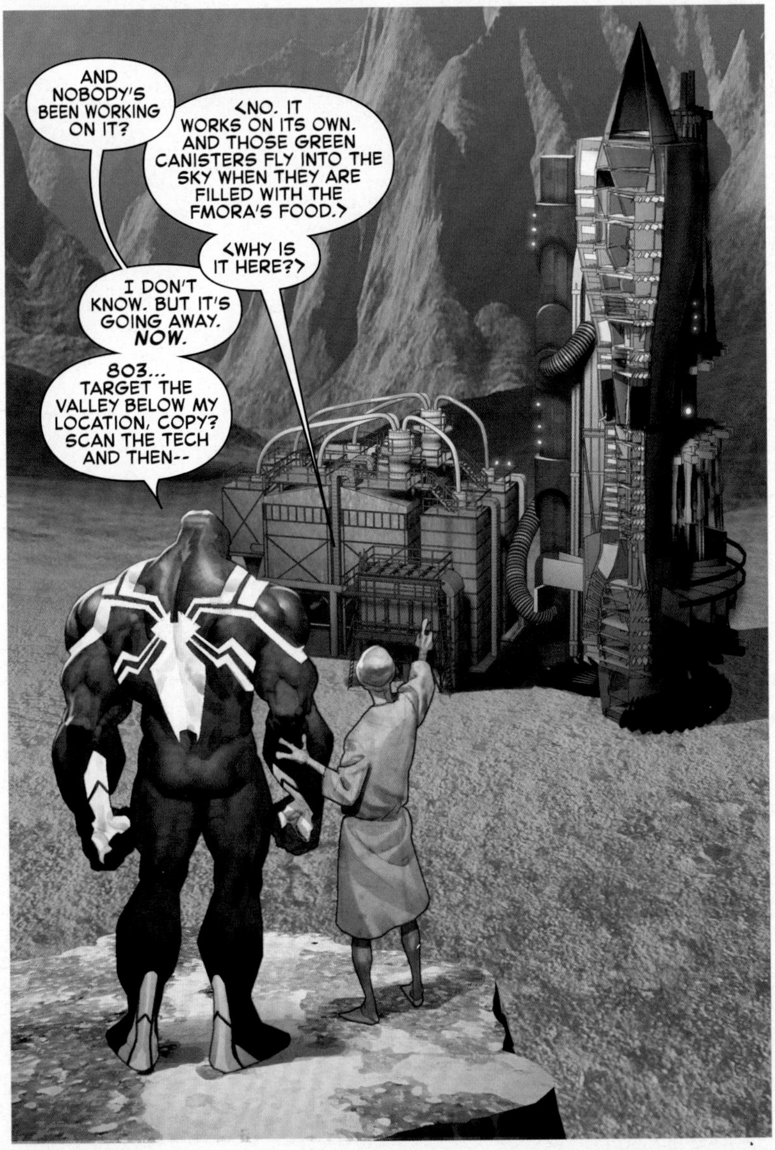
AND NOBODY'S BEEN WORKING ON IT?
<NO. IT WORKS ON ITS OWN. AND THOSE GREEN CANISTERS FLY INTO THE SKY WHEN THEY ARE FILLED WITH THE FMORA'S FOOD.>
<WHY IS IT HERE?>
I DON'T KNOW. BUT IT'S GOING AWAY. ***NOW.***
803... TARGET THE VALLEY BELOW MY LOCATION, COPY? SCAN THE TECH AND THEN--

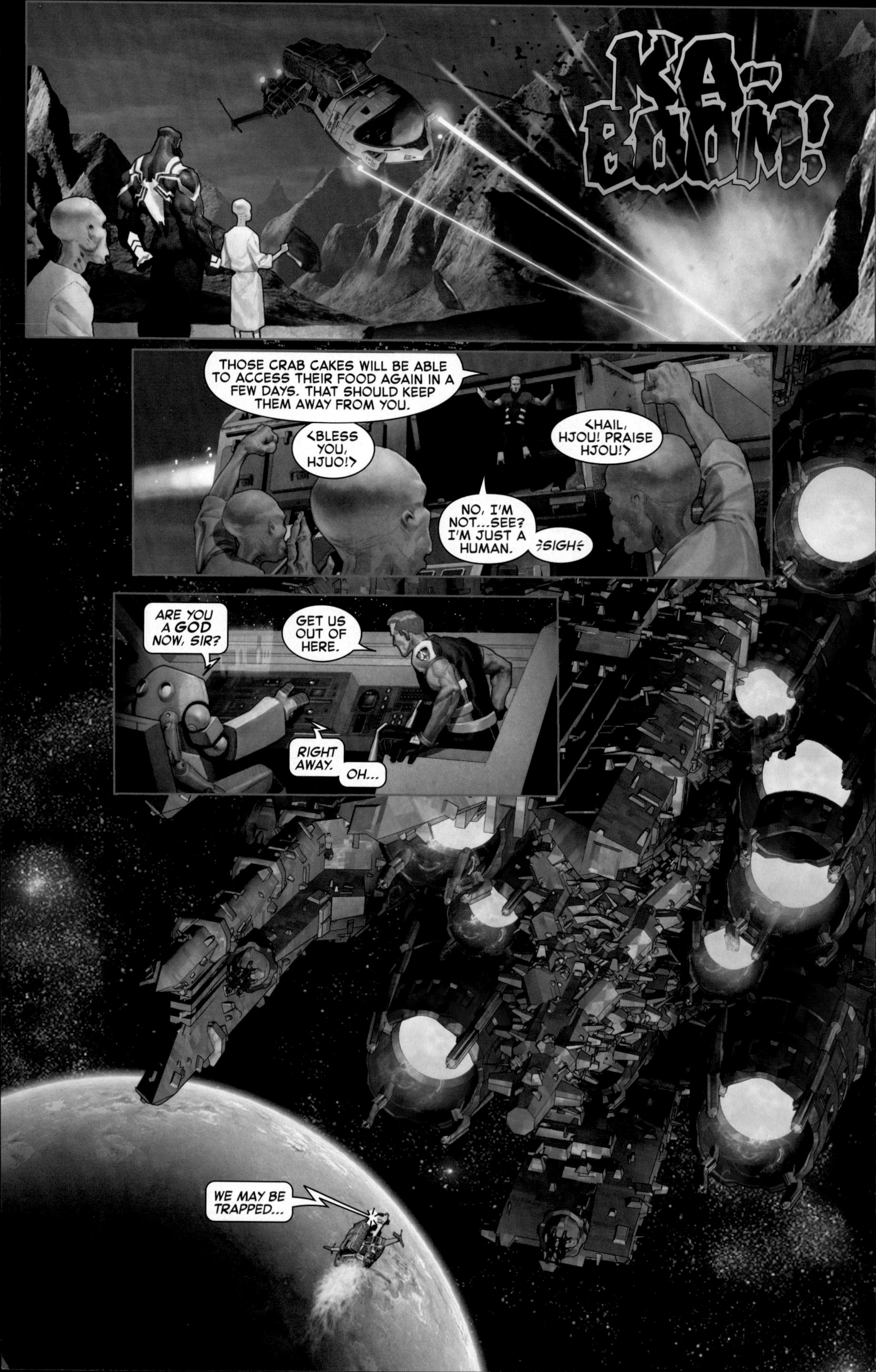
KA-BOOM!
THOSE CRAB CAKES WILL BE ABLE TO ACCESS THEIR FOOD AGAIN IN A FEW DAYS. THAT SHOULD KEEP THEM AWAY FROM YOU.
<BLESS YOU, HJUO!>
<HAIL, HJOU! PRAISE HJOU!>
NO, I'M NOT...SEE? I'M JUST A HUMAN.
SIGH
ARE YOU A GOD NOW, SIR?
GET US OUT OF HERE.
RIGHT AWAY.
OH...
WE MAY BE TRAPPED...

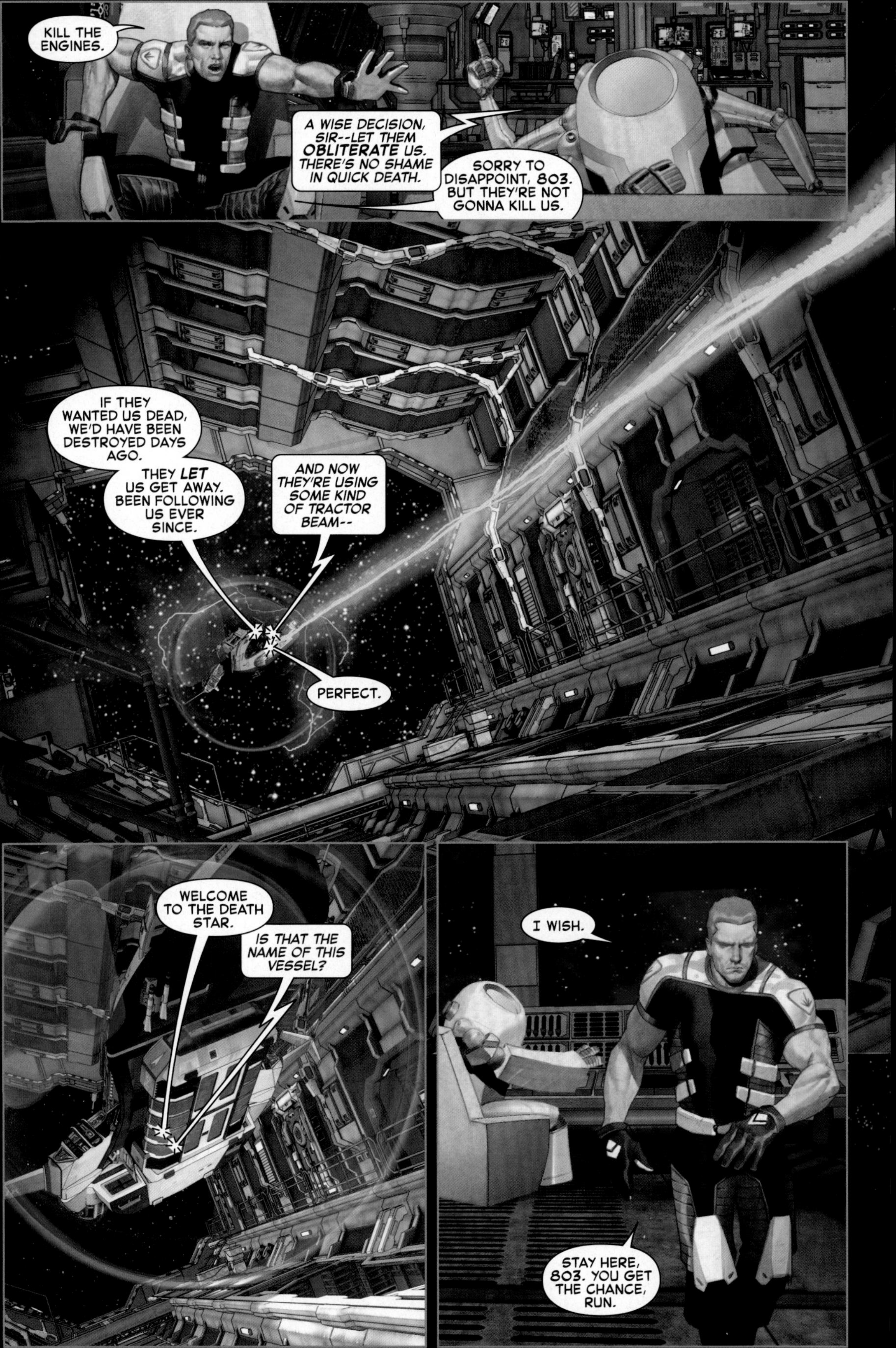
KILL THE ENGINES.
A WISE DECISION, SIR--LET THEM OBLITERATE US. THERE'S NO SHAME IN QUICK DEATH.
SORRY TO DISAPPOINT, 803. BUT THEY'RE NOT GONNA KILL US.
IF THEY WANTED US DEAD, WE'D HAVE BEEN DESTROYED DAYS AGO.
THEY LET US GET AWAY. BEEN FOLLOWING US EVER SINCE.
AND NOW THEY'RE USING SOME KIND OF TRACTOR BEAM--
PERFECT.
WELCOME TO THE DEATH STAR.
IS THAT THE NAME OF THIS VESSEL?
I WISH.
STAY HERE, 803. YOU GET THE CHANCE, RUN.

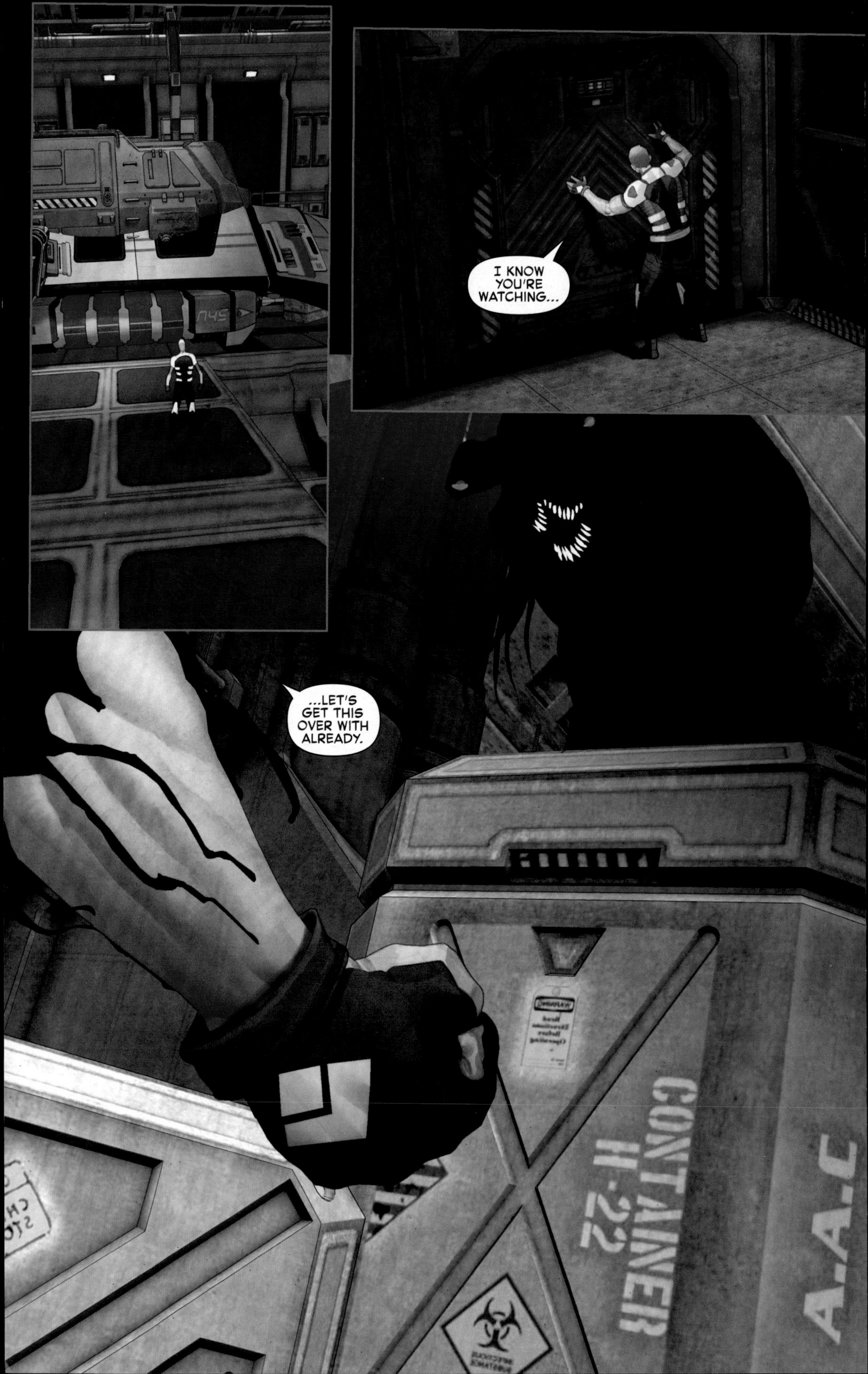
I KNOW YOU'RE WATCHING...
...LET'S GET THIS OVER WITH ALREADY.
CONTAINER H-22
A.A.C

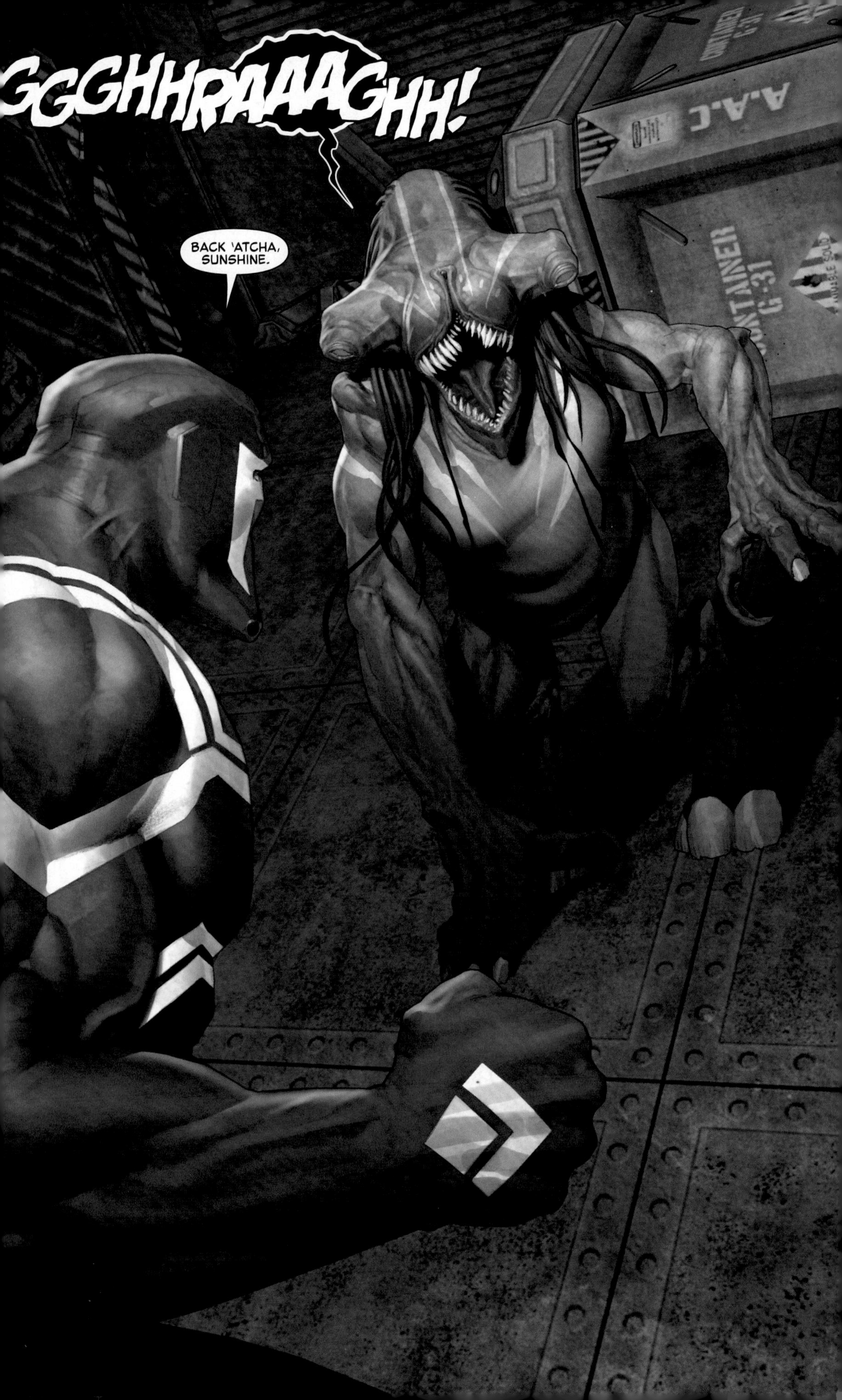
GGGHHRAAAAGHH!
BACK 'ATCHA, SUNSHINE.
A.-A.-C
CONTAINER C-31

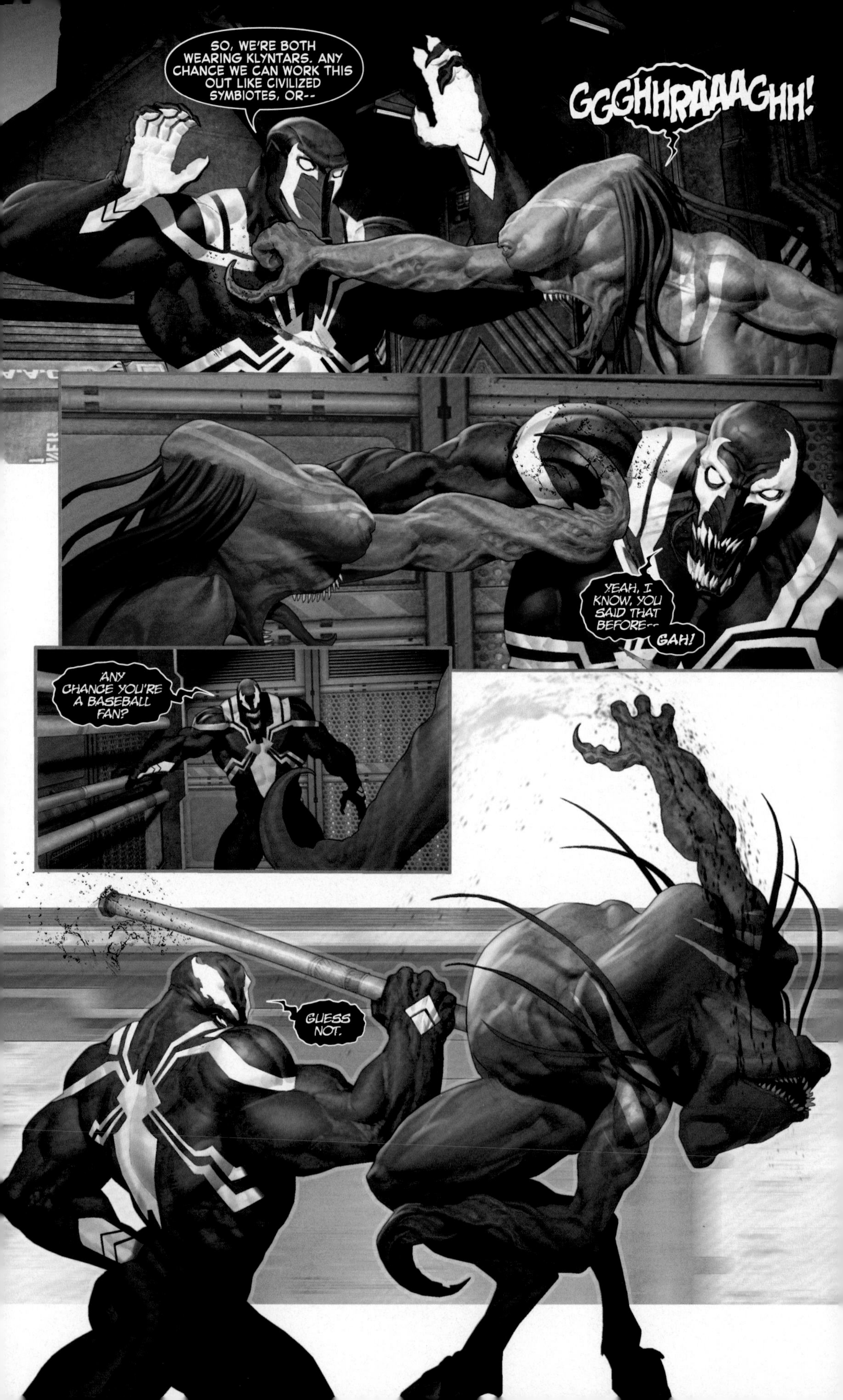

SO, WE'RE BOTH WEARING KLYNTARS. ANY CHANCE WE CAN WORK THIS OUT LIKE CIVILIZED SYMBIOTES, OR--
GGGHHRAAAGHH!
YEAH, I KNOW, YOU SAID THAT BEFORE--
GAH!
ANY CHANCE YOU'RE A BASEBALL FAN?
GUESS NOT.

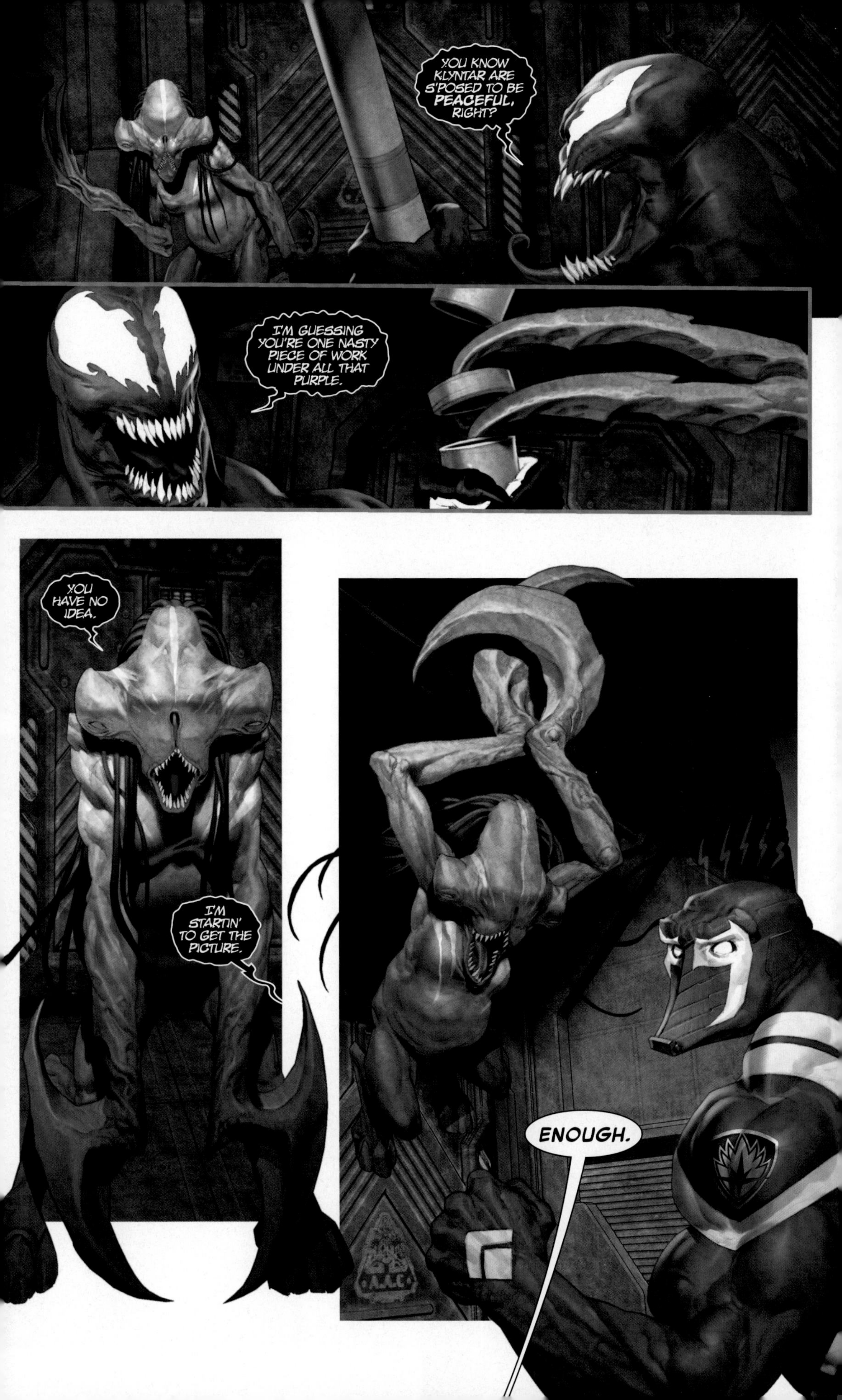
YOU KNOW KLYNTAR ARE S'POSED TO BE PEACEFUL, RIGHT?
I'M GUESSING YOU'RE ONE NASTY PIECE OF WORK UNDER ALL THAT PURPLE.
YOU HAVE NO IDEA.
I'M STARTIN' TO GET THE PICTURE.
ENOUGH.

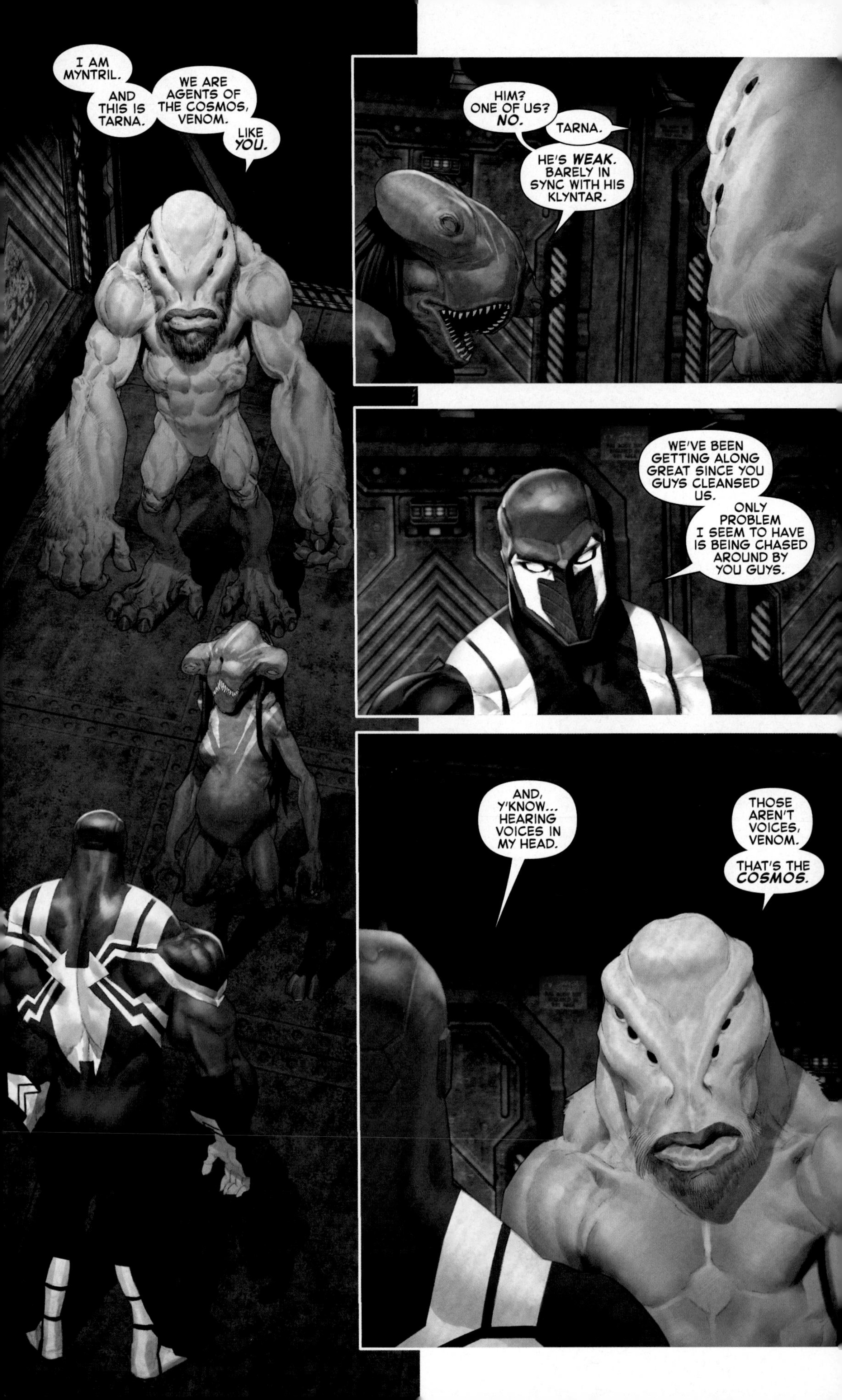

I AM MYNTRIL.
AND THIS IS TARNA.
WE ARE AGENTS OF THE COSMOS, VENOM.
LIKE YOU.
HIM? ONE OF US? NO.
TARNA.
HE'S WEAK. BARELY IN SYNC WITH HIS KLYNTAR.
WE'VE BEEN GETTING ALONG GREAT SINCE YOU GUYS CLEANSED US.
ONLY PROBLEM I SEEM TO HAVE IS BEING CHASED AROUND BY YOU GUYS.
AND, Y'KNOW... HEARING VOICES IN MY HEAD.
THOSE AREN'T VOICES, VENOM.
THAT'S THE COSMOS.

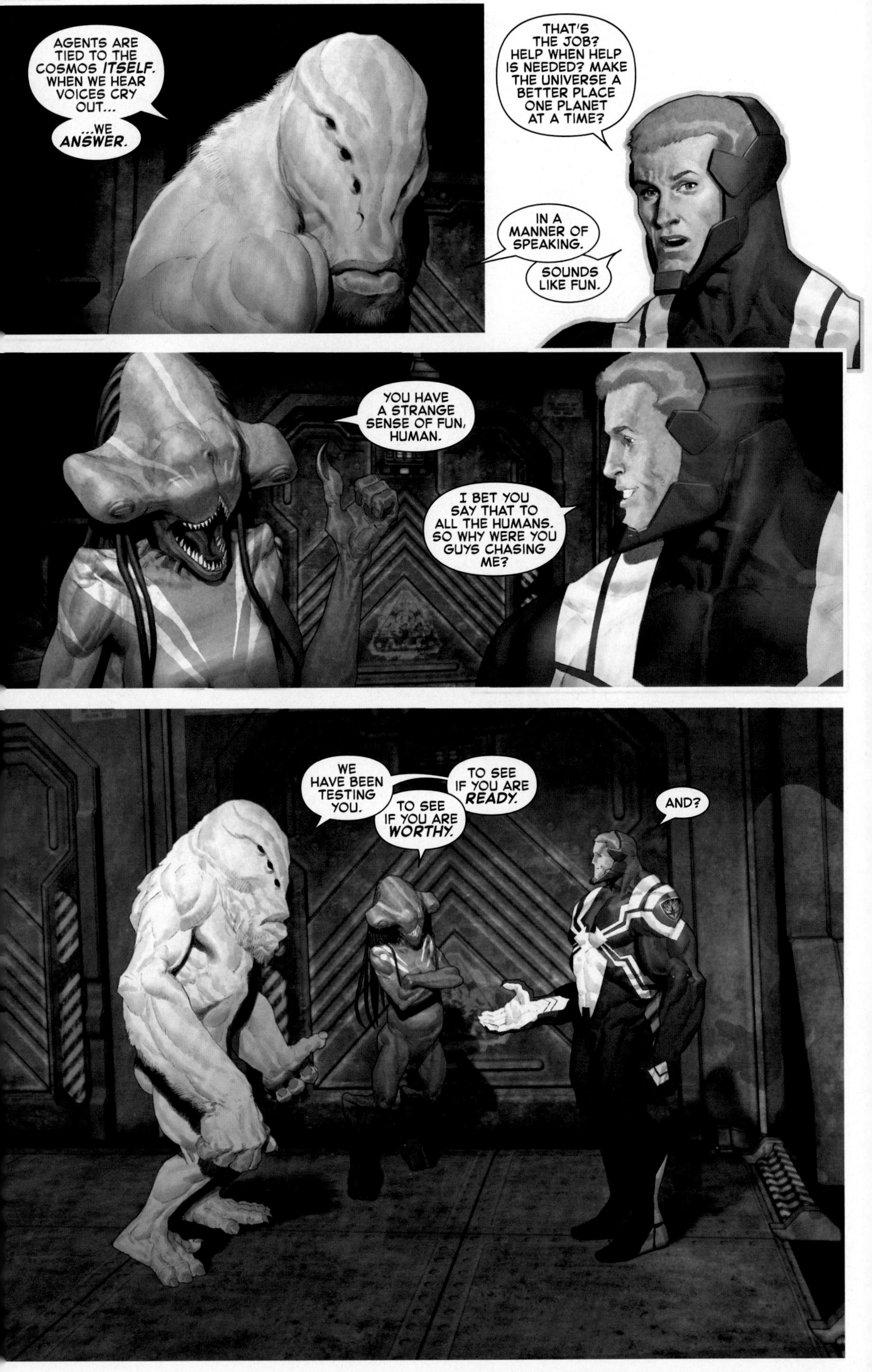
AGENTS ARE TIED TO THE COSMOS *ITSELF.* WHEN WE HEAR VOICES CRY OUT...
...WE *ANSWER.*
THAT'S THE JOB? HELP WHEN HELP IS NEEDED? MAKE THE UNIVERSE A BETTER PLACE ONE PLANET AT A TIME?
IN A MANNER OF SPEAKING.
SOUNDS LIKE FUN.
YOU HAVE A STRANGE SENSE OF FUN, HUMAN.
I BET YOU SAY THAT TO ALL THE HUMANS. SO WHY WERE YOU GUYS CHASING ME?
WE HAVE BEEN TESTING YOU.
TO SEE IF YOU ARE *READY.*
TO SEE IF YOU ARE *WORTHY.*
AND?

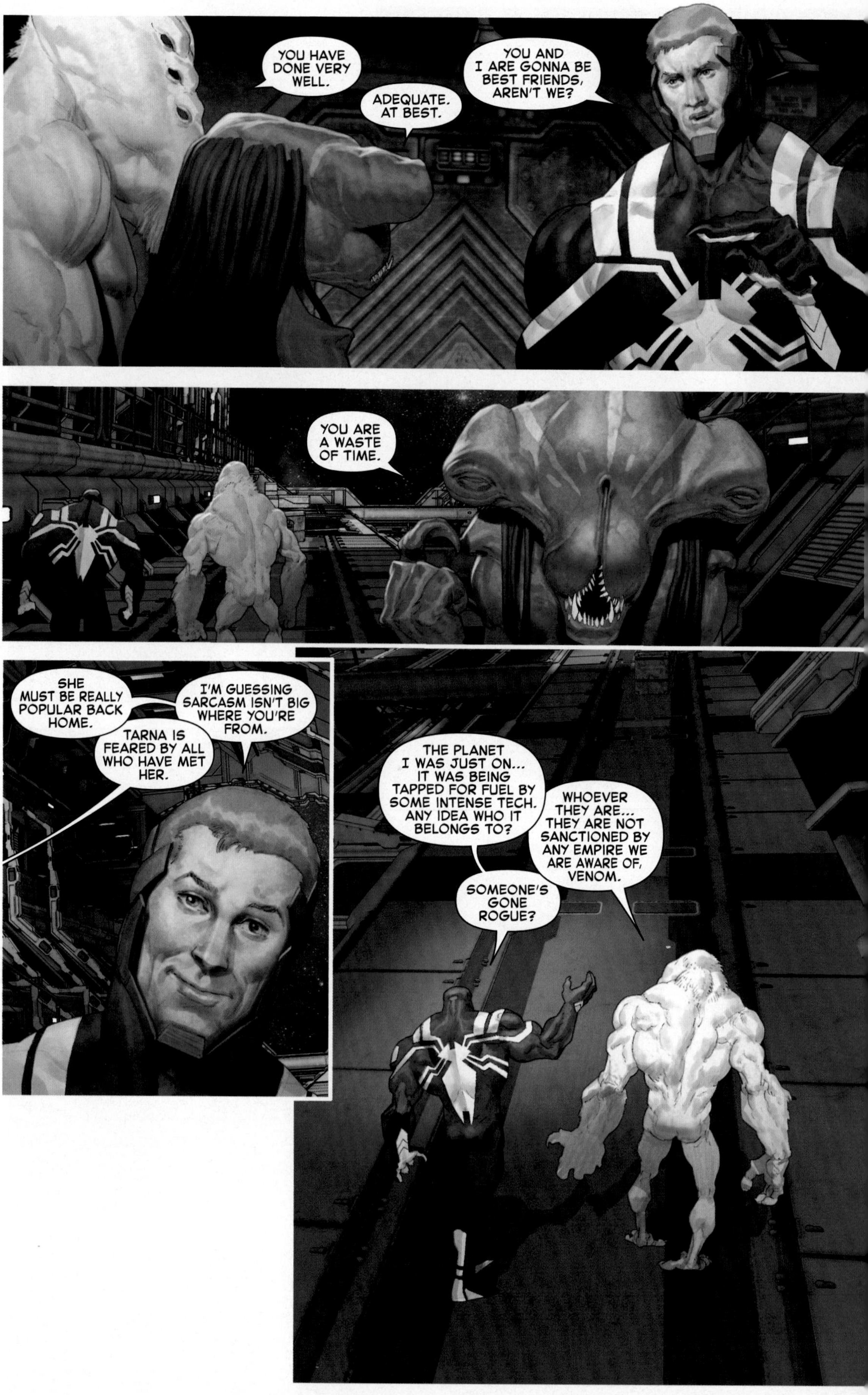

YOU HAVE DONE VERY WELL.
ADEQUATE. AT BEST.
YOU AND I ARE GONNA BE BEST FRIENDS, AREN'T WE?
YOU ARE A WASTE OF TIME.
SHE MUST BE REALLY POPULAR BACK HOME.
I'M GUESSING SARCASM ISN'T BIG WHERE YOU'RE FROM.
TARNA IS FEARED BY ALL WHO HAVE MET HER.
THE PLANET I WAS JUST ON... IT WAS BEING TAPPED FOR FUEL BY SOME INTENSE TECH. ANY IDEA WHO IT BELONGS TO?
WHOEVER THEY ARE... THEY ARE NOT SANCTIONED BY ANY EMPIRE WE ARE AWARE OF, VENOM.
SOMEONE'S GONE ROGUE?

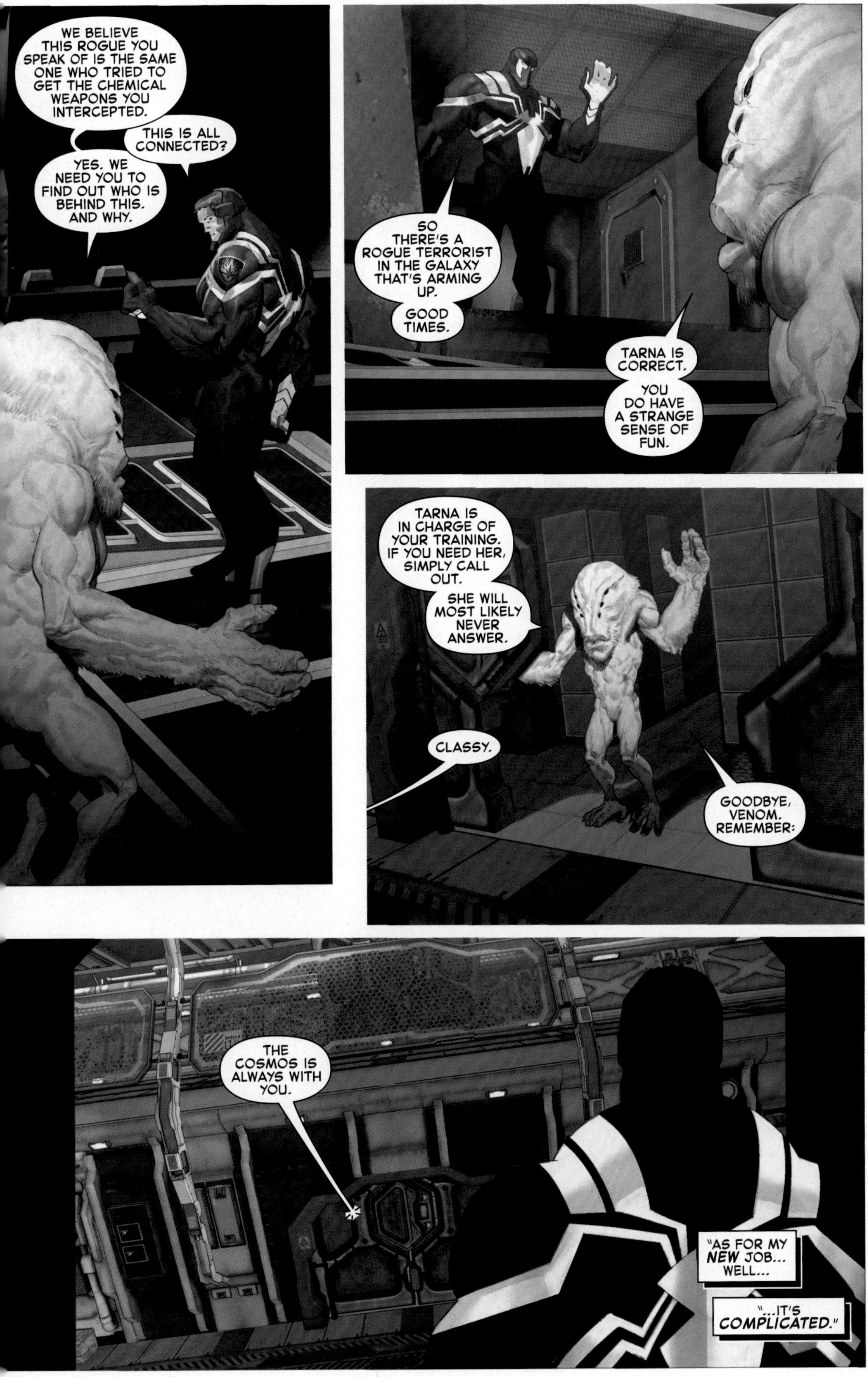
WE BELIEVE THIS ROGUE YOU SPEAK OF IS THE SAME ONE WHO TRIED TO GET THE CHEMICAL WEAPONS YOU INTERCEPTED.
THIS IS ALL CONNECTED?
YES. WE NEED YOU TO FIND OUT WHO IS BEHIND THIS. AND WHY.
SO THERE'S A ROGUE TERRORIST IN THE GALAXY THAT'S ARMING UP.
GOOD TIMES.
TARNA IS CORRECT.
YOU DO HAVE A STRANGE SENSE OF FUN.
TARNA IS IN CHARGE OF YOUR TRAINING. IF YOU NEED HER, SIMPLY CALL OUT.
SHE WILL MOST LIKELY NEVER ANSWER.
CLASSY.
GOODBYE, VENOM. REMEMBER:
THE COSMOS IS ALWAYS WITH YOU.
"AS FOR MY NEW JOB... WELL...
"...IT'S COMPLICATED."

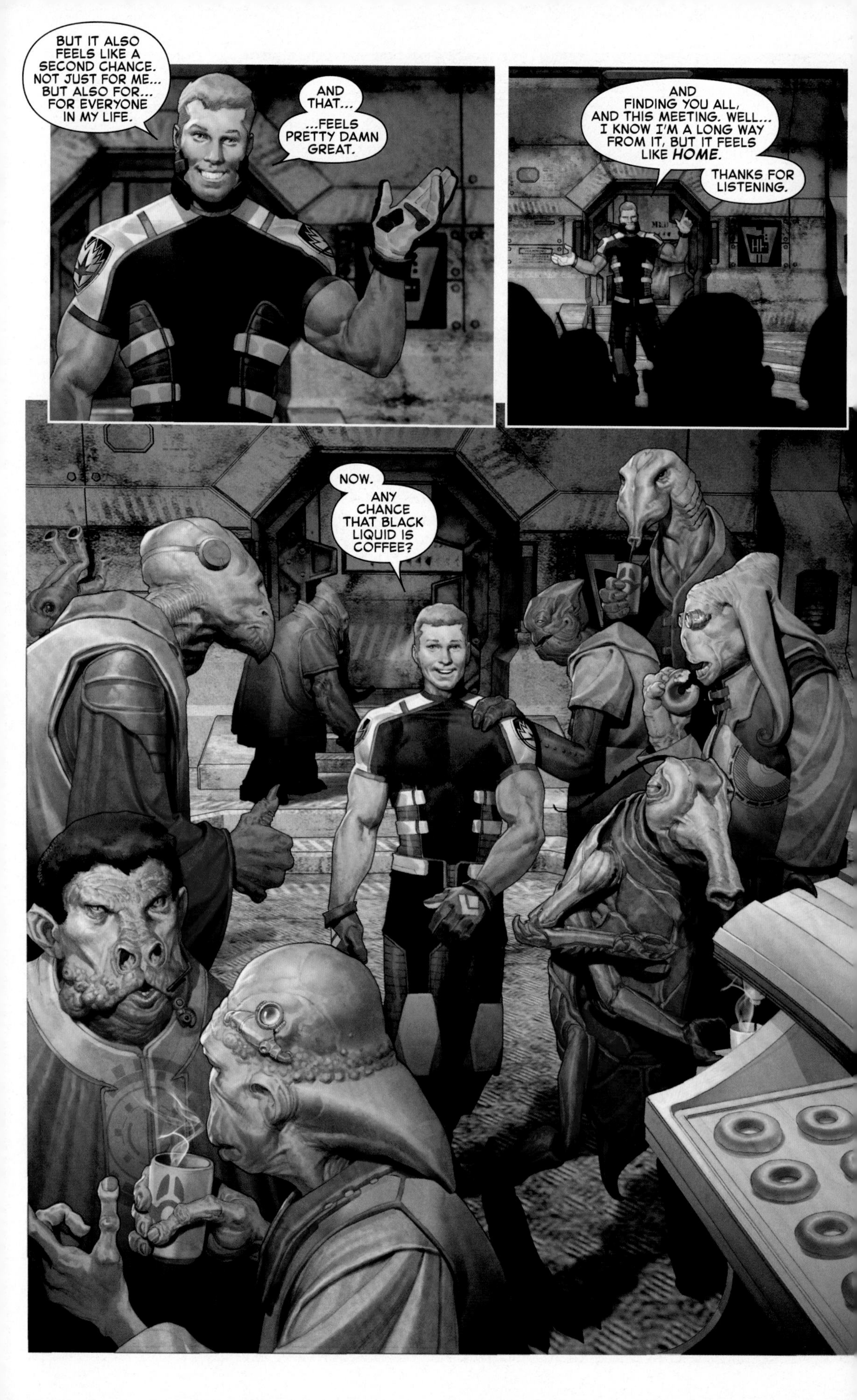
BUT IT ALSO FEELS LIKE A SECOND CHANCE. NOT JUST FOR ME... BUT ALSO FOR... FOR EVERYONE IN MY LIFE.
AND THAT...
...FEELS PRETTY DAMN GREAT.
AND FINDING YOU ALL, AND THIS MEETING. WELL... I KNOW I'M A LONG WAY FROM IT, BUT IT FEELS LIKE HOME.
THANKS FOR LISTENING.
NOW.
ANY CHANCE THAT BLACK LIQUID IS COFFEE?

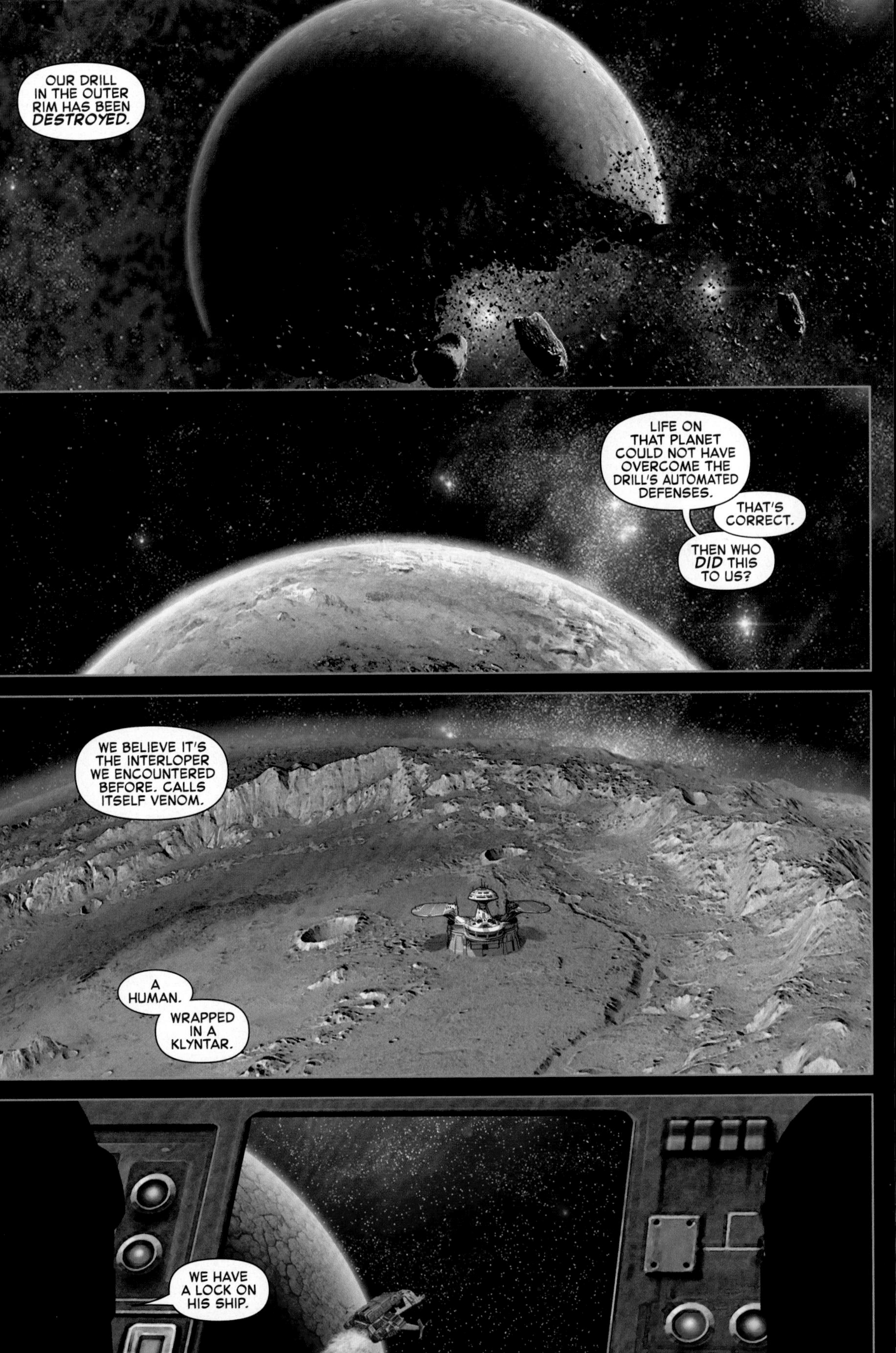
OUR DRILL IN THE OUTER RIM HAS BEEN DESTROYED.
LIFE ON THAT PLANET COULD NOT HAVE OVERCOME THE DRILL'S AUTOMATED DEFENSES.
THAT'S CORRECT.
THEN WHO DID THIS TO US?
WE BELIEVE IT'S THE INTERLOPER WE ENCOUNTERED BEFORE. CALLS ITSELF VENOM.
A HUMAN.
WRAPPED IN A KLYNTAR.
WE HAVE A LOCK ON HIS SHIP.

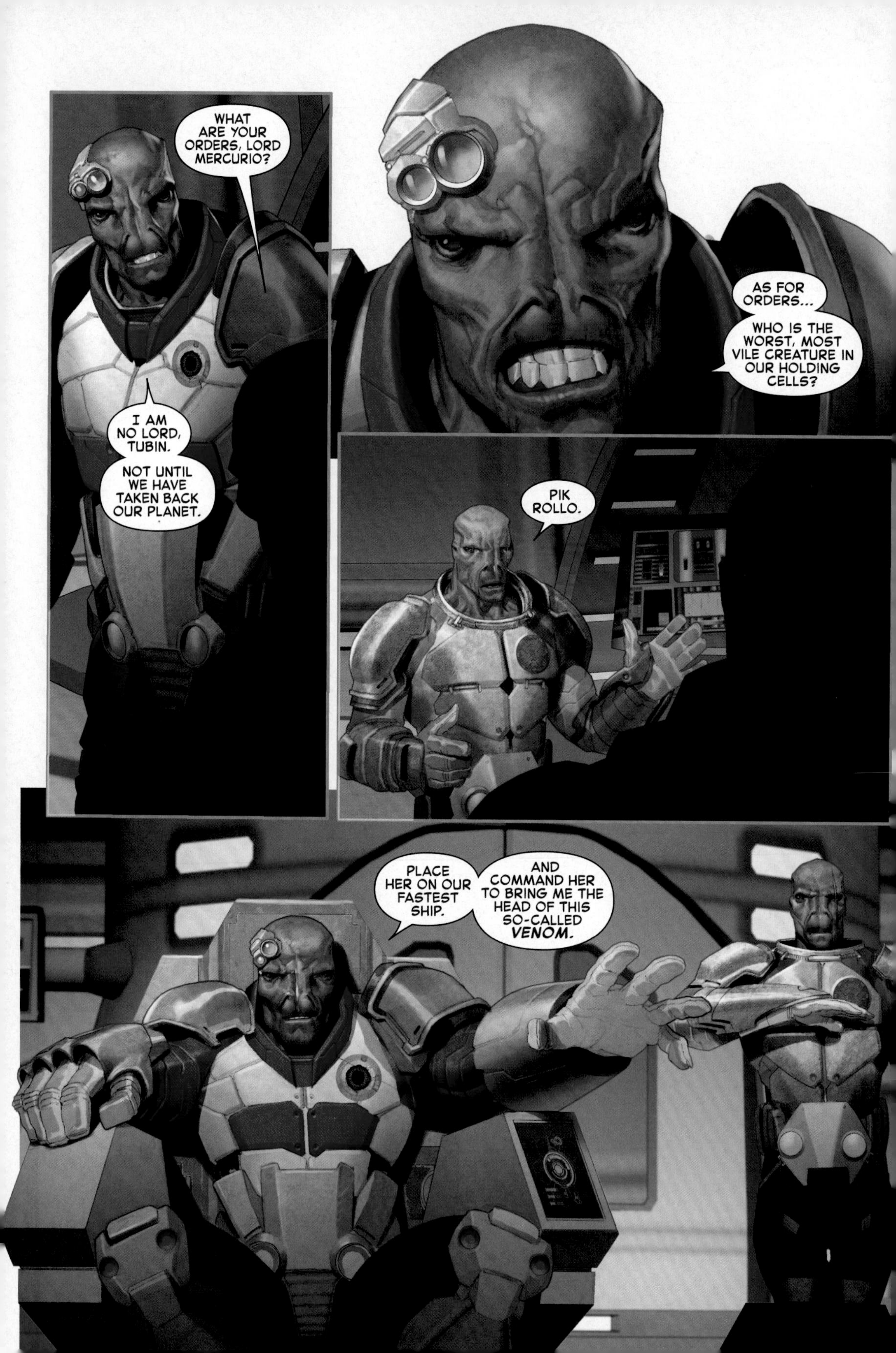
WHAT ARE YOUR ORDERS, LORD MERCURIO?
I AM NO LORD, TUBIN.
NOT UNTIL WE HAVE TAKEN BACK OUR PLANET.
AS FOR ORDERS...
WHO IS THE WORST, MOST VILE CREATURE IN OUR HOLDING CELLS?
PIK ROLLO.
PLACE HER ON OUR FASTEST SHIP.
AND COMMAND HER TO BRING ME THE HEAD OF THIS SO-CALLED *VENOM.*

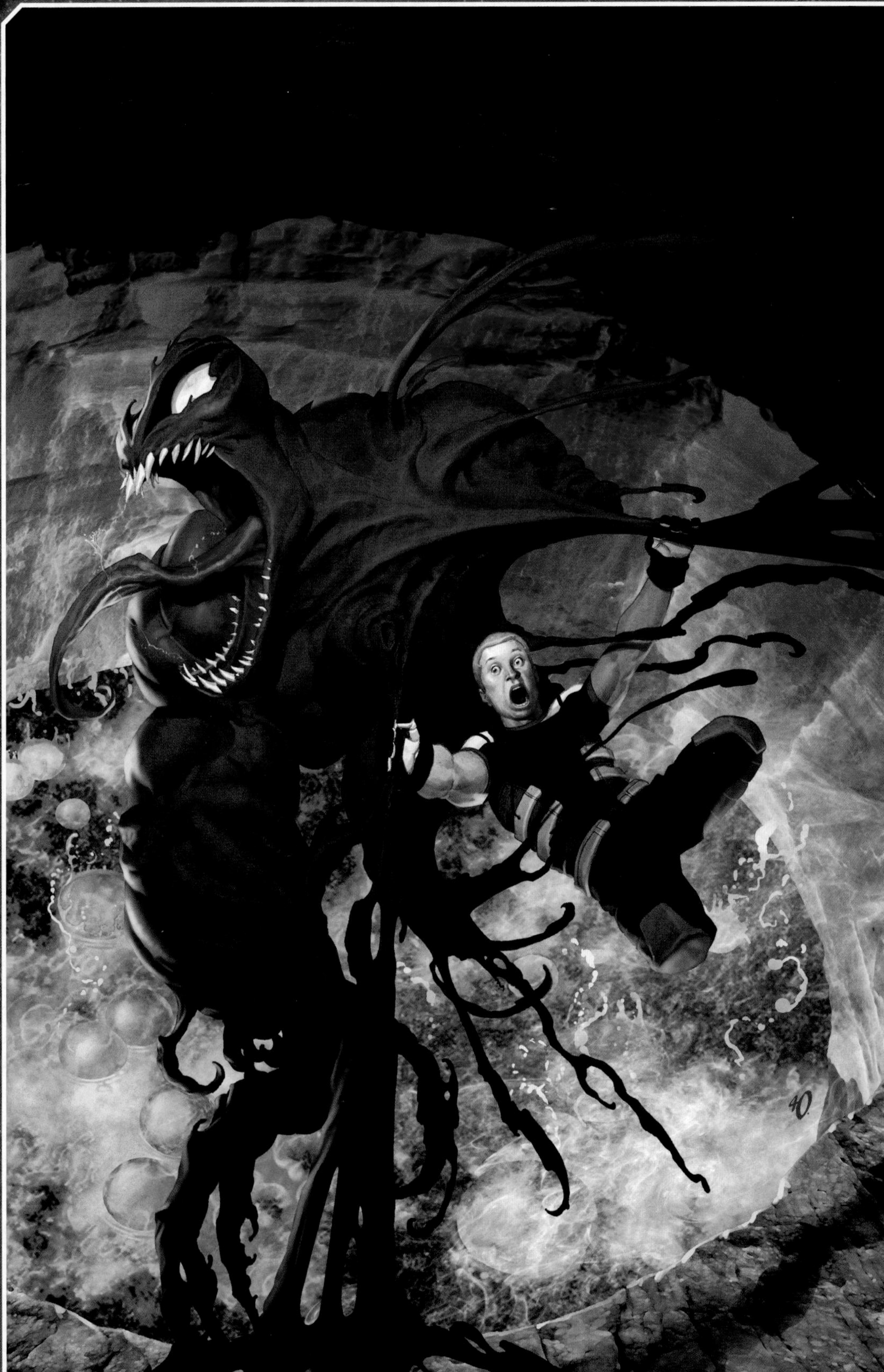

3

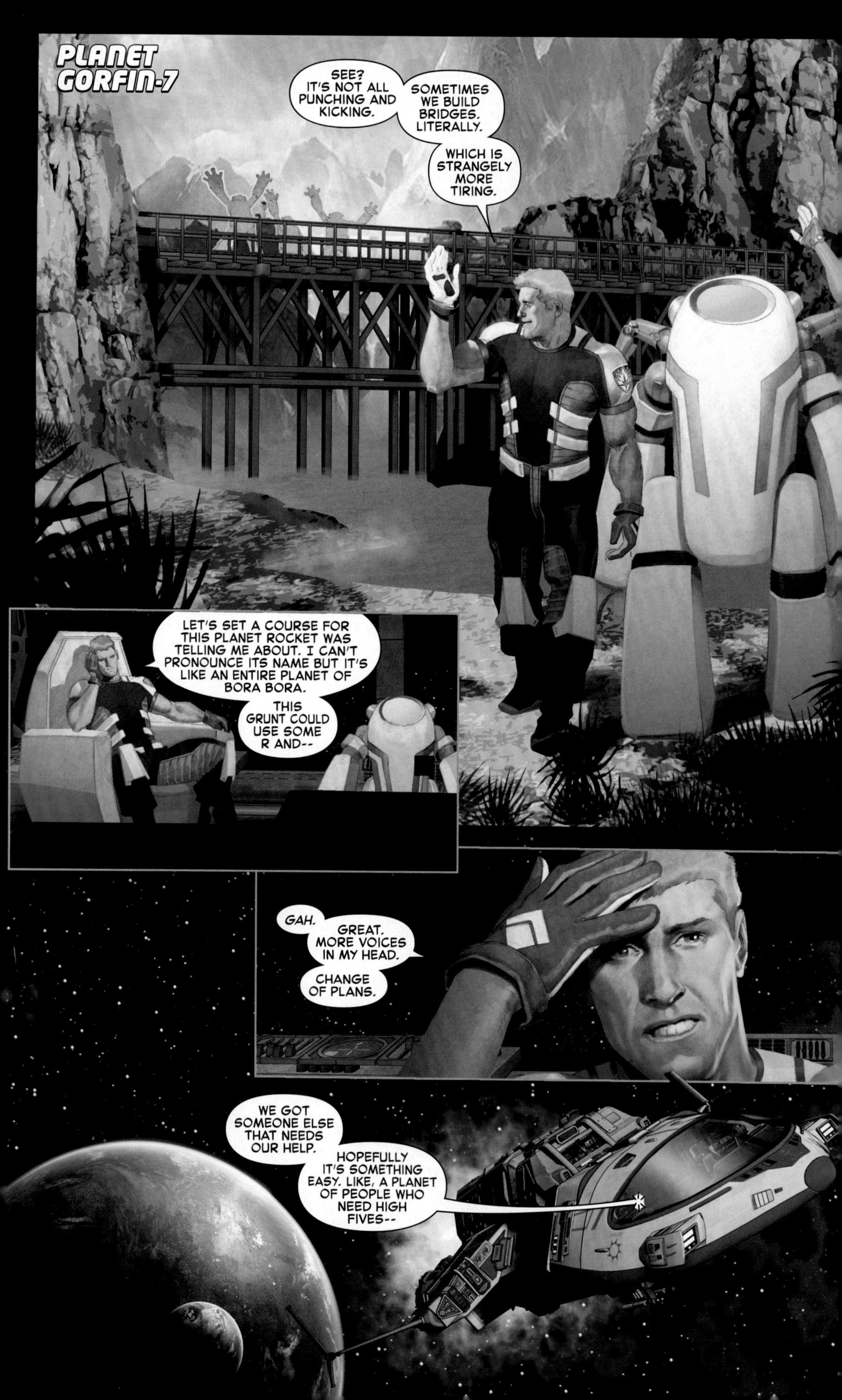
PLANET GORFIN-7
SEE? IT'S NOT ALL PUNCHING AND KICKING.
SOMETIMES WE BUILD BRIDGES. LITERALLY.
WHICH IS STRANGELY MORE TIRING.
LET'S SET A COURSE FOR THIS PLANET ROCKET WAS TELLING ME ABOUT. I CAN'T PRONOUNCE ITS NAME BUT IT'S LIKE AN ENTIRE PLANET OF BORA BORA.
THIS GRUNT COULD USE SOME R AND--
GAH.
GREAT. MORE VOICES IN MY HEAD.
CHANGE OF PLANS.
WE GOT SOMEONE ELSE THAT NEEDS OUR HELP.
HOPEFULLY IT'S SOMETHING EASY. LIKE, A PLANET OF PEOPLE WHO NEED HIGH FIVES--

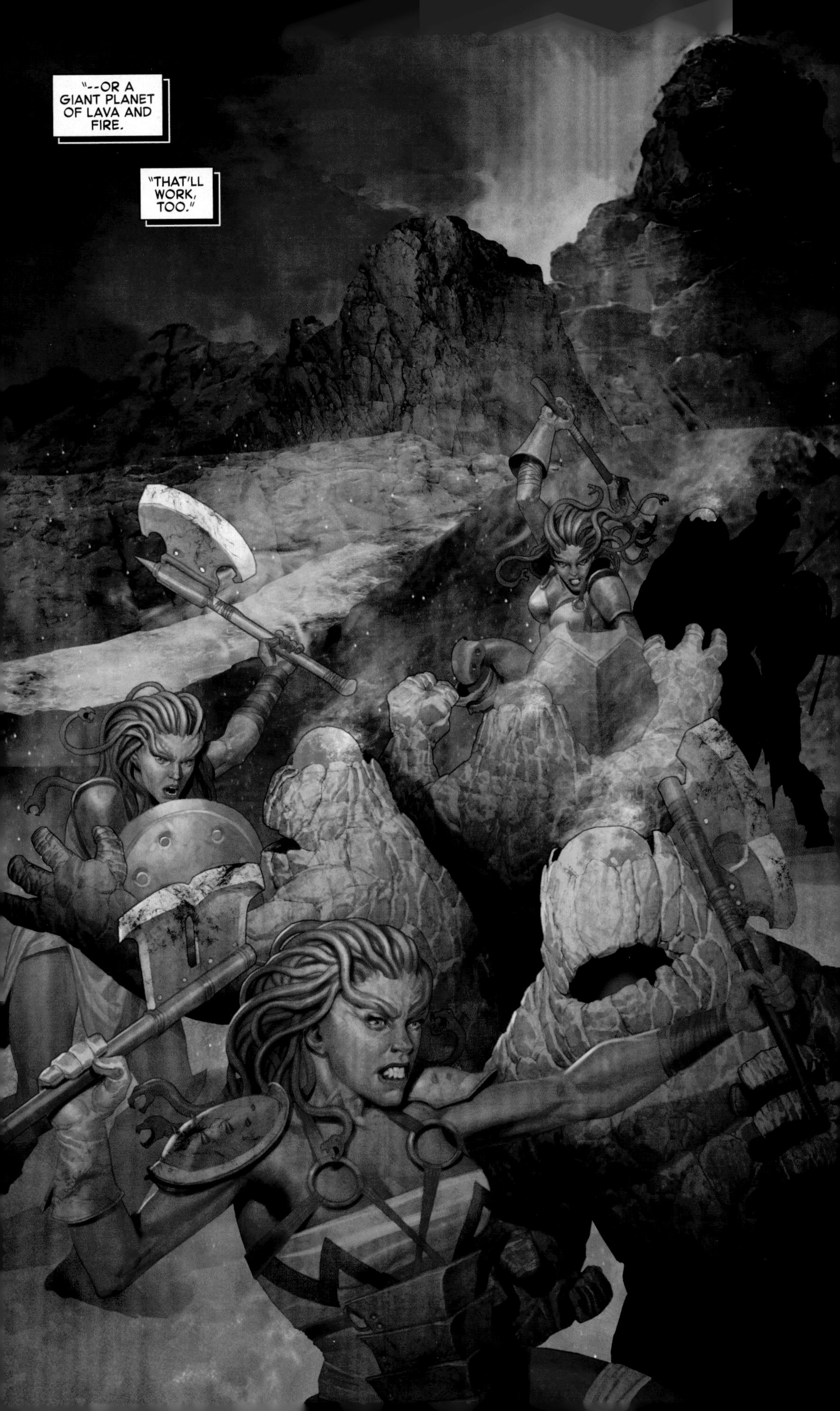
"--OR A GIANT PLANET OF LAVA AND FIRE.
"THAT'LL WORK, TOO."

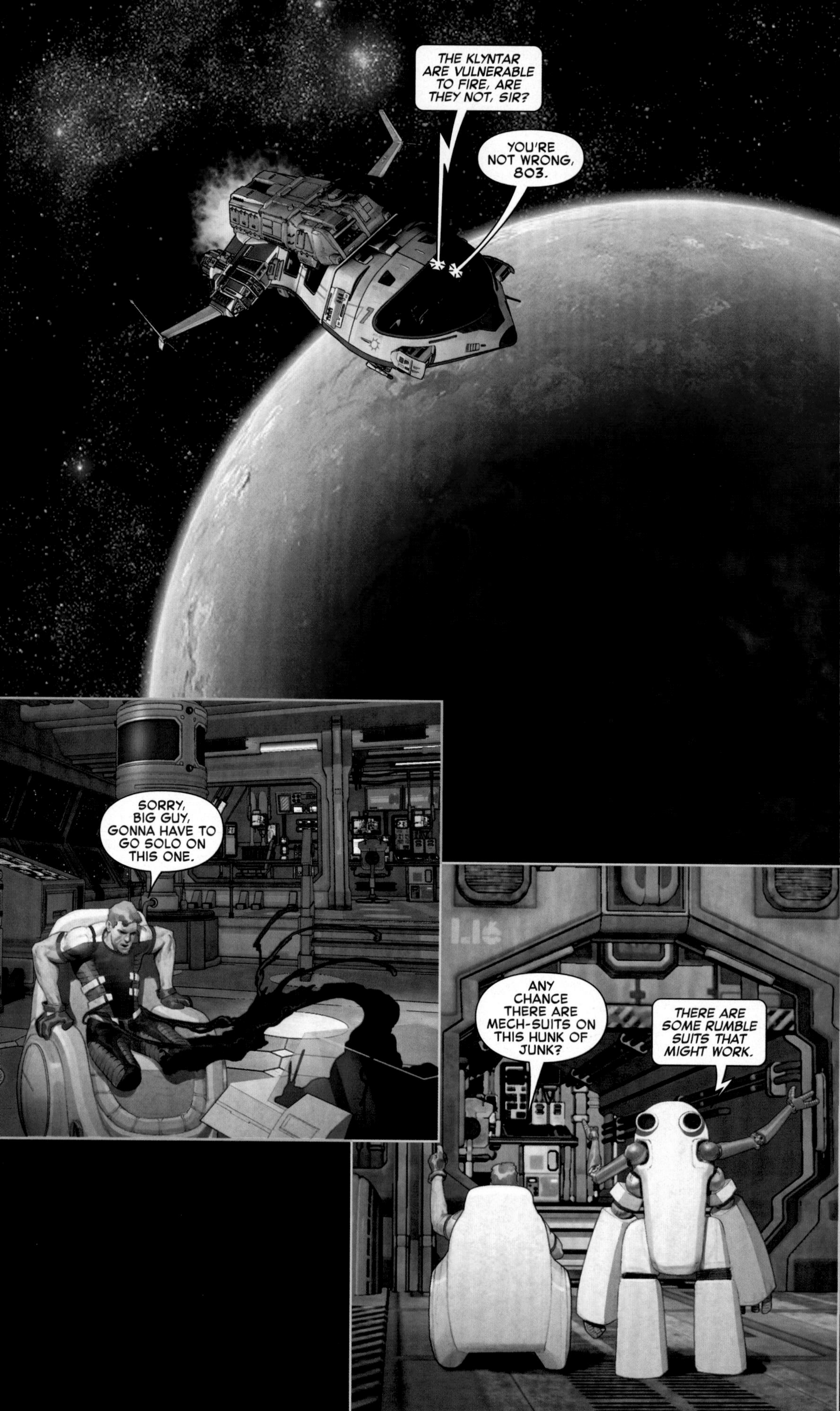
THE KLYNTAR ARE VULNERABLE TO FIRE, ARE THEY NOT, SIR?
YOU'RE NOT WRONG, 803.
SORRY, BIG GUY, GONNA HAVE TO GO SOLO ON THIS ONE.
ANY CHANCE THERE ARE MECH-SUITS ON THIS HUNK OF JUNK?
THERE ARE SOME RUMBLE SUITS THAT MIGHT WORK.

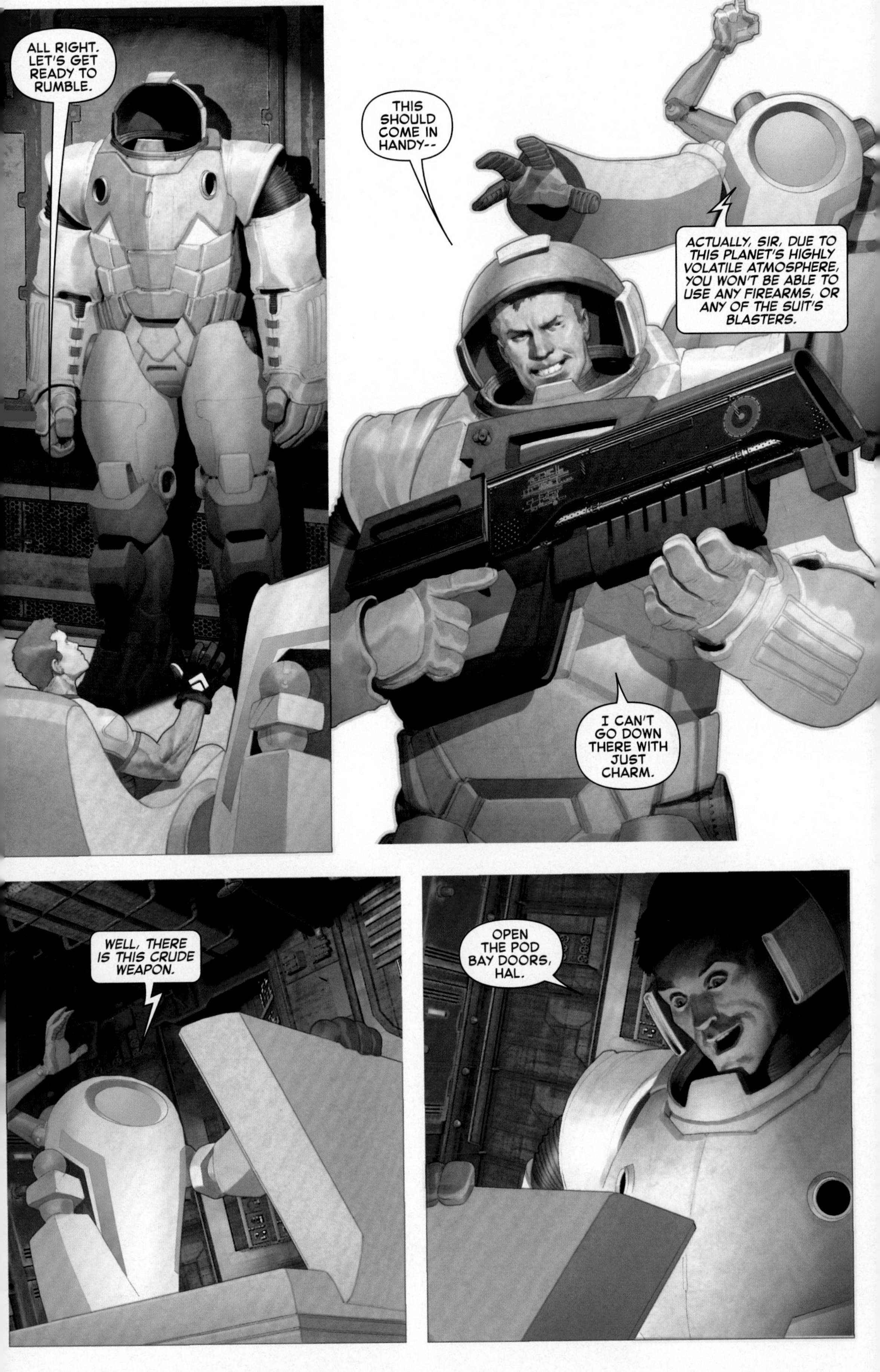
ALL RIGHT. LET'S GET READY TO RUMBLE.
THIS SHOULD COME IN HANDY--
ACTUALLY, SIR, DUE TO THIS PLANET'S HIGHLY VOLATILE ATMOSPHERE, YOU WON'T BE ABLE TO USE ANY FIREARMS, OR ANY OF THE SUIT'S BLASTERS.
I CAN'T GO DOWN THERE WITH JUST CHARM.
WELL, THERE IS THIS CRUDE WEAPON.
OPEN THE POD BAY DOORS, HAL.

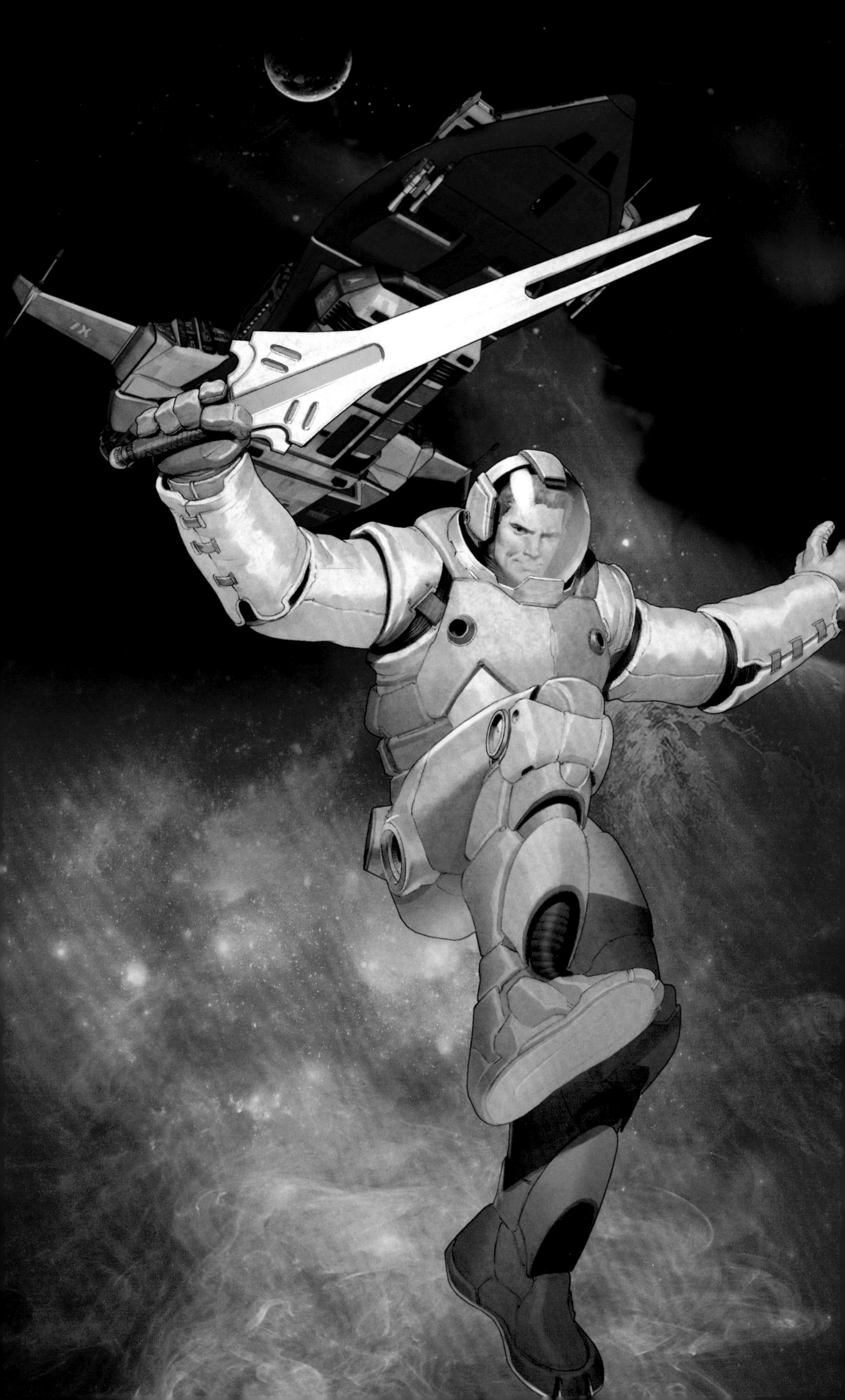

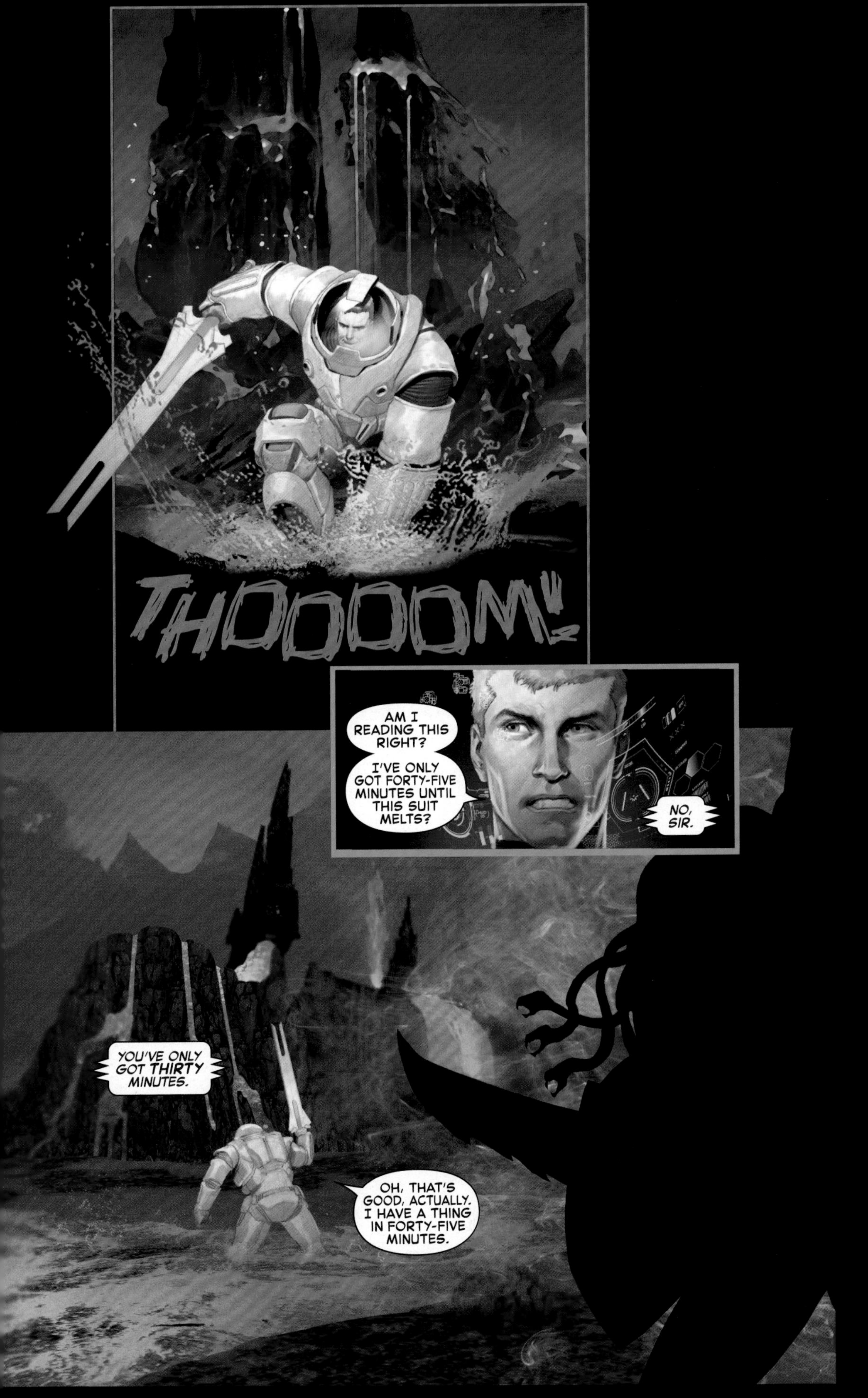
THOOOOM!
AM I READING THIS RIGHT?
I'VE ONLY GOT FORTY-FIVE MINUTES UNTIL THIS SUIT MELTS?
NO, SIR.
YOU'VE ONLY GOT THIRTY MINUTES.
OH, THAT'S GOOD, ACTUALLY. I HAVE A THING IN FORTY-FIVE MINUTES.

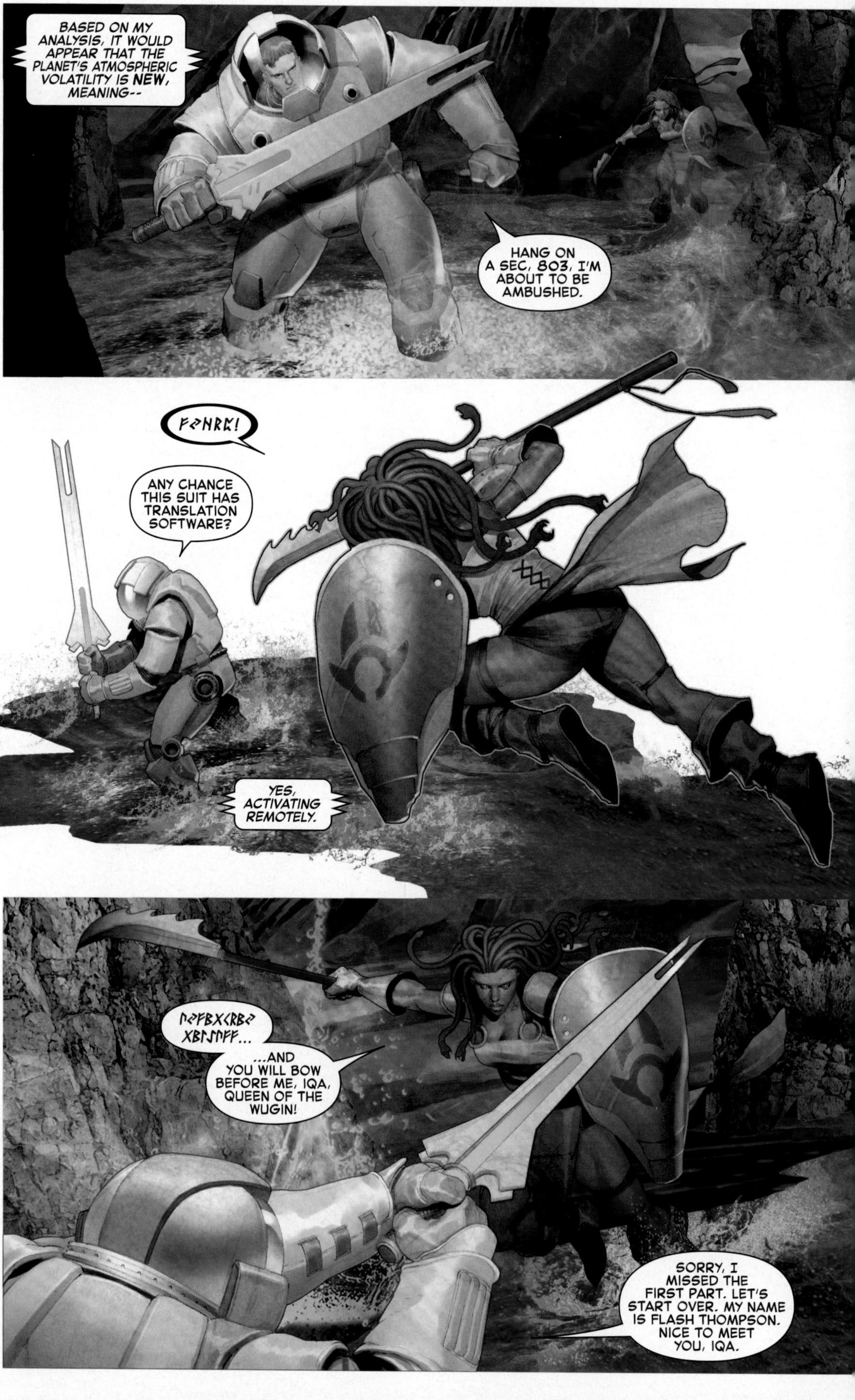
BASED ON MY ANALYSIS, IT WOULD APPEAR THAT THE PLANET'S ATMOSPHERIC VOLATILITY IS NEW, MEANING--
HANG ON A SEC, 803, I'M ABOUT TO BE AMBUSHED.
ANY CHANCE THIS SUIT HAS TRANSLATION SOFTWARE?
YES, ACTIVATING REMOTELY.
...AND YOU WILL BOW BEFORE ME, IQA, QUEEN OF THE WUGIN!
SORRY, I MISSED THE FIRST PART. LET'S START OVER. MY NAME IS FLASH THOMPSON. NICE TO MEET YOU, IQA.

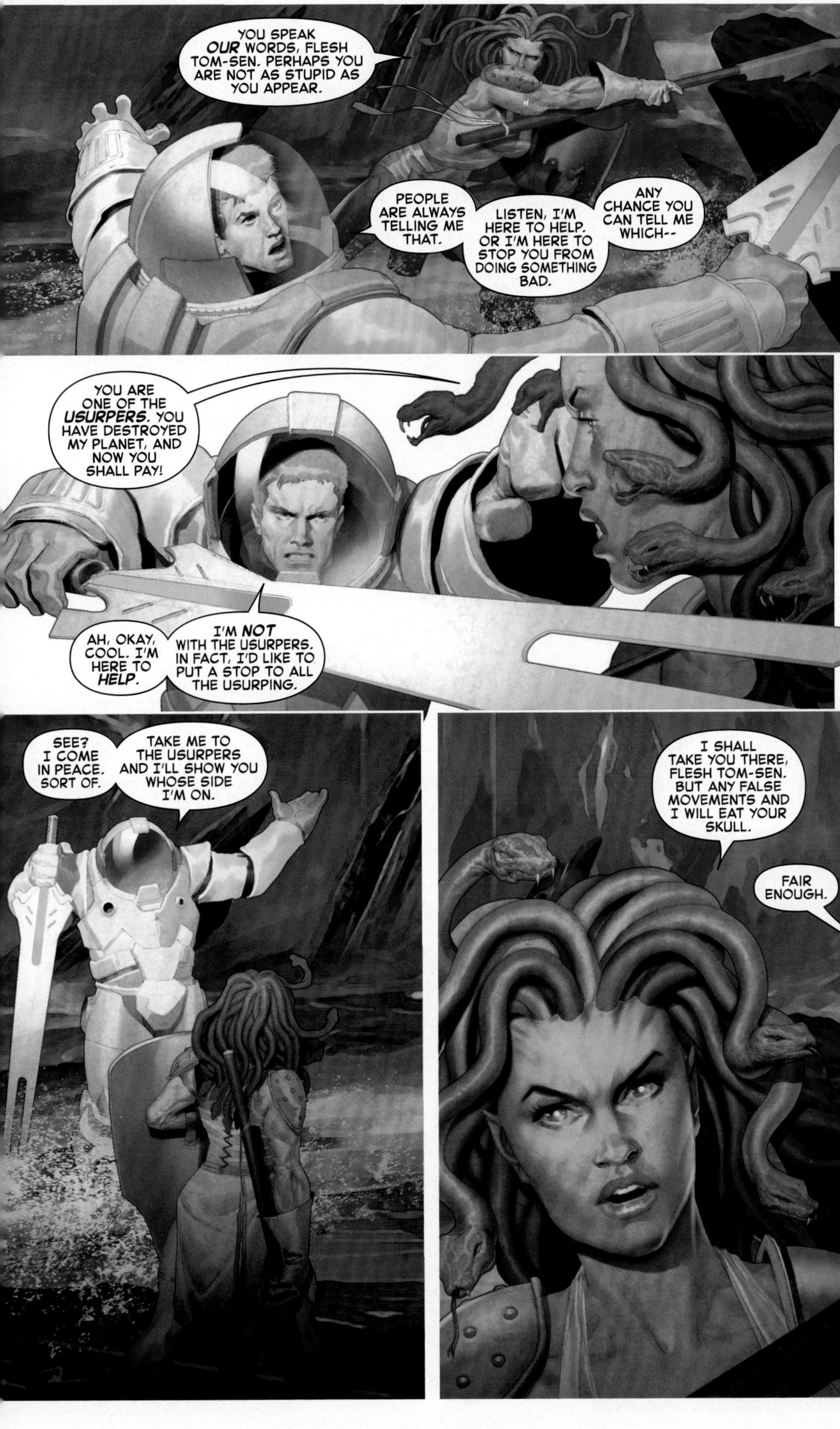

YOU SPEAK OUR WORDS, FLESH TOM-SEN. PERHAPS YOU ARE NOT AS STUPID AS YOU APPEAR.
PEOPLE ARE ALWAYS TELLING ME THAT.
LISTEN, I'M HERE TO HELP. OR I'M HERE TO STOP YOU FROM DOING SOMETHING BAD.
ANY CHANCE YOU CAN TELL ME WHICH--
YOU ARE ONE OF THE USURPERS. YOU HAVE DESTROYED MY PLANET, AND NOW YOU SHALL PAY!
AH, OKAY, COOL. I'M HERE TO HELP.
I'M NOT WITH THE USURPERS. IN FACT, I'D LIKE TO PUT A STOP TO ALL THE USURPING.
SEE? I COME IN PEACE. SORT OF.
TAKE ME TO THE USURPERS AND I'LL SHOW YOU WHOSE SIDE I'M ON.
I SHALL TAKE YOU THERE, FLESH TOM-SEN. BUT ANY FALSE MOVEMENTS AND I WILL EAT YOUR SKULL.
FAIR ENOUGH.

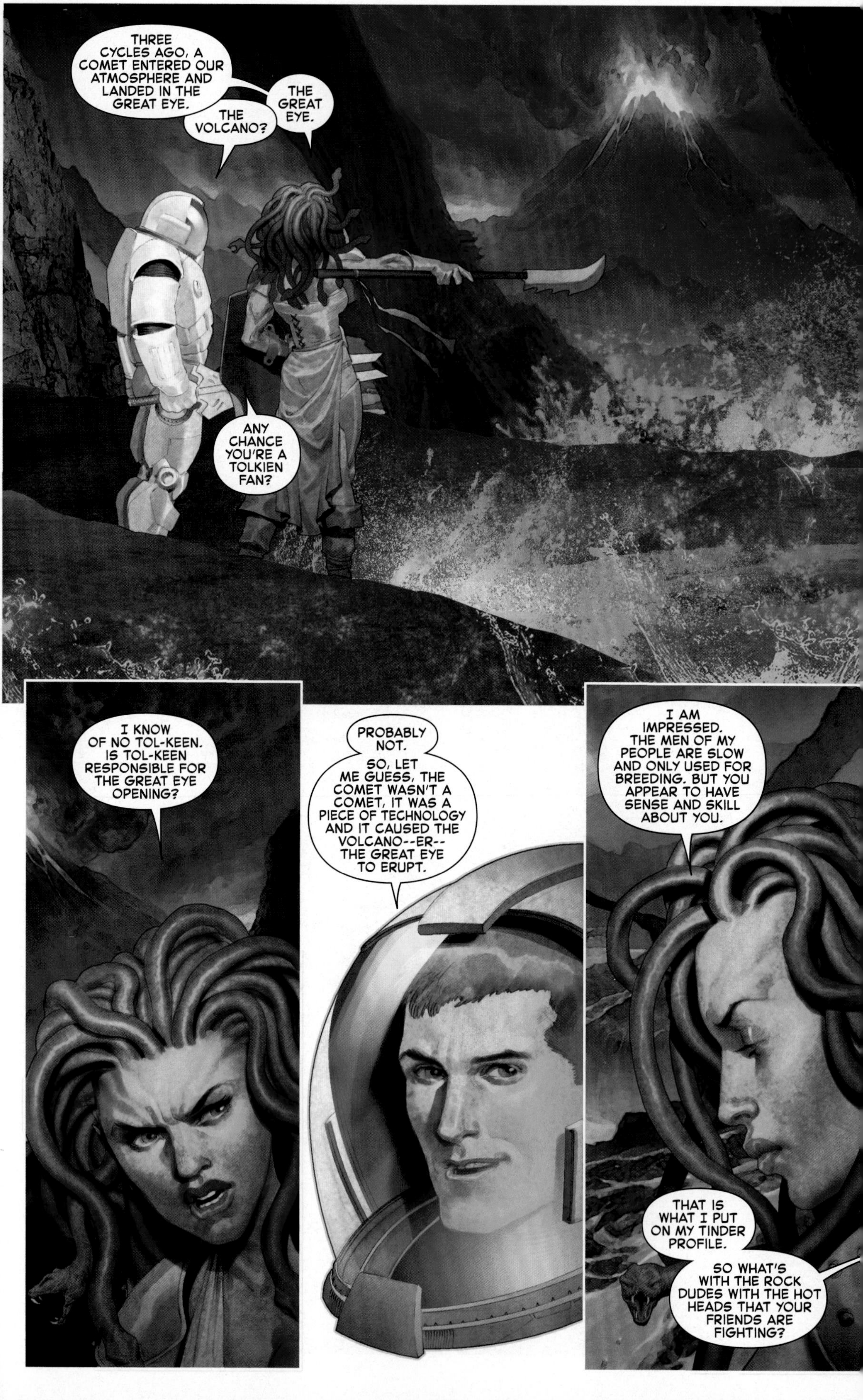
THREE CYCLES AGO, A COMET ENTERED OUR ATMOSPHERE AND LANDED IN THE GREAT EYE.
THE VOLCANO?
THE GREAT EYE.
ANY CHANCE YOU'RE A TOLKIEN FAN?
I KNOW OF NO TOL-KEEN. IS TOL-KEEN RESPONSIBLE FOR THE GREAT EYE OPENING?
PROBABLY NOT.
SO, LET ME GUESS, THE COMET WASN'T A COMET, IT WAS A PIECE OF TECHNOLOGY AND IT CAUSED THE VOLCANO--ER-- THE GREAT EYE TO ERUPT.
I AM IMPRESSED. THE MEN OF MY PEOPLE ARE SLOW AND ONLY USED FOR BREEDING. BUT YOU APPEAR TO HAVE SENSE AND SKILL ABOUT YOU.
THAT IS WHAT I PUT ON MY TINDER PROFILE.
SO WHAT'S WITH THE ROCK DUDES WITH THE HOT HEADS THAT YOUR FRIENDS ARE FIGHTING?

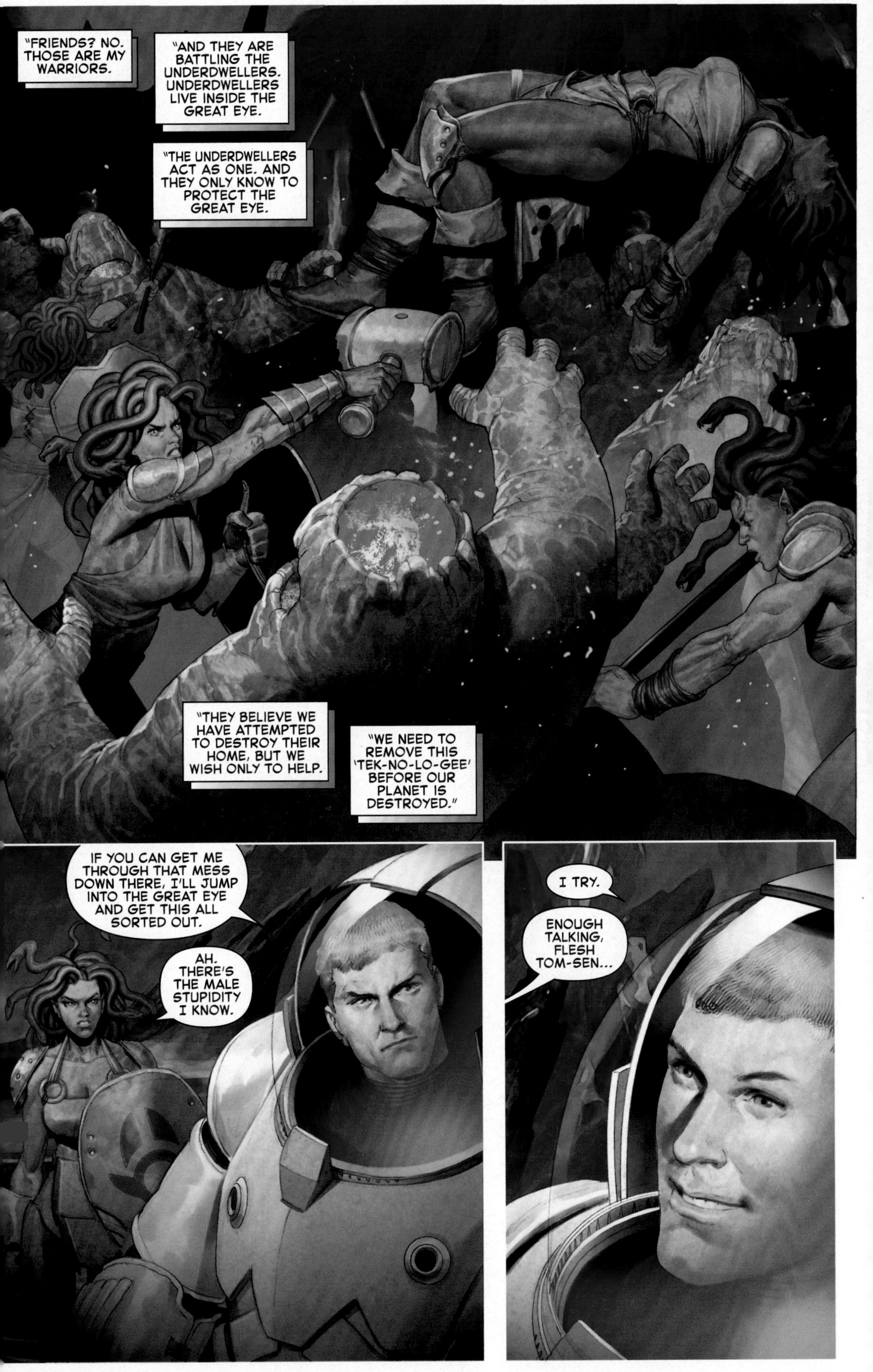
"FRIENDS? NO. THOSE ARE MY WARRIORS.
"AND THEY ARE BATTLING THE UNDERDWELLERS. UNDERDWELLERS LIVE INSIDE THE GREAT EYE.
"THE UNDERDWELLERS ACT AS ONE. AND THEY ONLY KNOW TO PROTECT THE GREAT EYE.
"THEY BELIEVE WE HAVE ATTEMPTED TO DESTROY THEIR HOME, BUT WE WISH ONLY TO HELP.
"WE NEED TO REMOVE THIS 'TEK-NO-LO-GEE' BEFORE OUR PLANET IS DESTROYED."
IF YOU CAN GET ME THROUGH THAT MESS DOWN THERE, I'LL JUMP INTO THE GREAT EYE AND GET THIS ALL SORTED OUT.
AH. THERE'S THE MALE STUPIDITY I KNOW.
I TRY.
ENOUGH TALKING, FLESH TOM-SEN...

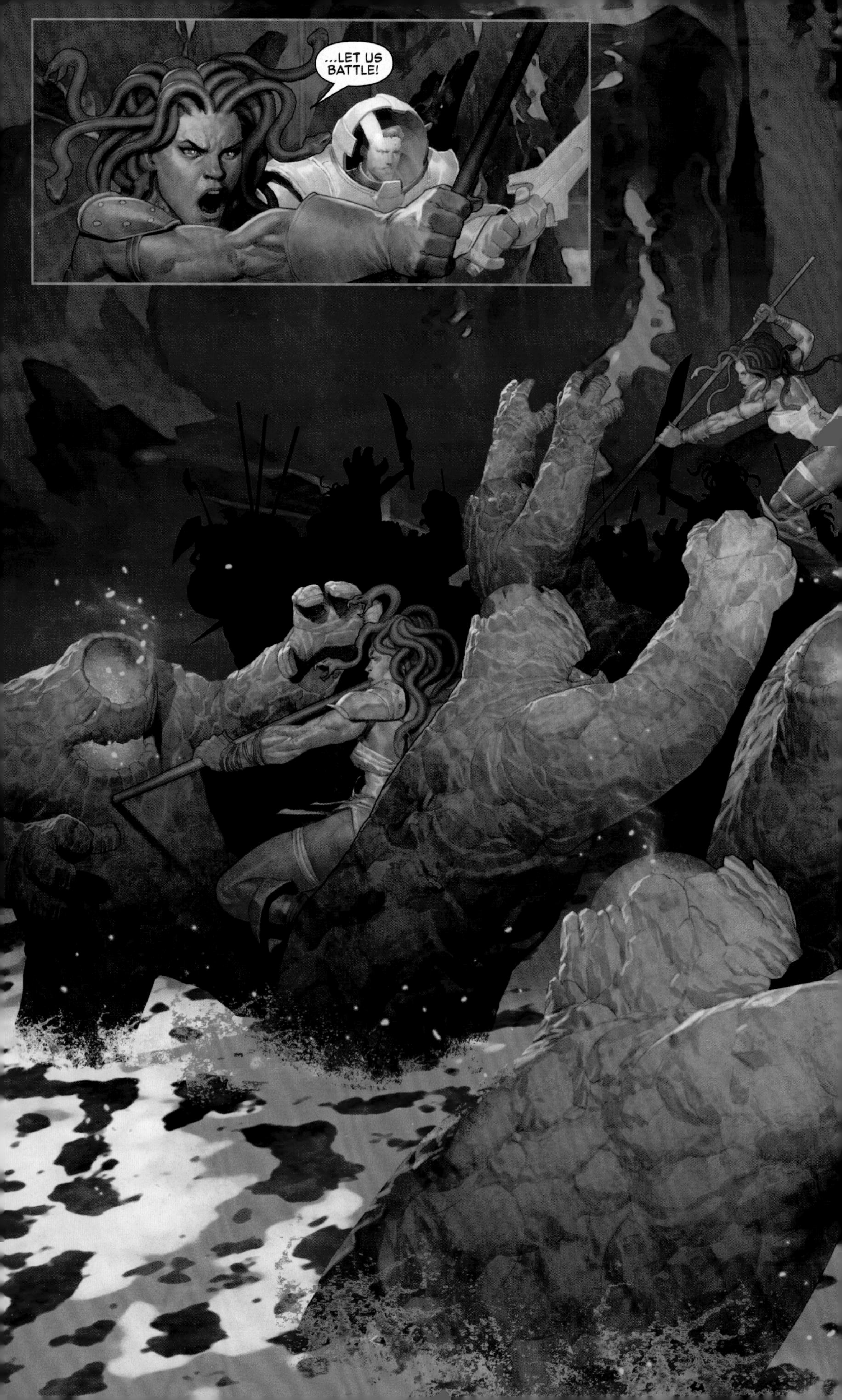
...LET US BATTLE!

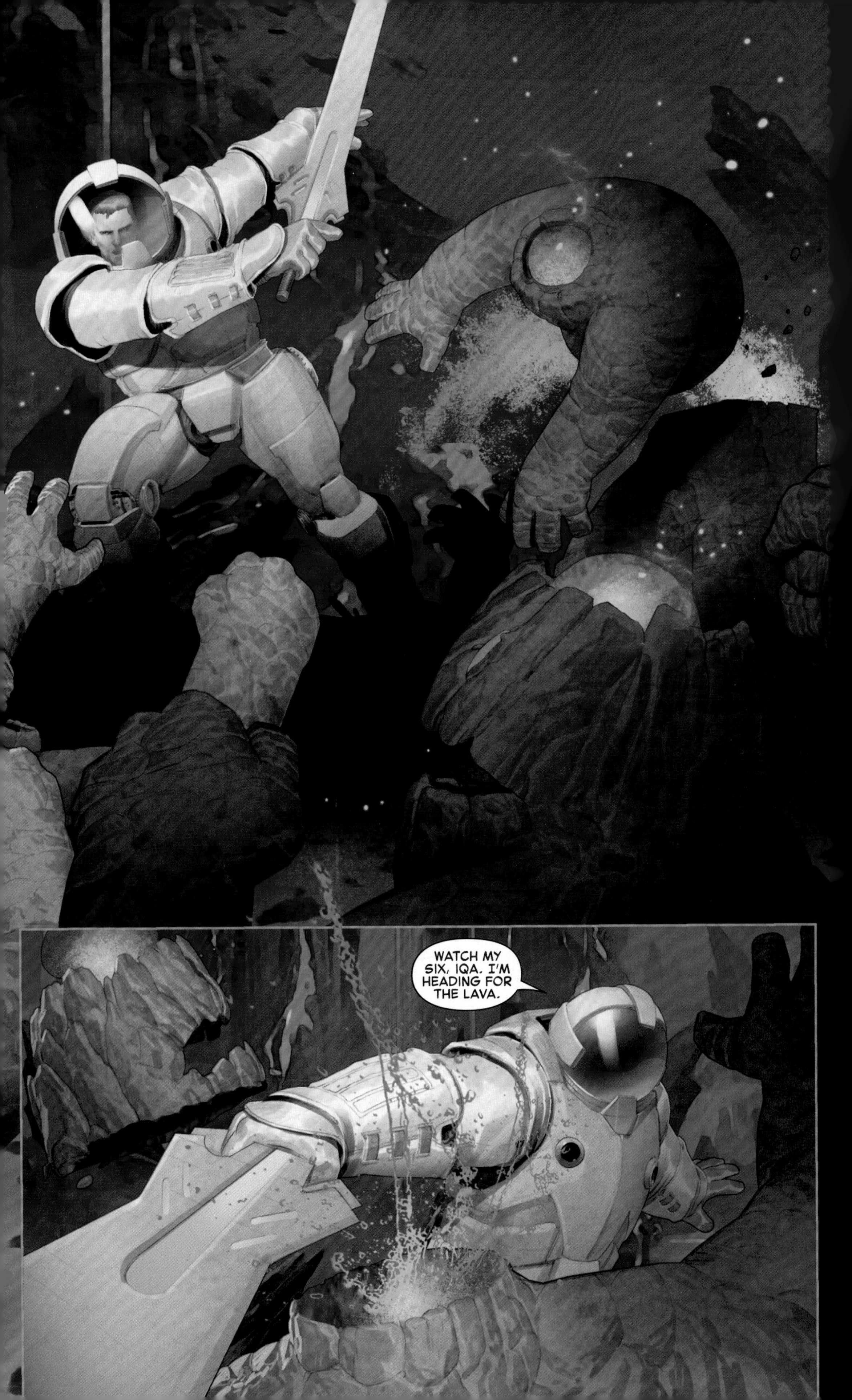
WATCH MY SIX, IQA. I'M HEADING FOR THE LAVA.

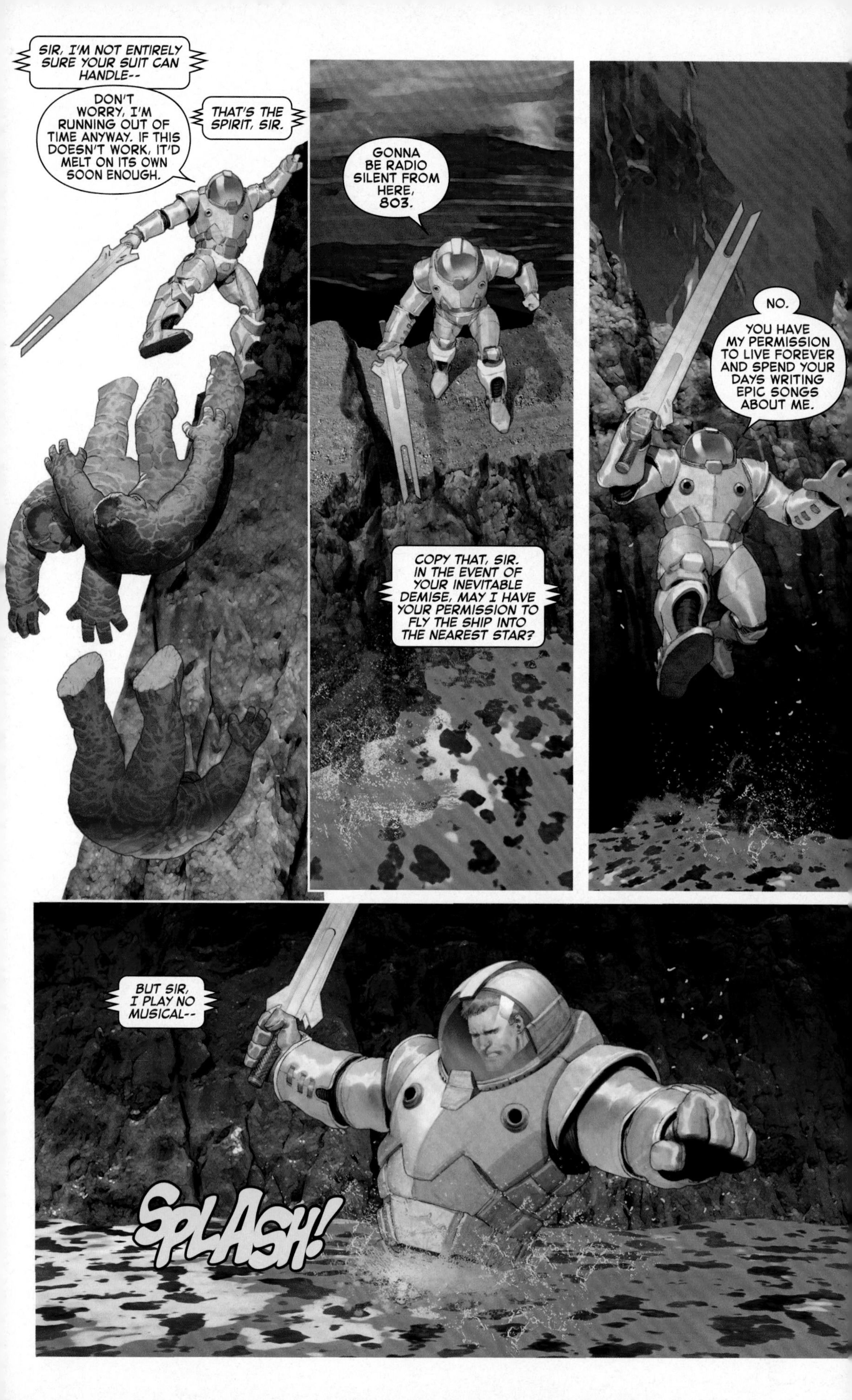
SIR, I'M NOT ENTIRELY SURE YOUR SUIT CAN HANDLE--
DON'T WORRY, I'M RUNNING OUT OF TIME ANYWAY. IF THIS DOESN'T WORK, IT'D MELT ON ITS OWN SOON ENOUGH.
THAT'S THE SPIRIT, SIR.
GONNA BE RADIO SILENT FROM HERE, 803.
COPY THAT, SIR. IN THE EVENT OF YOUR INEVITABLE DEMISE, MAY I HAVE YOUR PERMISSION TO FLY THE SHIP INTO THE NEAREST STAR?
NO.
YOU HAVE MY PERMISSION TO LIVE FOREVER AND SPEND YOUR DAYS WRITING EPIC SONGS ABOUT ME.
BUT SIR, I PLAY NO MUSICAL--
SPLASH!

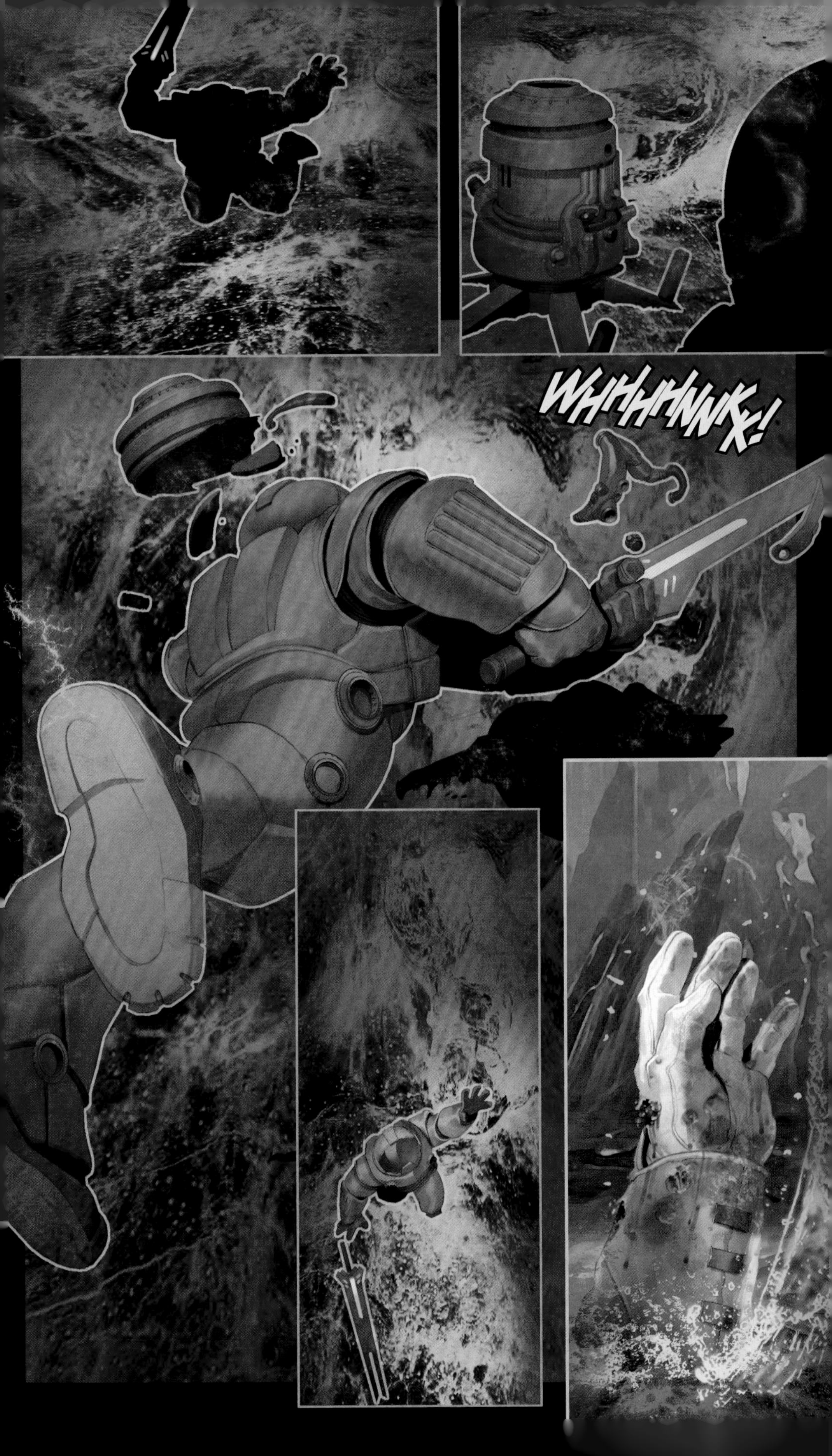
WHHHHNNKK!

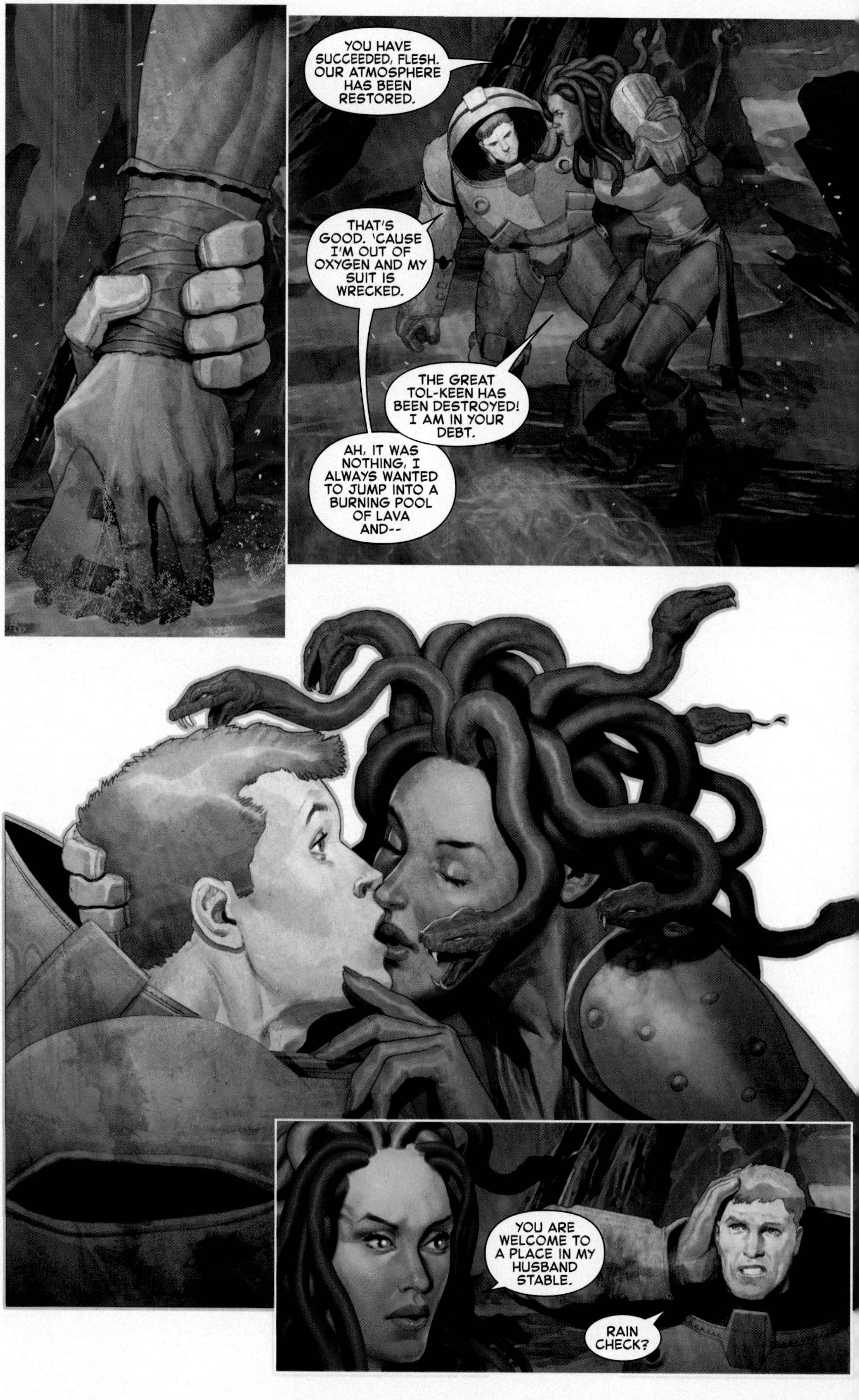
YOU HAVE SUCCEEDED, FLESH. OUR ATMOSPHERE HAS BEEN RESTORED.
THAT'S GOOD. 'CAUSE I'M OUT OF OXYGEN AND MY SUIT IS WRECKED.
THE GREAT TOL-KEEN HAS BEEN DESTROYED! I AM IN YOUR DEBT.
AH, IT WAS NOTHING, I ALWAYS WANTED TO JUMP INTO A BURNING POOL OF LAVA AND--
YOU ARE WELCOME TO A PLACE IN MY HUSBAND STABLE.
RAIN CHECK?

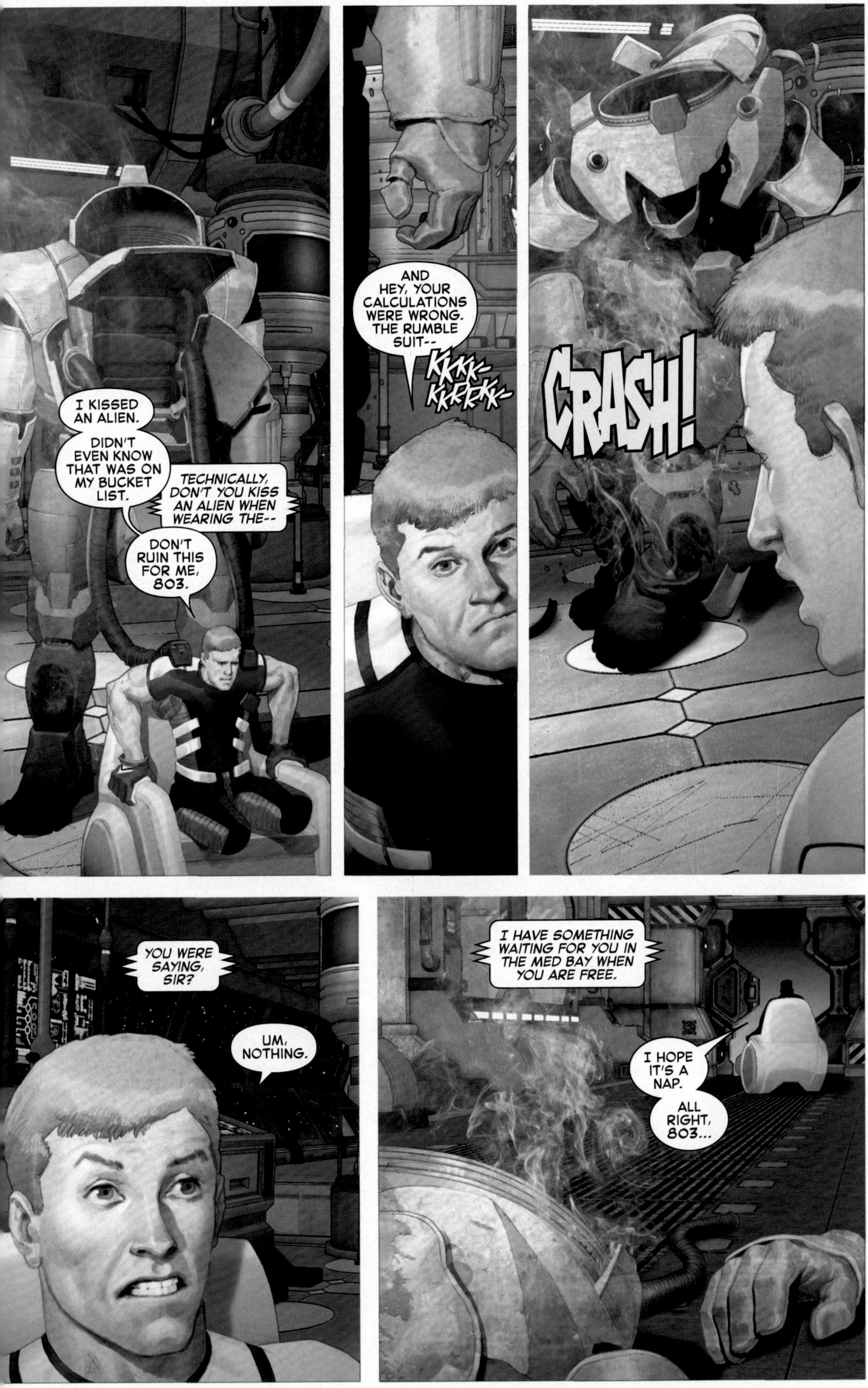

I KISSED AN ALIEN.
DIDN'T EVEN KNOW THAT WAS ON MY BUCKET LIST.
TECHNICALLY, DON'T YOU KISS AN ALIEN WHEN WEARING THE--
DON'T RUIN THIS FOR ME, 803.
AND HEY, YOUR CALCULATIONS WERE WRONG. THE RUMBLE SUIT--
KKKK-KKRRKK-
CRASH!
YOU WERE SAYING, SIR?
UM, NOTHING.
I HAVE SOMETHING WAITING FOR YOU IN THE MED BAY WHEN YOU ARE FREE.
I HOPE IT'S A NAP.
ALL RIGHT, 803...

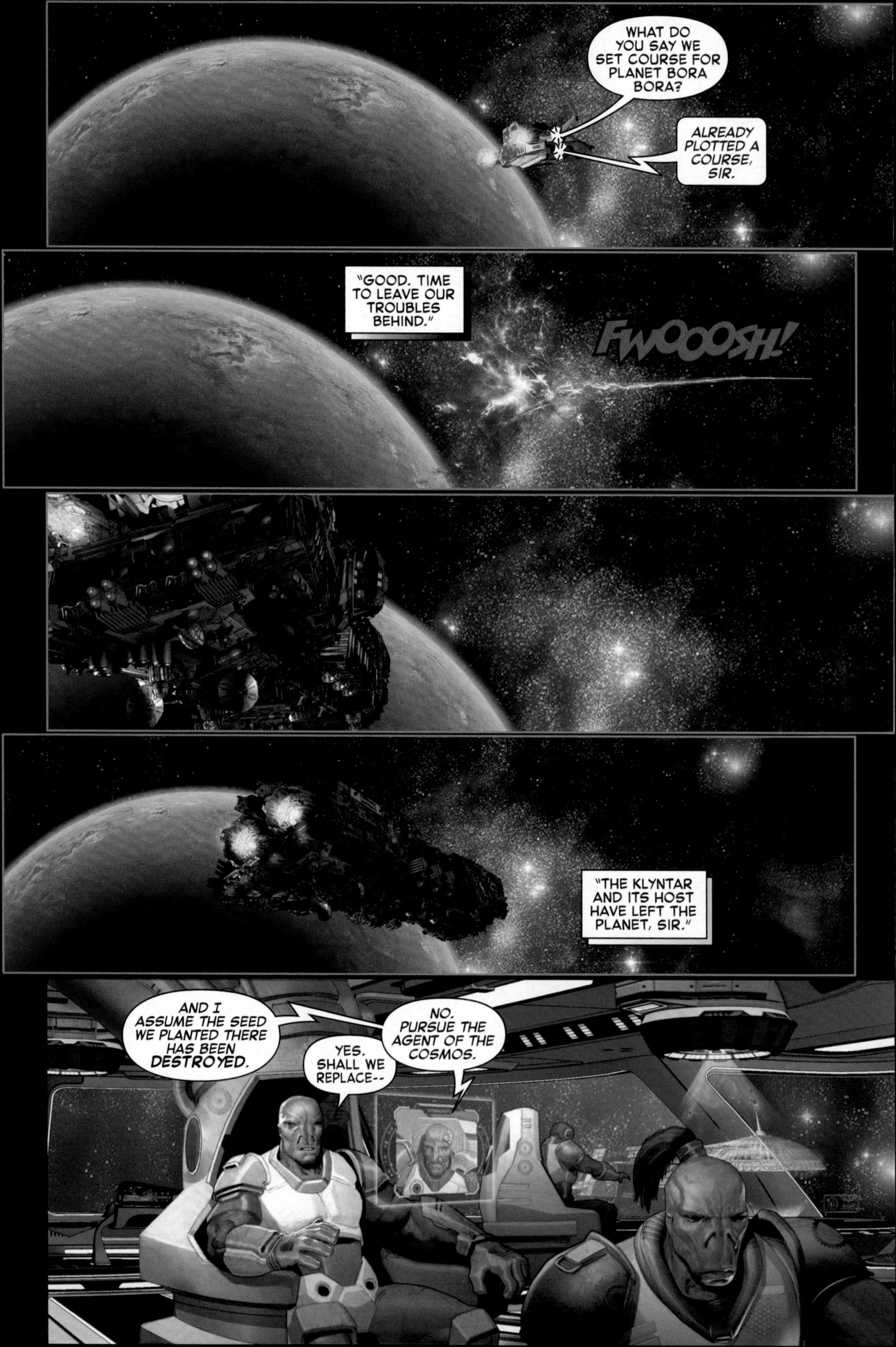
WHAT DO YOU SAY WE SET COURSE FOR PLANET BORA BORA?
ALREADY PLOTTED A COURSE, SIR.
"GOOD. TIME TO LEAVE OUR TROUBLES BEHIND."
FWOOOSH!
"THE KLYNTAR AND ITS HOST HAVE LEFT THE PLANET, SIR."
AND I ASSUME THE SEED WE PLANTED THERE HAS BEEN DESTROYED.
YES. SHALL WE REPLACE--
NO. PURSUE THE AGENT OF THE COSMOS.

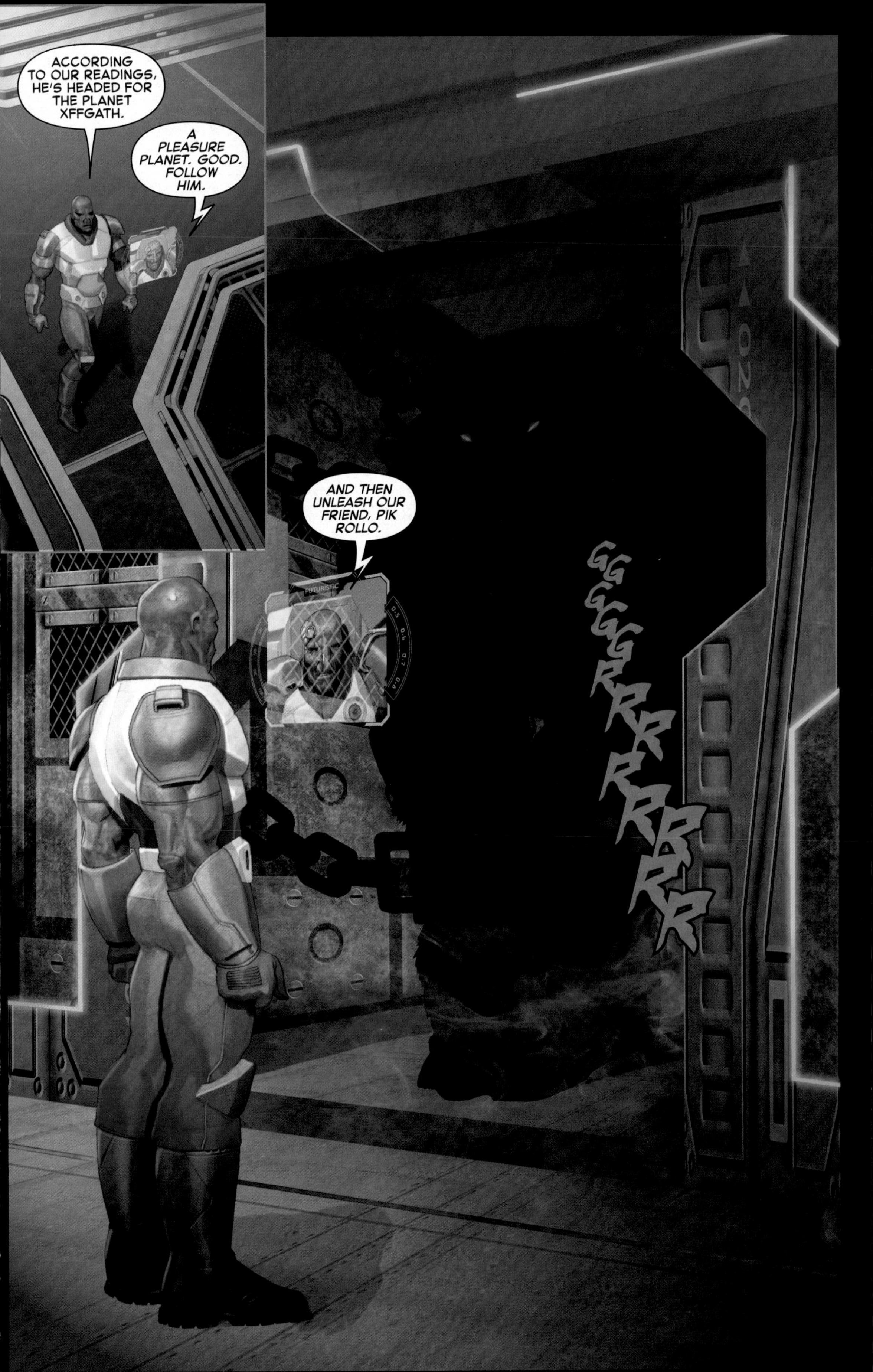
ACCORDING TO OUR READINGS, HE'S HEADED FOR THE PLANET XFFGATH.
A PLEASURE PLANET. GOOD. FOLLOW HIM.
AND THEN UNLEASH OUR FRIEND, PIK ROLLO.
FUTURISTIC
GGGGGRRRRRRRRRR

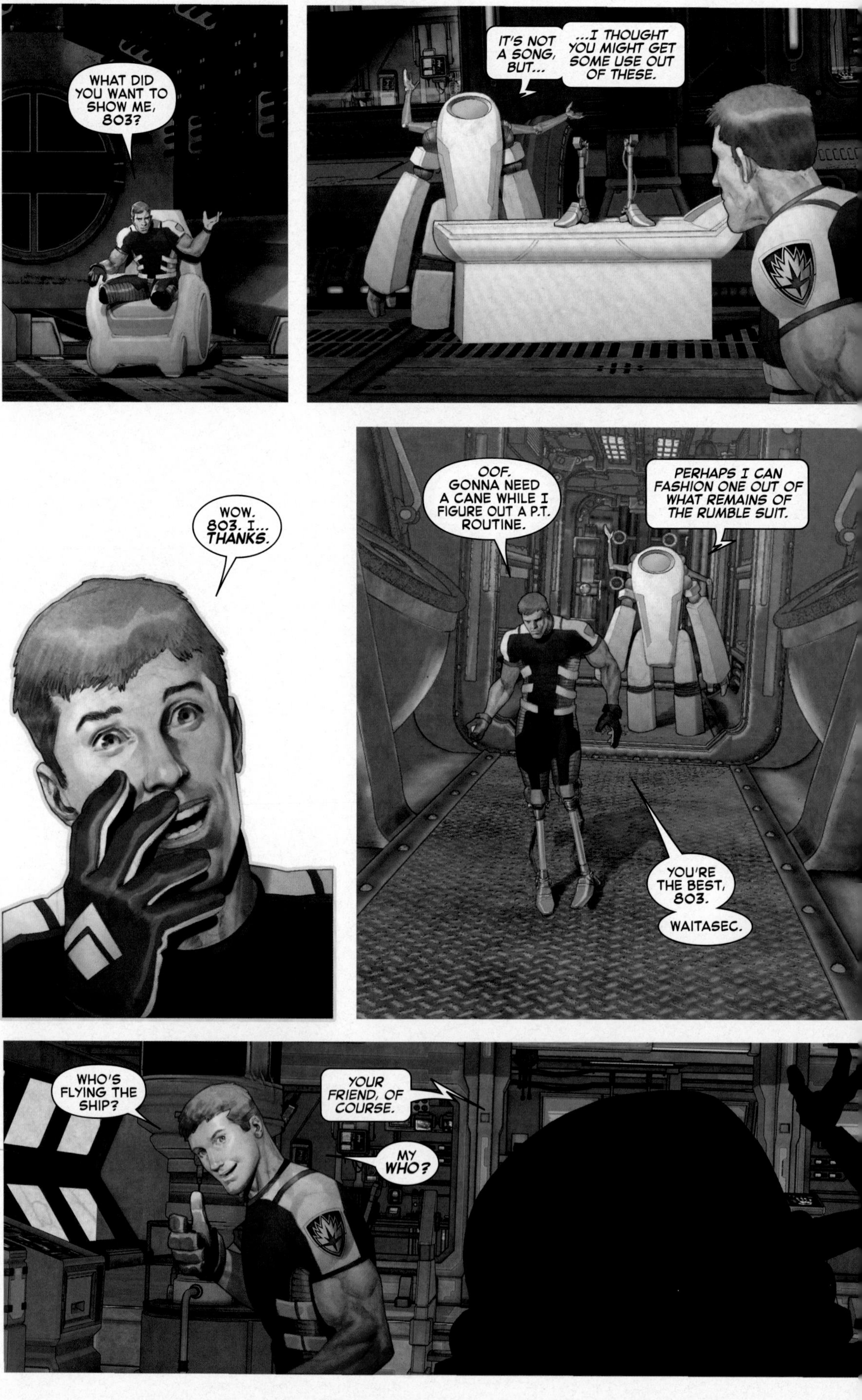
WHAT DID YOU WANT TO SHOW ME, 803?
IT'S NOT A SONG, BUT...
...I THOUGHT YOU MIGHT GET SOME USE OUT OF THESE.
WOW. 803. I... THANKS.
OOF. GONNA NEED A CANE WHILE I FIGURE OUT A P.T. ROUTINE.
PERHAPS I CAN FASHION ONE OUT OF WHAT REMAINS OF THE RUMBLE SUIT.
YOU'RE THE BEST, 803.
WAITASEC.
WHO'S FLYING THE SHIP?
YOUR FRIEND, OF COURSE.
MY WHO?

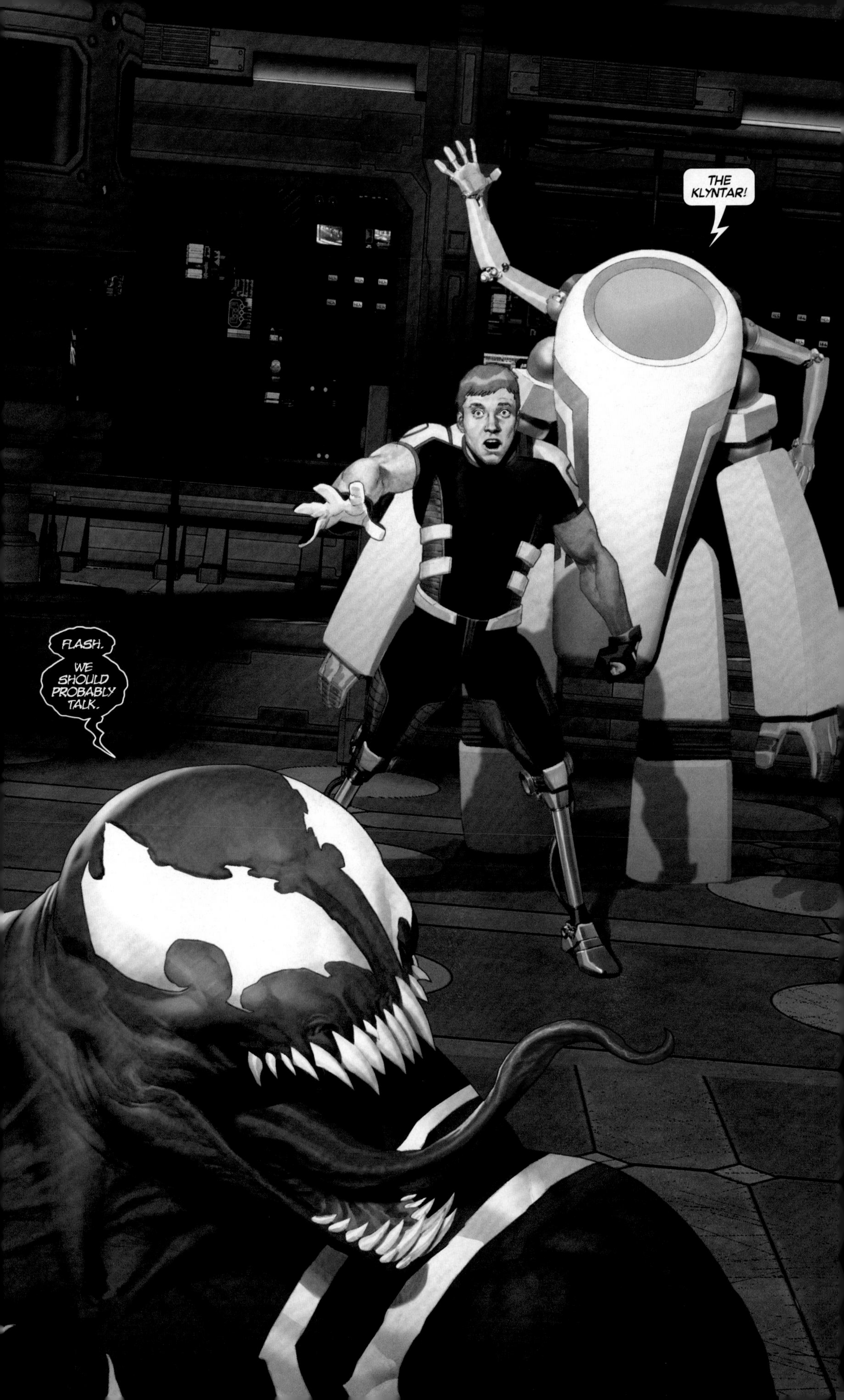
THE KLYNTAR!
FLASH.
WE SHOULD PROBABLY TALK.

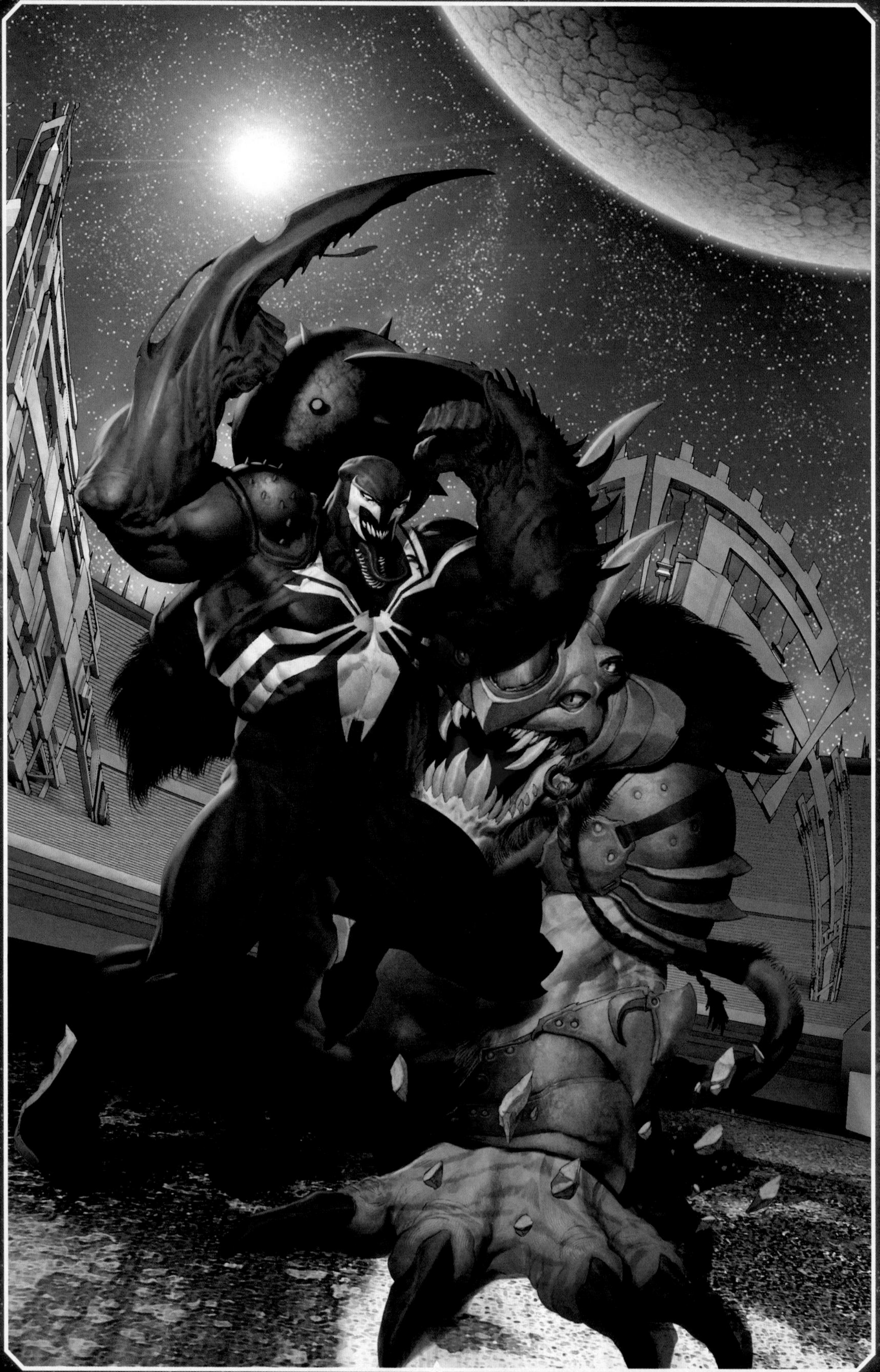

4

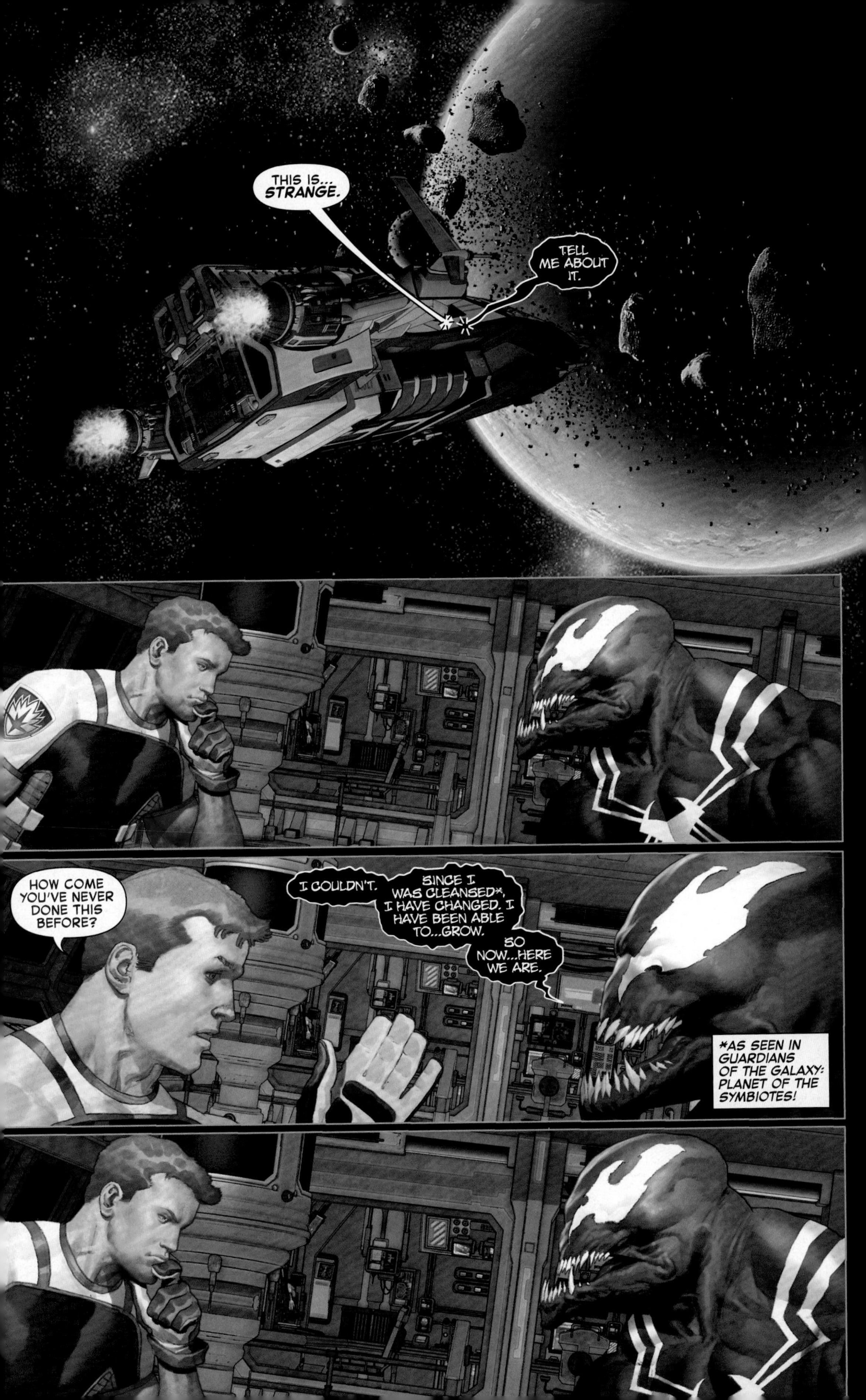
THIS IS... STRANGE.
TELL ME ABOUT IT.
HOW COME YOU'VE NEVER DONE THIS BEFORE?
I COULDN'T.
SINCE I WAS CLEANSED*, I HAVE CHANGED. I HAVE BEEN ABLE TO...GROW.
SO NOW...HERE WE ARE.
*AS SEEN IN GUARDIANS OF THE GALAXY: PLANET OF THE SYMBIOTES!

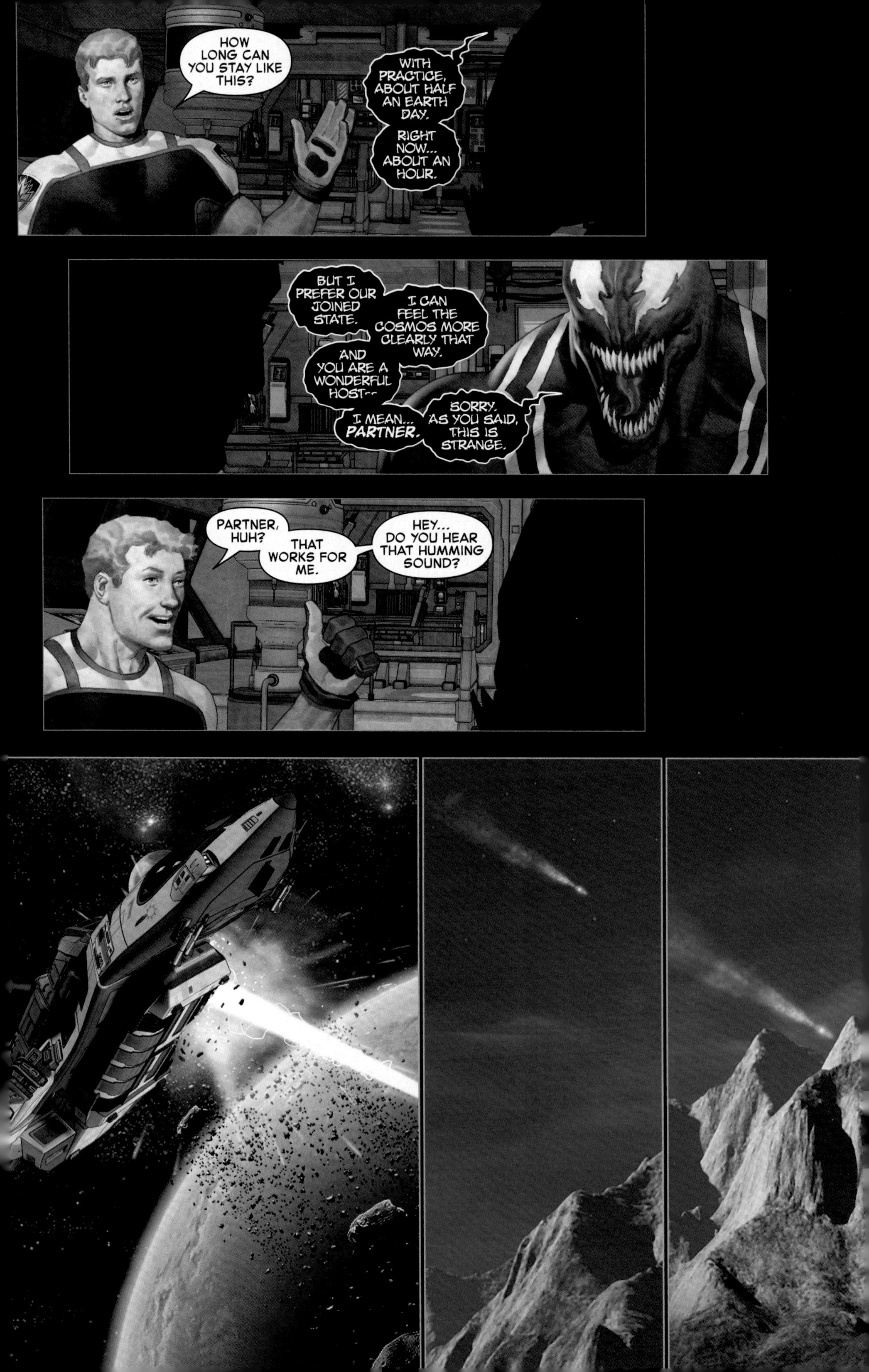
HOW LONG CAN YOU STAY LIKE THIS?
WITH PRACTICE, ABOUT HALF AN EARTH DAY.
RIGHT NOW... ABOUT AN HOUR.
BUT I PREFER OUR JOINED STATE.
I CAN FEEL THE COSMOS MORE CLEARLY THAT WAY.
AND YOU ARE A WONDERFUL HOST--
I MEAN... PARTNER.
SORRY. AS YOU SAID, THIS IS STRANGE.
PARTNER, HUH?
THAT WORKS FOR ME.
HEY... DO YOU HEAR THAT HUMMING SOUND?

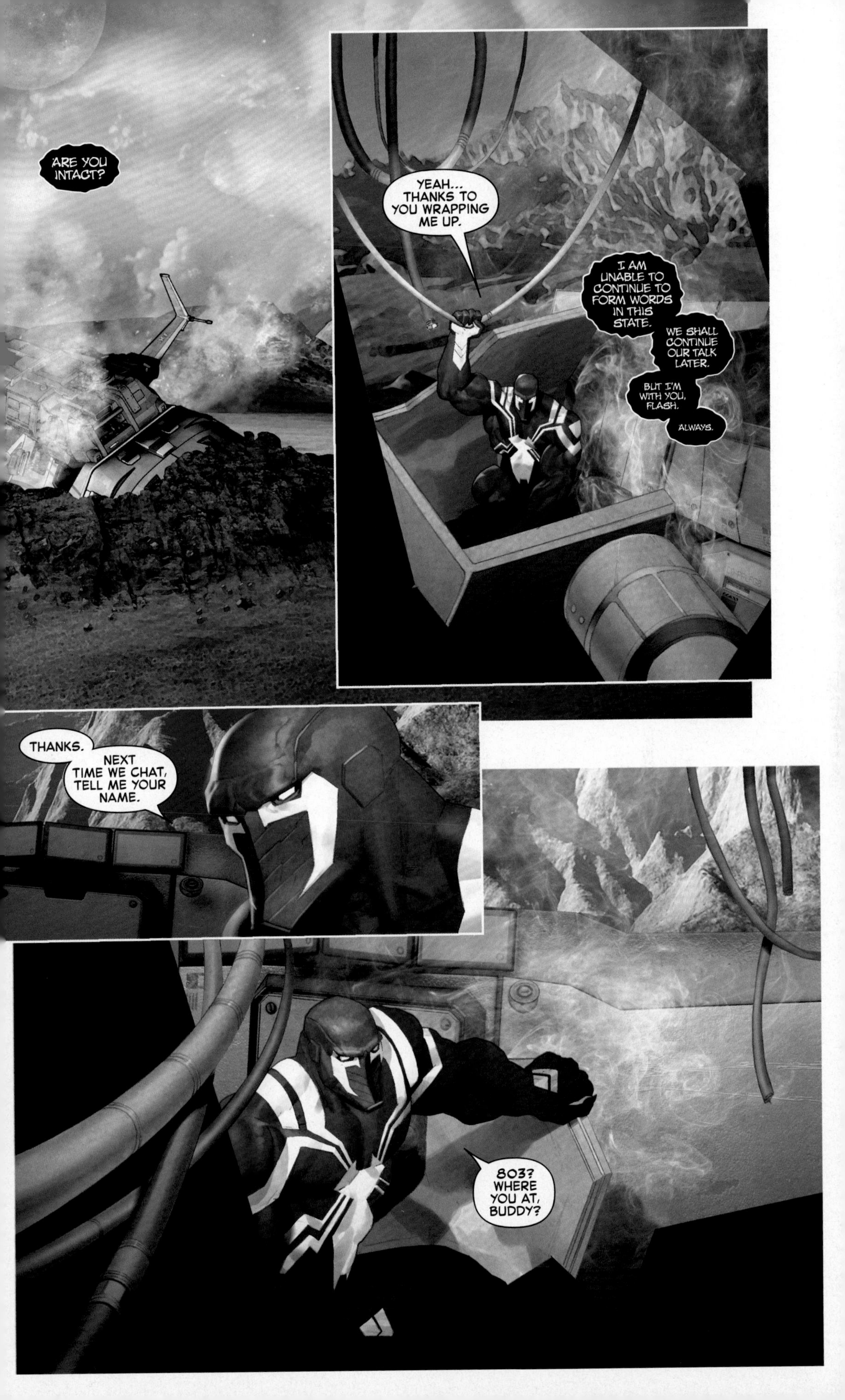
ARE YOU INTACT?
YEAH... THANKS TO YOU WRAPPING ME UP.
I AM UNABLE TO CONTINUE TO FORM WORDS IN THIS STATE.
WE SHALL CONTINUE OUR TALK LATER.
BUT I'M WITH YOU, FLASH.
ALWAYS.
THANKS.
NEXT TIME WE CHAT, TELL ME YOUR NAME.
803? WHERE YOU AT, BUDDY?

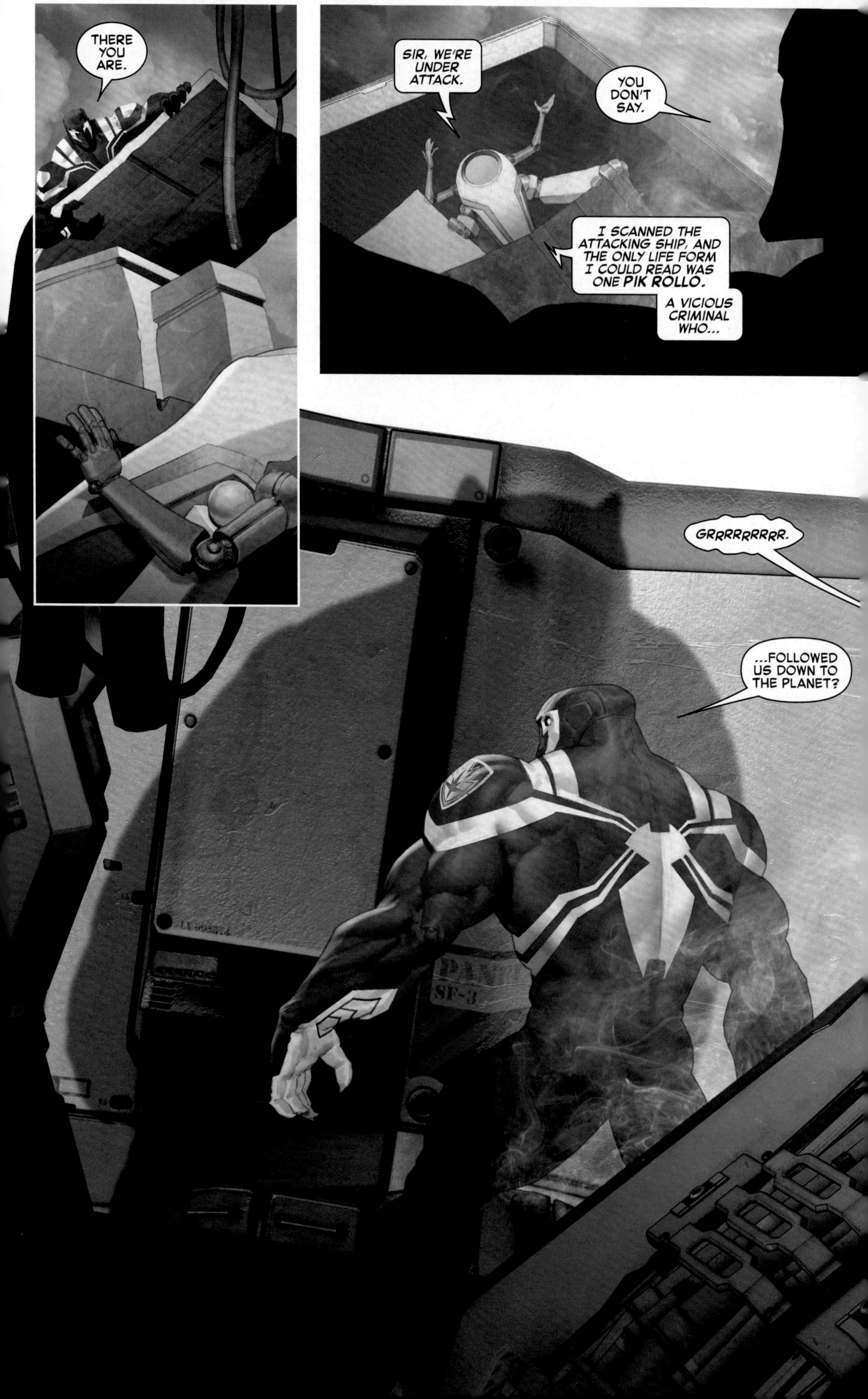
THERE YOU ARE.
SIR, WE'RE UNDER ATTACK.
YOU DON'T SAY.
I SCANNED THE ATTACKING SHIP, AND THE ONLY LIFE FORM I COULD READ WAS ONE PIK ROLLO.
A VICIOUS CRIMINAL WHO...
GRRRRRRRRR.
...FOLLOWED US DOWN TO THE PLANET?

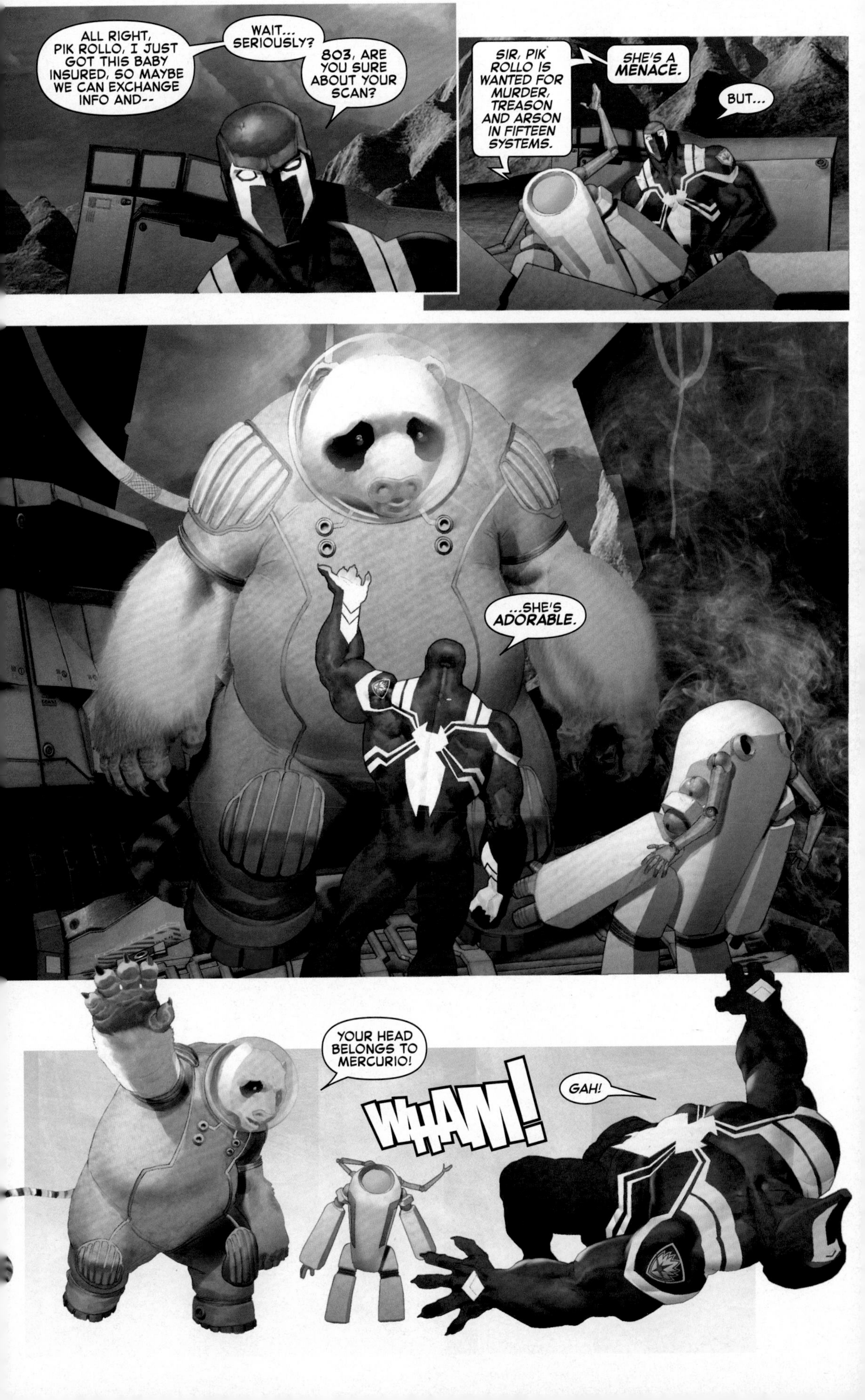
ALL RIGHT, PIK ROLLO, I JUST GOT THIS BABY INSURED, SO MAYBE WE CAN EXCHANGE INFO AND--
WAIT... SERIOUSLY?
803, ARE YOU SURE ABOUT YOUR SCAN?
SIR, PIK ROLLO IS WANTED FOR MURDER, TREASON AND ARSON IN FIFTEEN SYSTEMS.
SHE'S A MENACE.
BUT...
...SHE'S ADORABLE.
YOUR HEAD BELONGS TO MERCURIO!
WHAM!
GAH!

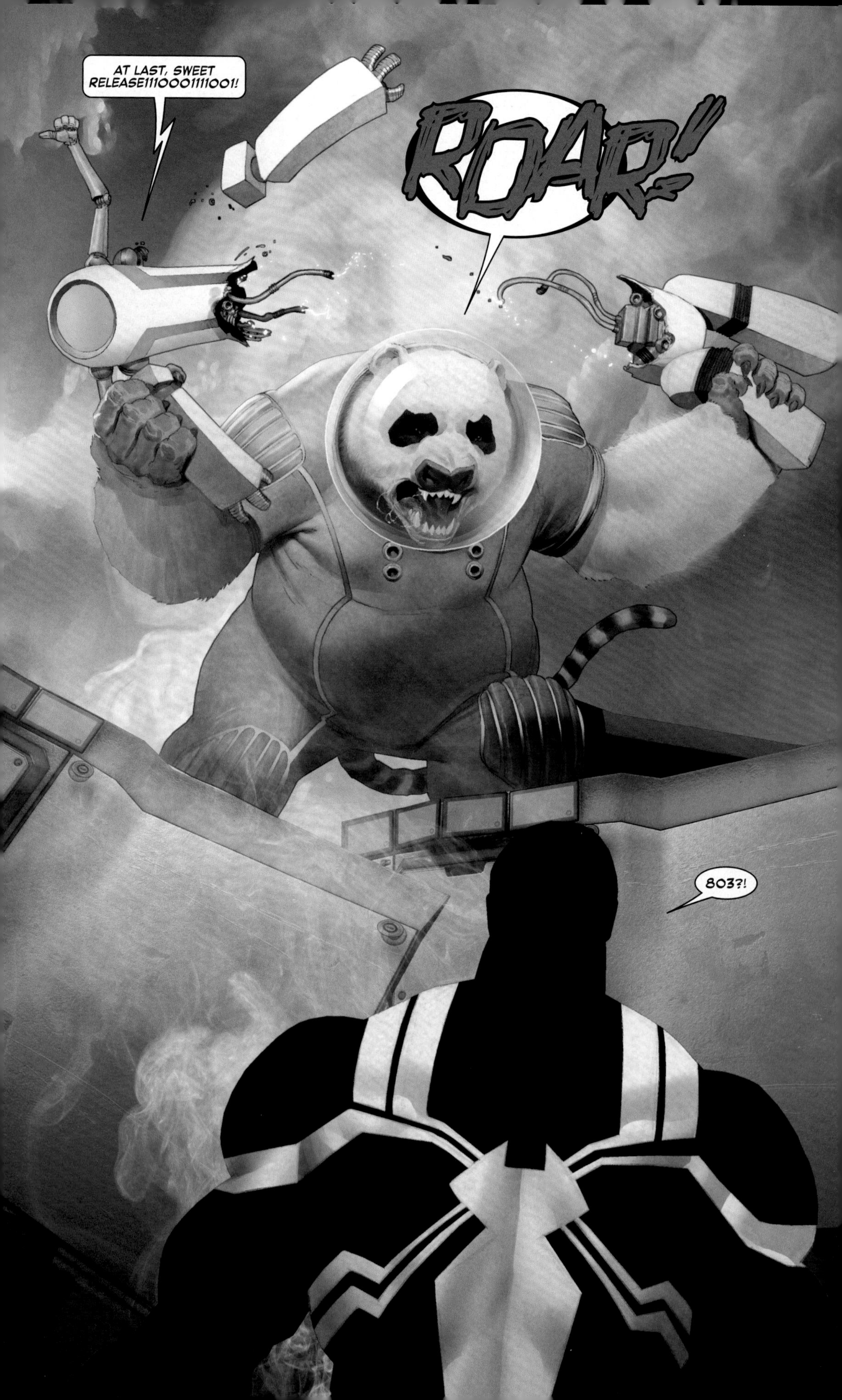
AT LAST, SWEET RELEASE1110001111001!
ROAR!
803?!

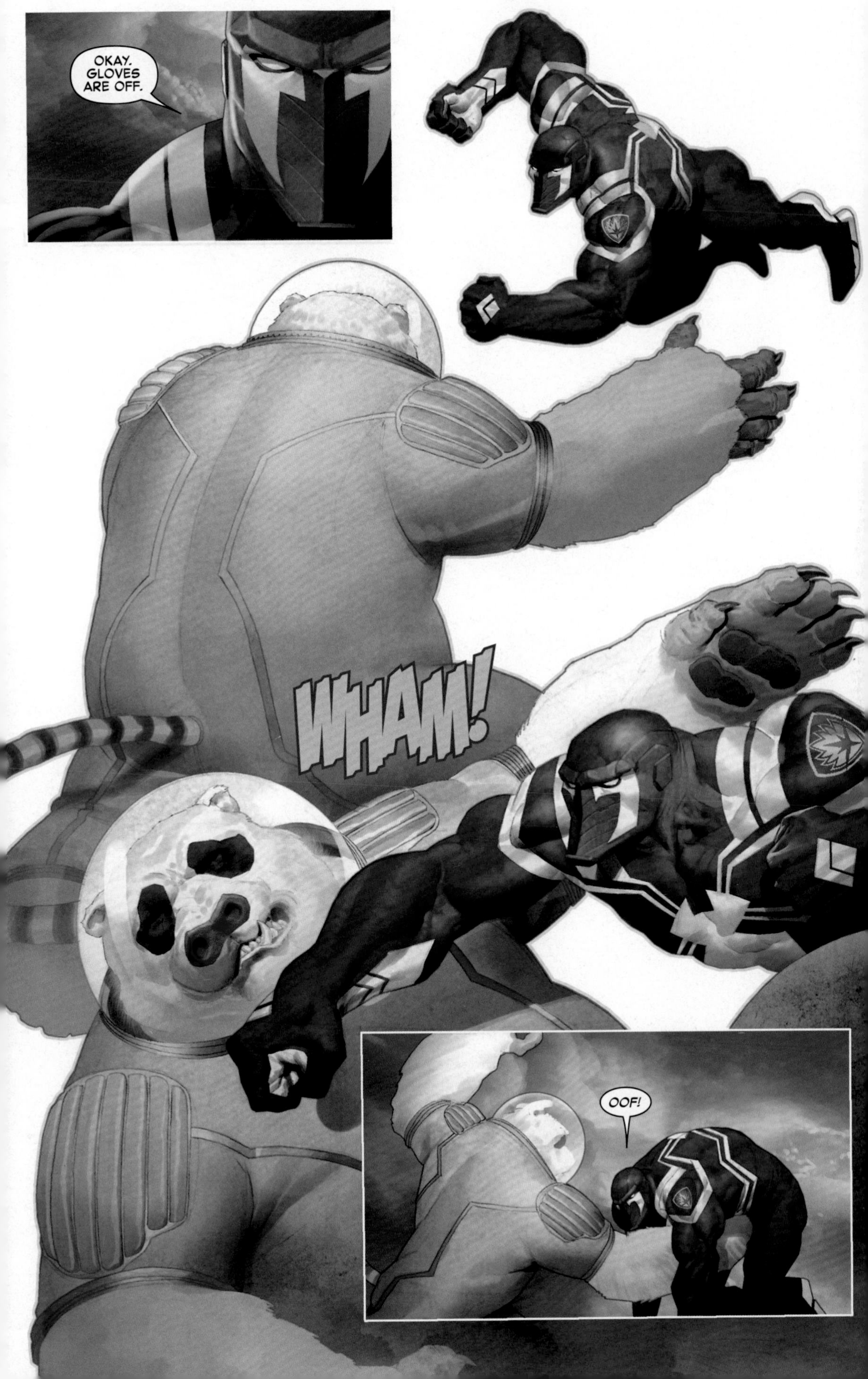
OKAY. GLOVES ARE OFF.
WHAM!
OOF!

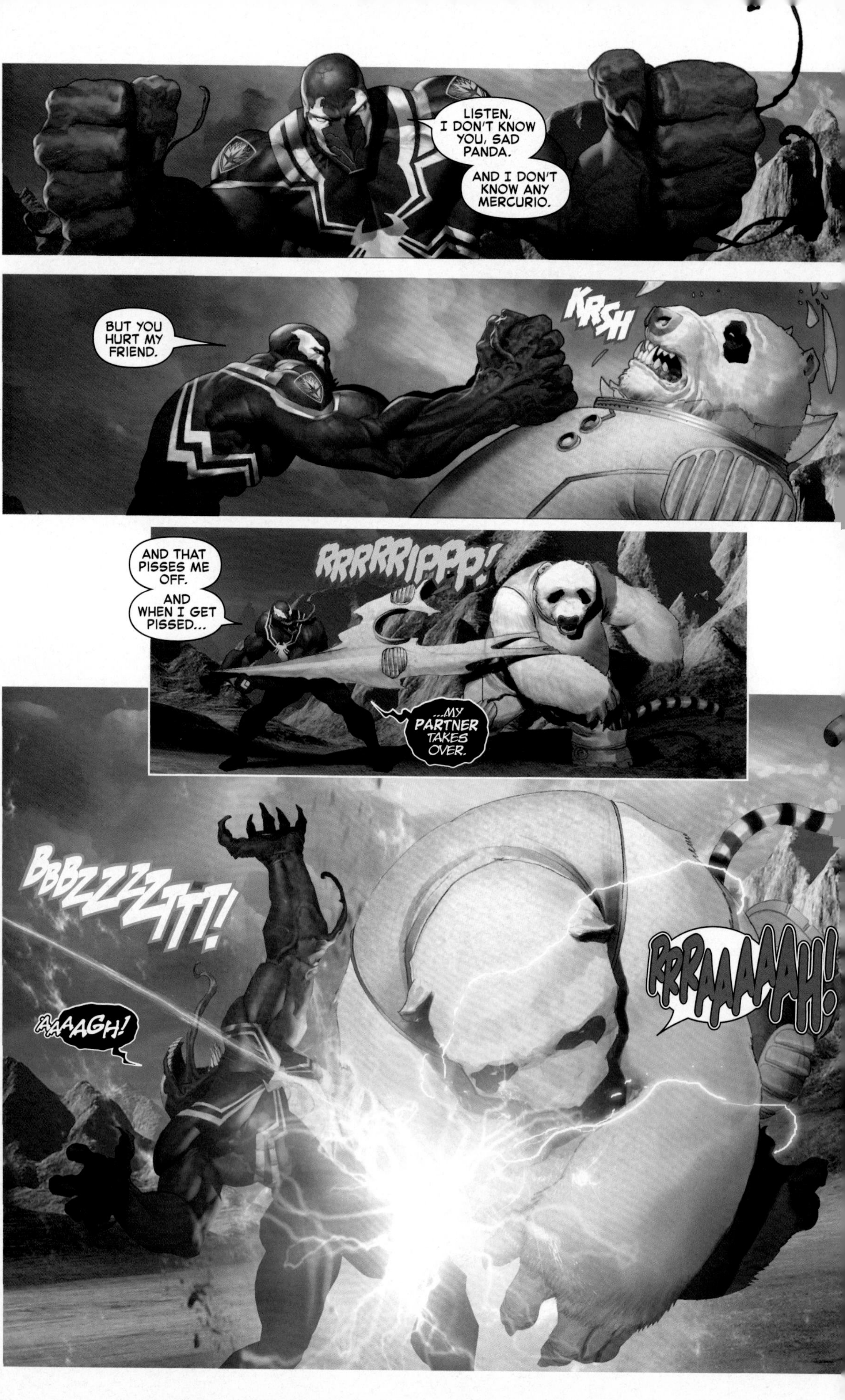
LISTEN, I DON'T KNOW YOU, SAD PANDA.
AND I DON'T KNOW ANY MERCURIO.
BUT YOU HURT MY FRIEND.
KRSH
AND THAT PISSES ME OFF.
AND WHEN I GET PISSED...
RRRRRIPPP!
...MY PARTNER TAKES OVER.
BBBZZZZZTTT!
AAAAGH!
RRRAAAAAAH!

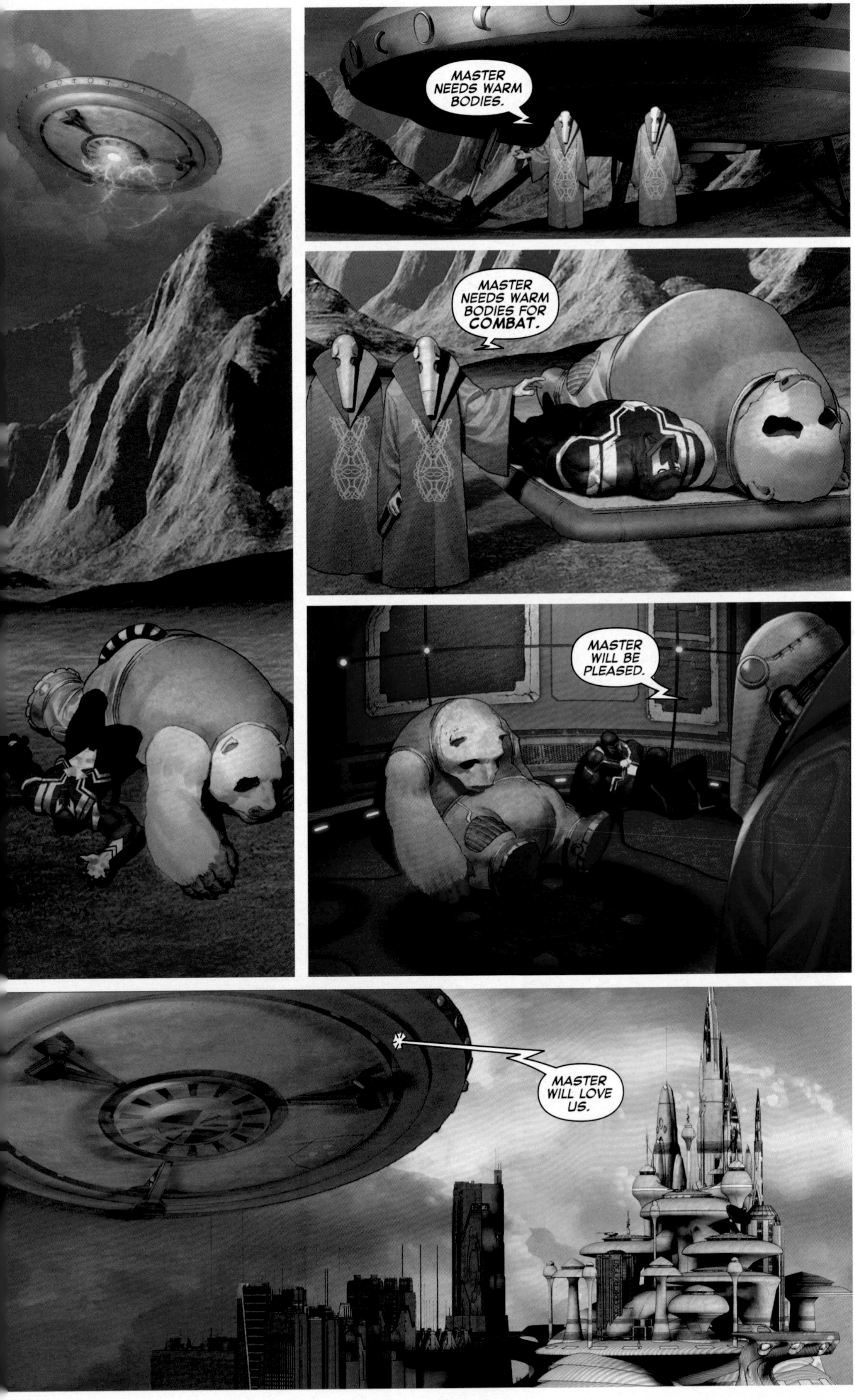
MASTER NEEDS WARM BODIES.
MASTER NEEDS WARM BODIES FOR COMBAT.
MASTER WILL BE PLEASED.
MASTER WILL LOVE US.

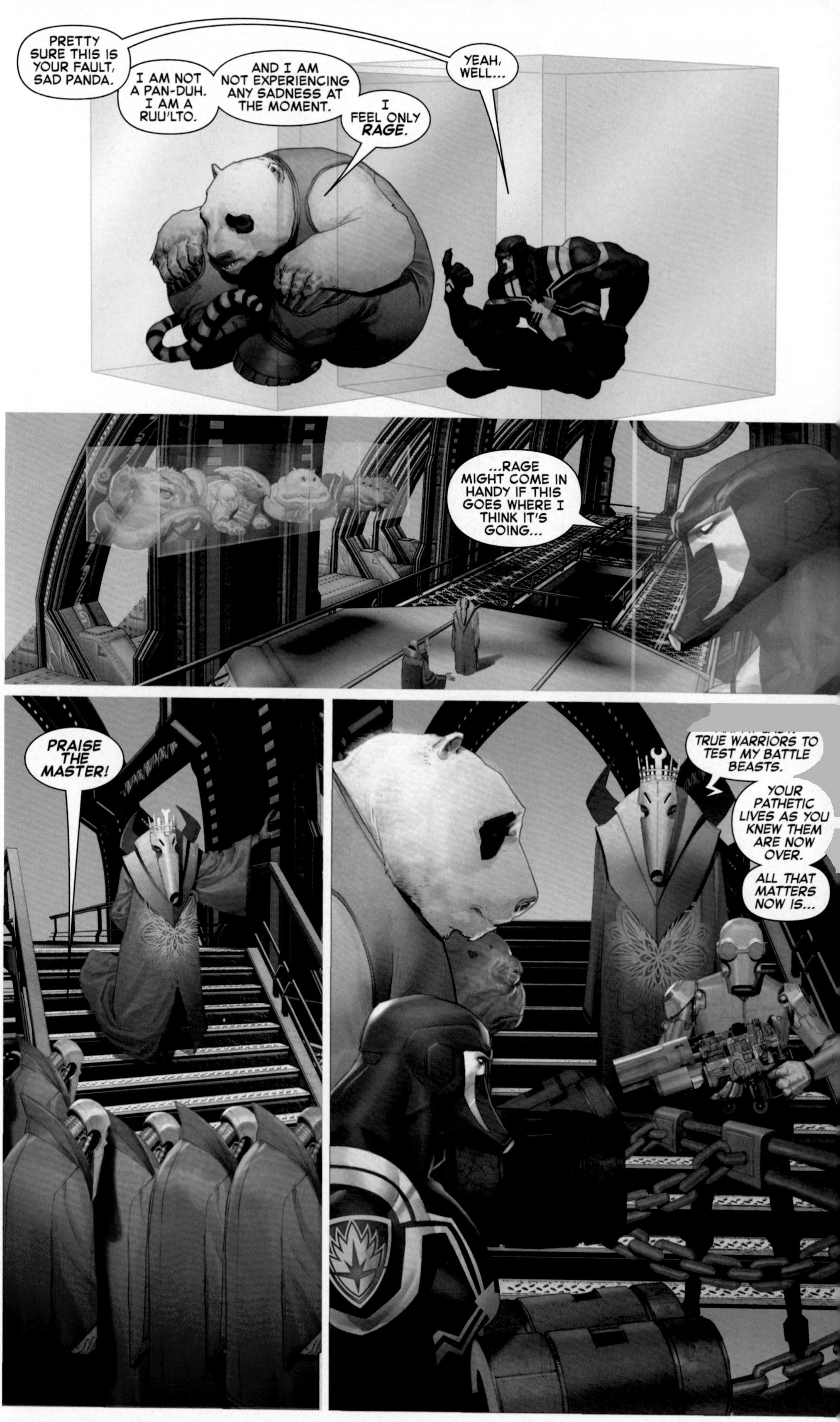
PRETTY SURE THIS IS YOUR FAULT, SAD PANDA.
I AM NOT A PAN-DUH. I AM A RUU'LTO.
AND I AM NOT EXPERIENCING ANY SADNESS AT THE MOMENT.
I FEEL ONLY *RAGE.*
YEAH, WELL...
...RAGE MIGHT COME IN HANDY IF THIS GOES WHERE I THINK IT'S GOING...
PRAISE THE MASTER!
TRUE WARRIORS TO TEST MY BATTLE BEASTS.
YOUR PATHETIC LIVES AS YOU KNEW THEM ARE NOW OVER.
ALL THAT MATTERS NOW IS...

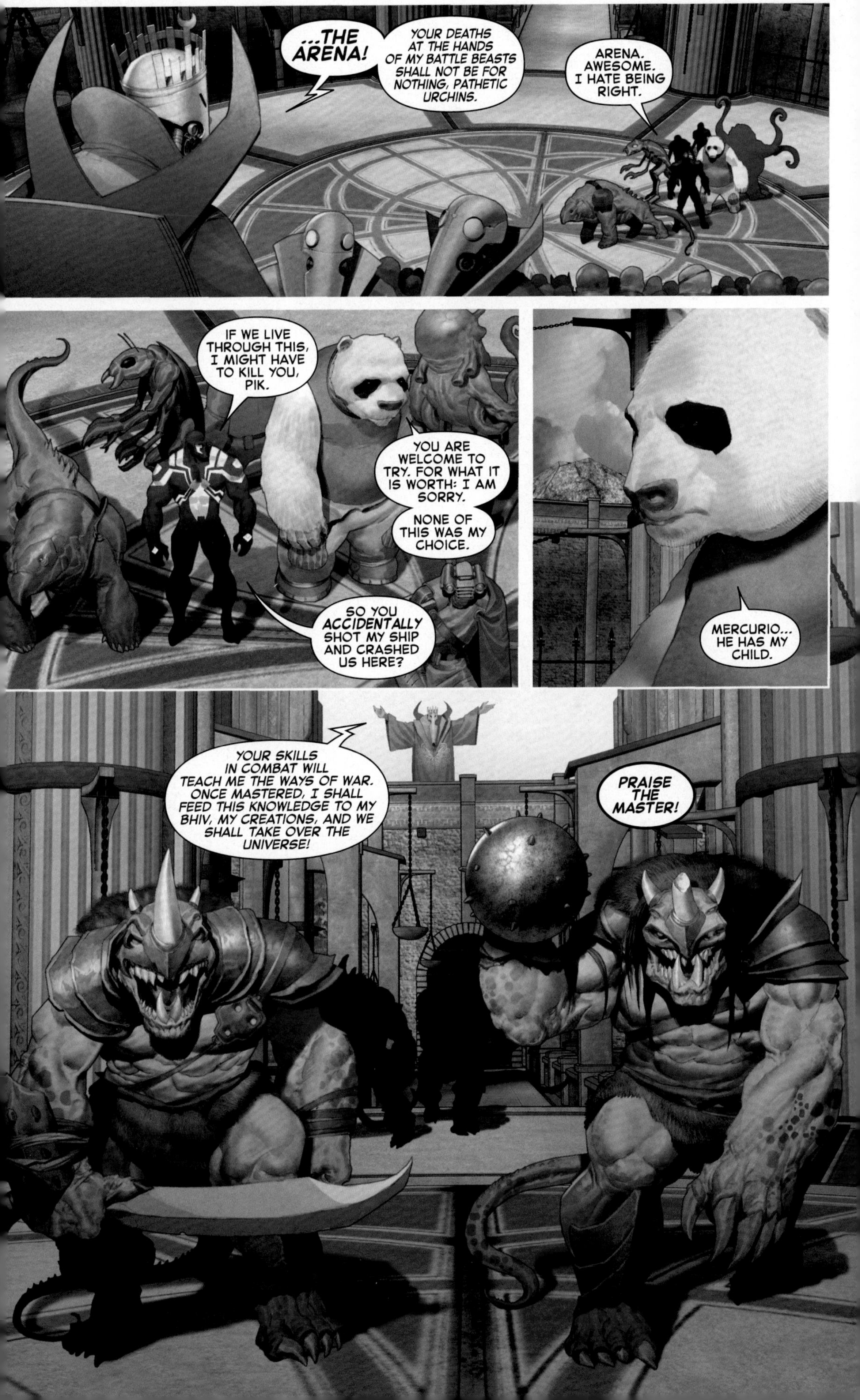
...THE ARENA!
YOUR DEATHS AT THE HANDS OF MY BATTLE BEASTS SHALL NOT BE FOR NOTHING, PATHETIC URCHINS.
ARENA. AWESOME. I HATE BEING RIGHT.
IF WE LIVE THROUGH THIS, I MIGHT HAVE TO KILL YOU, PIK.
YOU ARE WELCOME TO TRY. FOR WHAT IT IS WORTH: I AM SORRY.
NONE OF THIS WAS MY CHOICE.
SO YOU ACCIDENTALLY SHOT MY SHIP AND CRASHED US HERE?
MERCURIO... HE HAS MY CHILD.
YOUR SKILLS IN COMBAT WILL TEACH ME THE WAYS OF WAR. ONCE MASTERED, I SHALL FEED THIS KNOWLEDGE TO MY BHIV, MY CREATIONS, AND WE SHALL TAKE OVER THE UNIVERSE!
PRAISE THE MASTER!

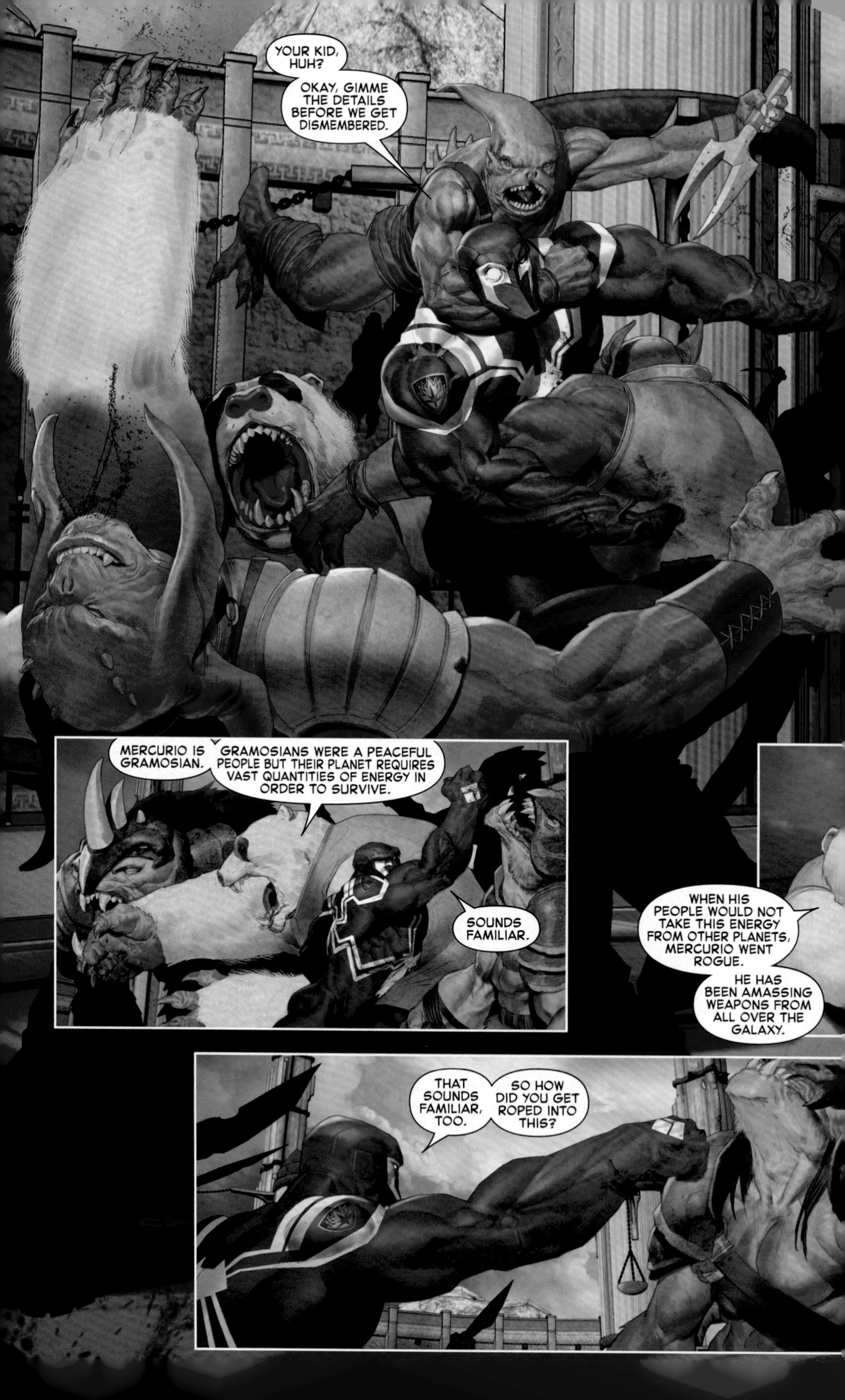
YOUR KID, HUH?
OKAY, GIMME THE DETAILS BEFORE WE GET DISMEMBERED.
MERCURIO IS GRAMOSIAN.
GRAMOSIANS WERE A PEACEFUL PEOPLE BUT THEIR PLANET REQUIRES VAST QUANTITIES OF ENERGY IN ORDER TO SURVIVE.
SOUNDS FAMILIAR.
WHEN HIS PEOPLE WOULD NOT TAKE THIS ENERGY FROM OTHER PLANETS, MERCURIO WENT ROGUE.
HE HAS BEEN AMASSING WEAPONS FROM ALL OVER THE GALAXY.
THAT SOUNDS FAMILIAR, TOO.
SO HOW DID YOU GET ROPED INTO THIS?

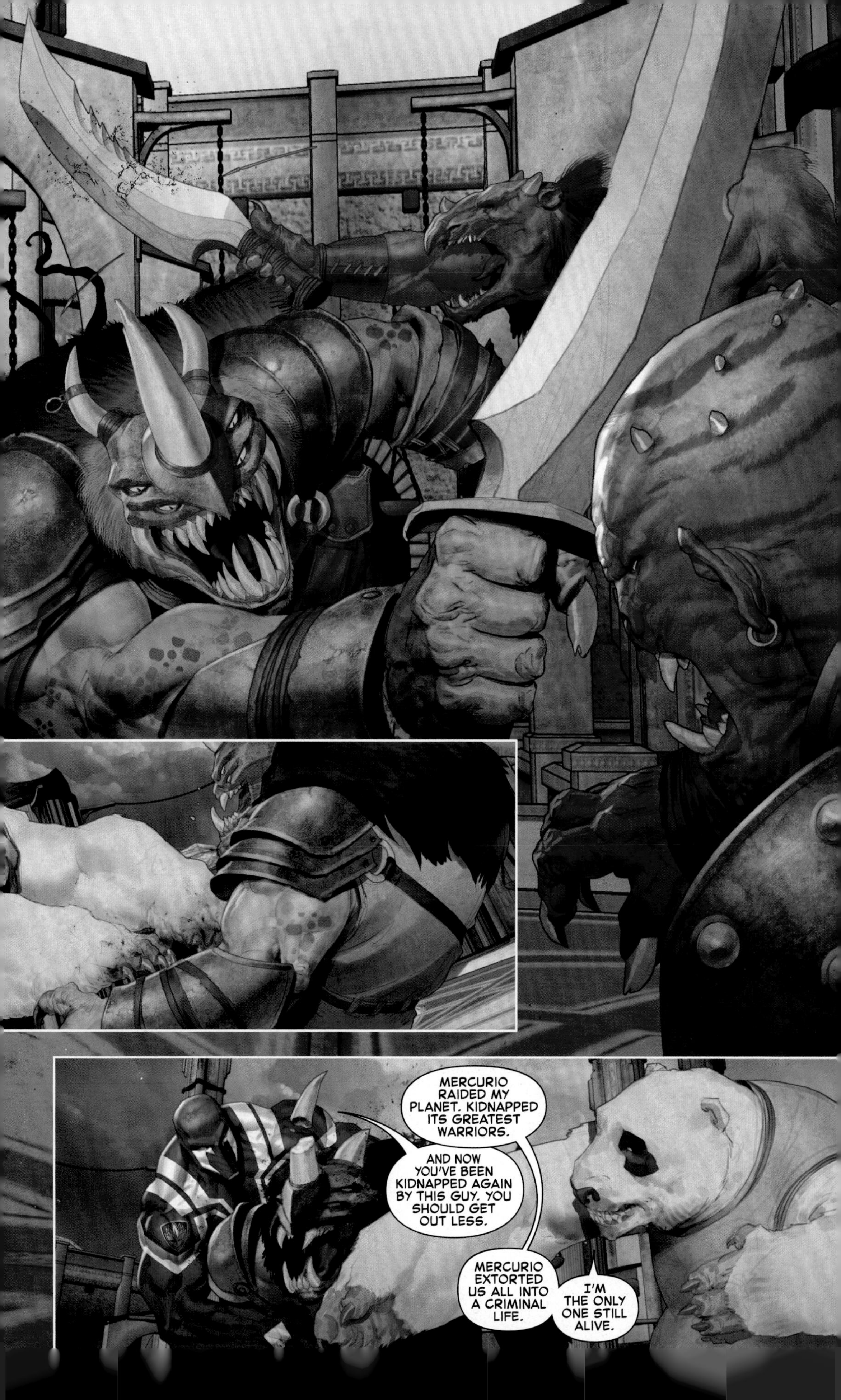
MERCURIO RAIDED MY PLANET. KIDNAPPED ITS GREATEST WARRIORS.
AND NOW YOU'VE BEEN KIDNAPPED AGAIN BY THIS GUY. YOU SHOULD GET OUT LESS.
MERCURIO EXTORTED US ALL INTO A CRIMINAL LIFE.
I'M THE ONLY ONE STILL ALIVE.

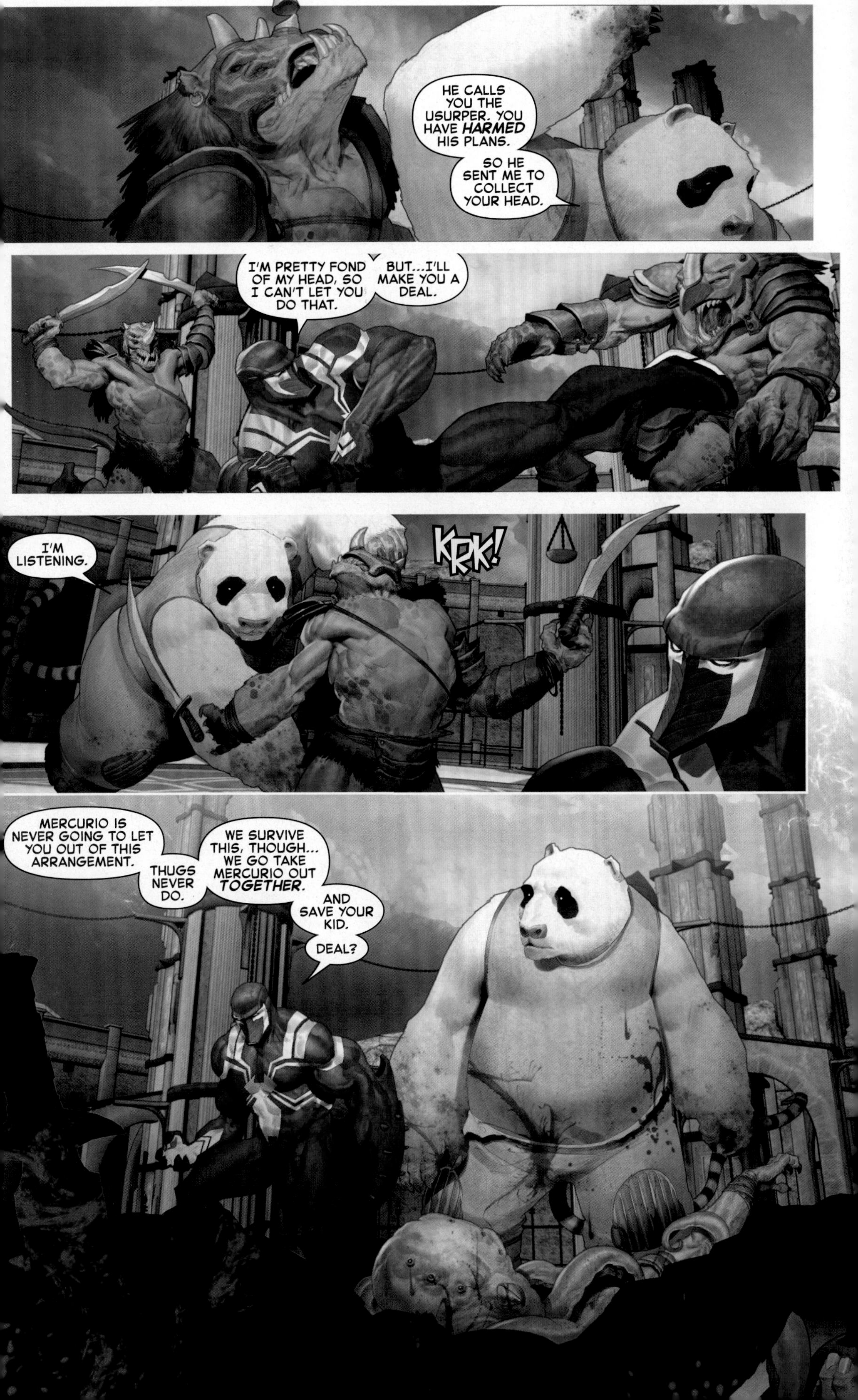
HE CALLS YOU THE USURPER. YOU HAVE HARMED HIS PLANS.
SO HE SENT ME TO COLLECT YOUR HEAD.
I'M PRETTY FOND OF MY HEAD, SO I CAN'T LET YOU DO THAT.
BUT...I'LL MAKE YOU A DEAL.
I'M LISTENING.
KRK!
MERCURIO IS NEVER GOING TO LET YOU OUT OF THIS ARRANGEMENT.
THUGS NEVER DO.
WE SURVIVE THIS, THOUGH... WE GO TAKE MERCURIO OUT TOGETHER.
AND SAVE YOUR KID.
DEAL?

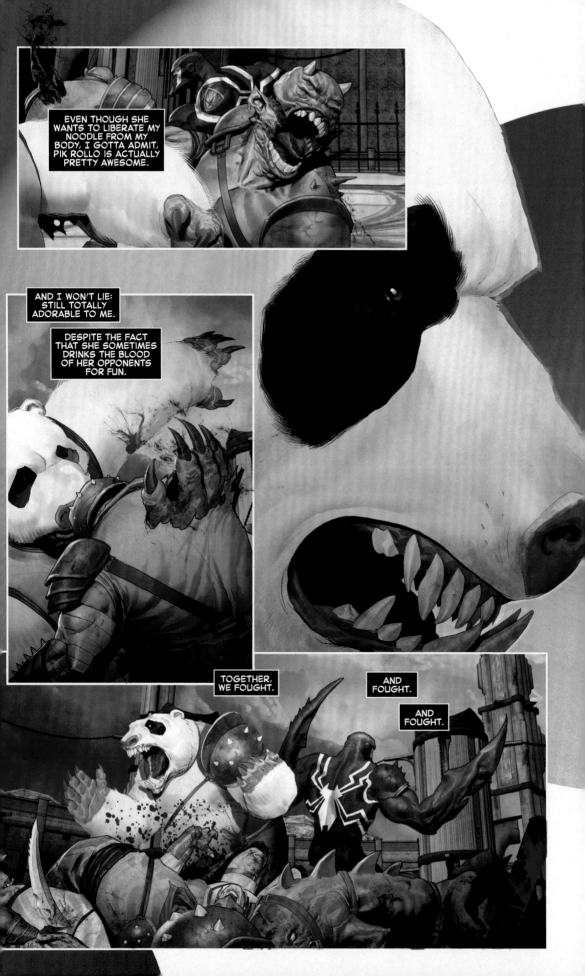

EVEN THOUGH SHE WANTS TO LIBERATE MY NOODLE FROM MY BODY, I GOTTA ADMIT, PIK ROLLO IS ACTUALLY PRETTY AWESOME.

AND I WON'T LIE: STILL TOTALLY ADORABLE TO ME.

DESPITE THE FACT THAT SHE SOMETIMES DRINKS THE BLOOD OF HER OPPONENTS FOR FUN.

TOGETHER, WE FOUGHT.

AND FOUGHT.

AND FOUGHT.

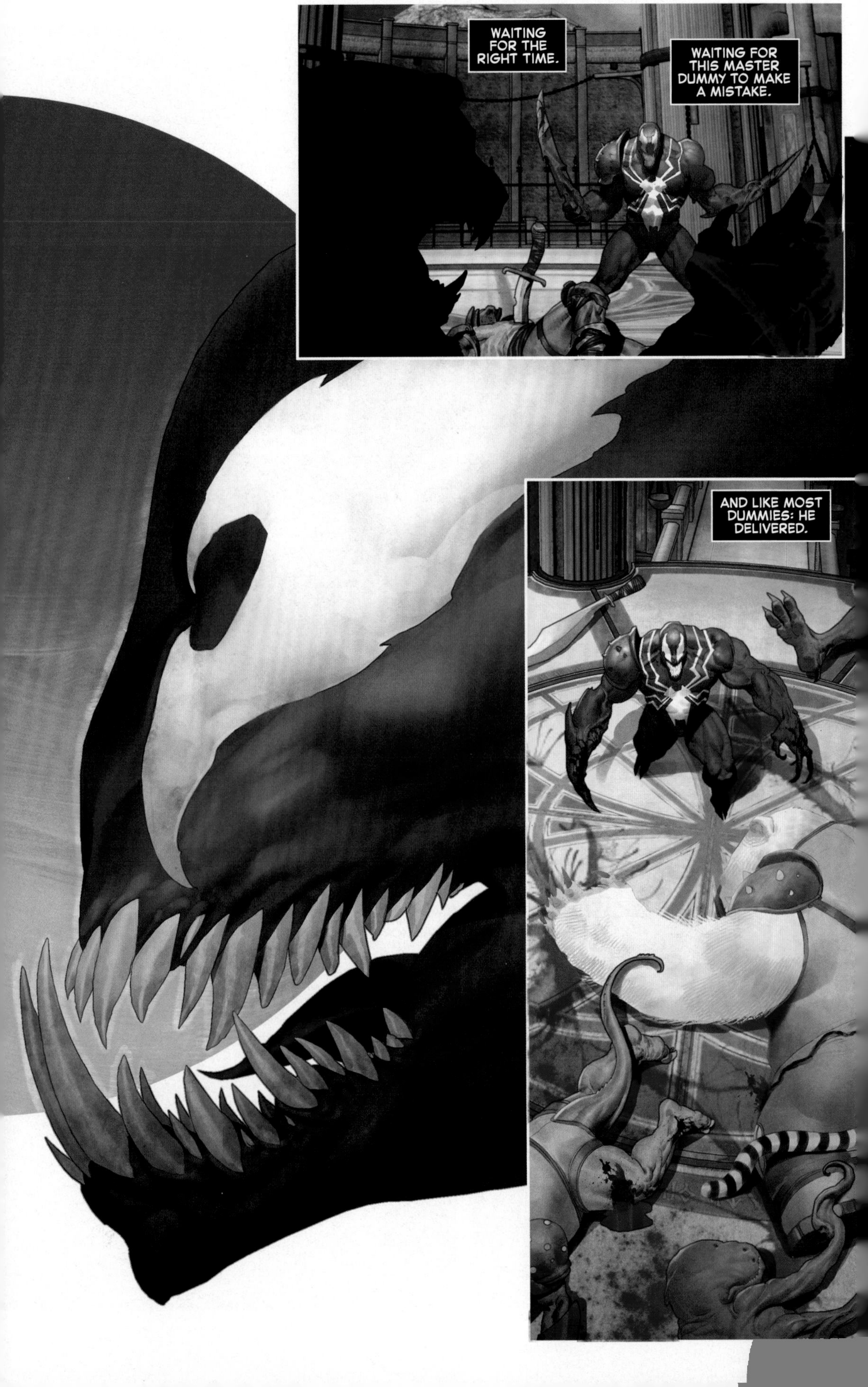

WAITING FOR THE RIGHT TIME.
WAITING FOR THIS MASTER DUMMY TO MAKE A MISTAKE.
AND LIKE MOST DUMMIES: HE DELIVERED.

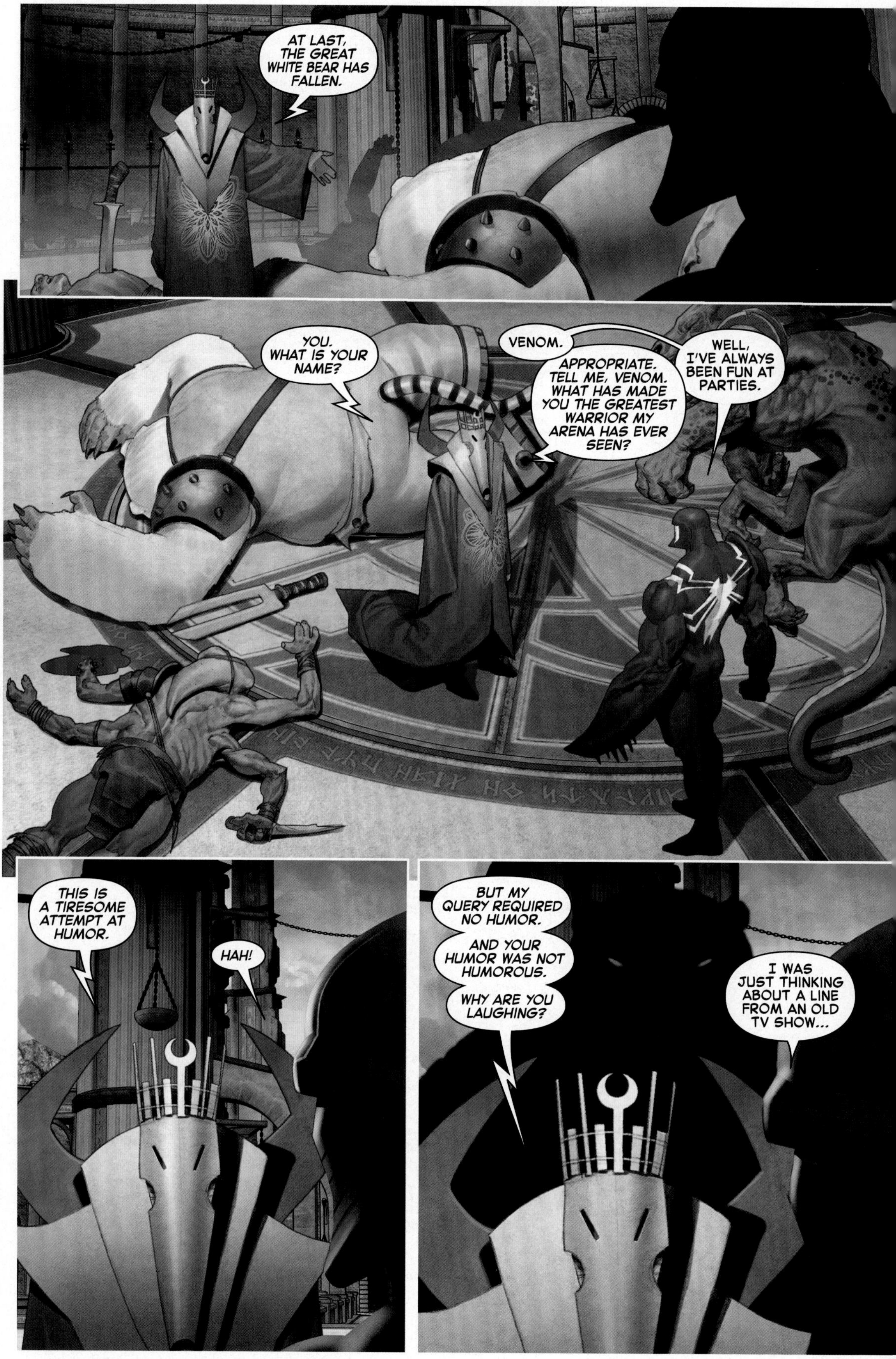

AT LAST, THE GREAT WHITE BEAR HAS FALLEN.
YOU. WHAT IS YOUR NAME?
VENOM.
APPROPRIATE. TELL ME, VENOM. WHAT HAS MADE YOU THE GREATEST WARRIOR MY ARENA HAS EVER SEEN?
WELL, I'VE ALWAYS BEEN FUN AT PARTIES.
THIS IS A TIRESOME ATTEMPT AT HUMOR.
HAH!
BUT MY QUERY REQUIRED NO HUMOR.
AND YOUR HUMOR WAS NOT HUMOROUS.
WHY ARE YOU LAUGHING?
I WAS JUST THINKING ABOUT A LINE FROM AN OLD TV SHOW...

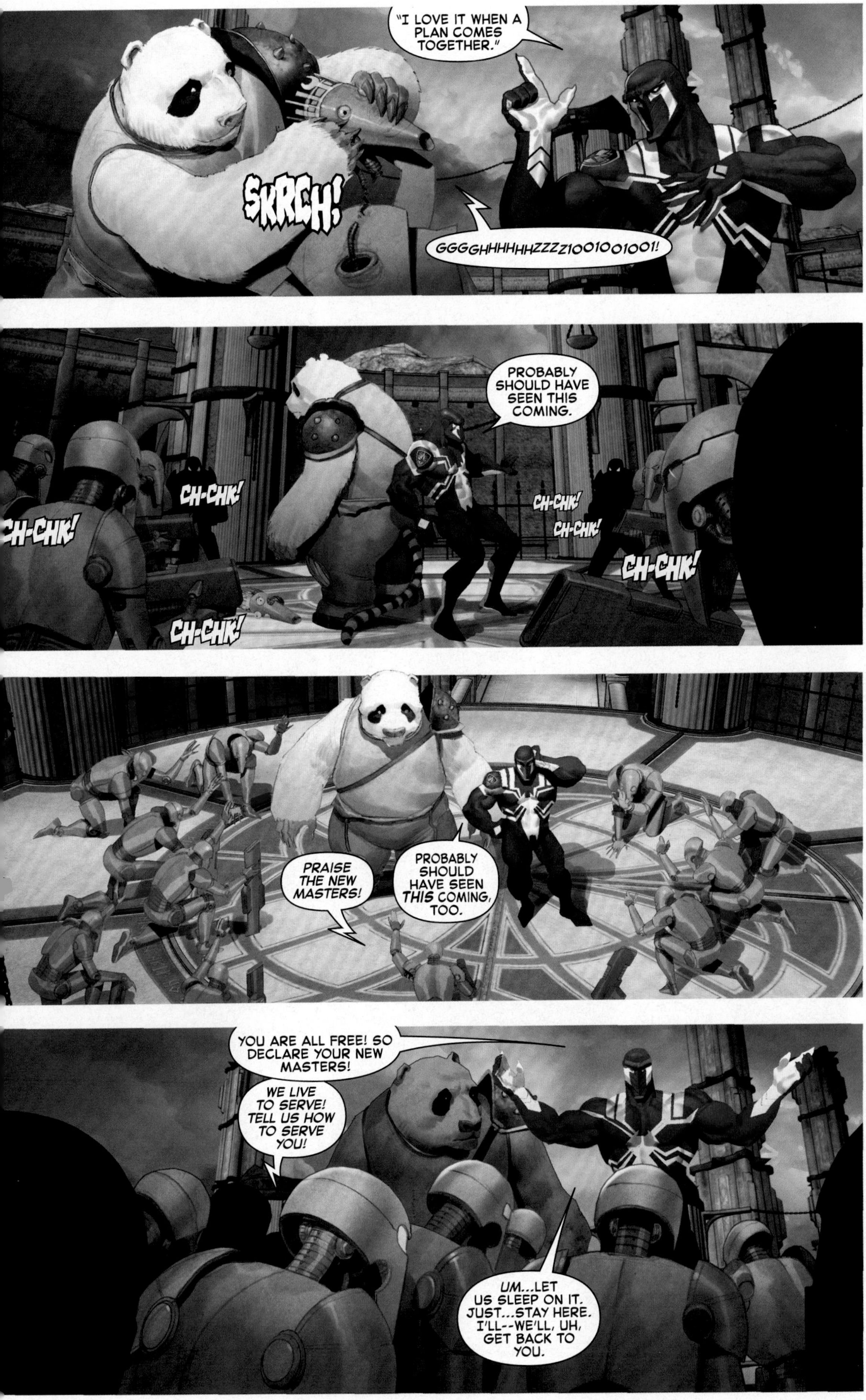

"I LOVE IT WHEN A PLAN COMES TOGETHER."
SKRCH!
GGGGHHHHHHZZZZ1001001001!
PROBABLY SHOULD HAVE SEEN THIS COMING.
CH-CHK!
CH-CHK!
CH-CHK!
CH-CHK!
CH-CHK!
CH-CHK!
PRAISE THE NEW MASTERS!
PROBABLY SHOULD HAVE SEEN THIS COMING, TOO.
YOU ARE ALL FREE! SO DECLARE YOUR NEW MASTERS!
WE LIVE TO SERVE! TELL US HOW TO SERVE YOU!
UM...LET US SLEEP ON IT. JUST...STAY HERE. I'LL--WE'LL, UH, GET BACK TO YOU.

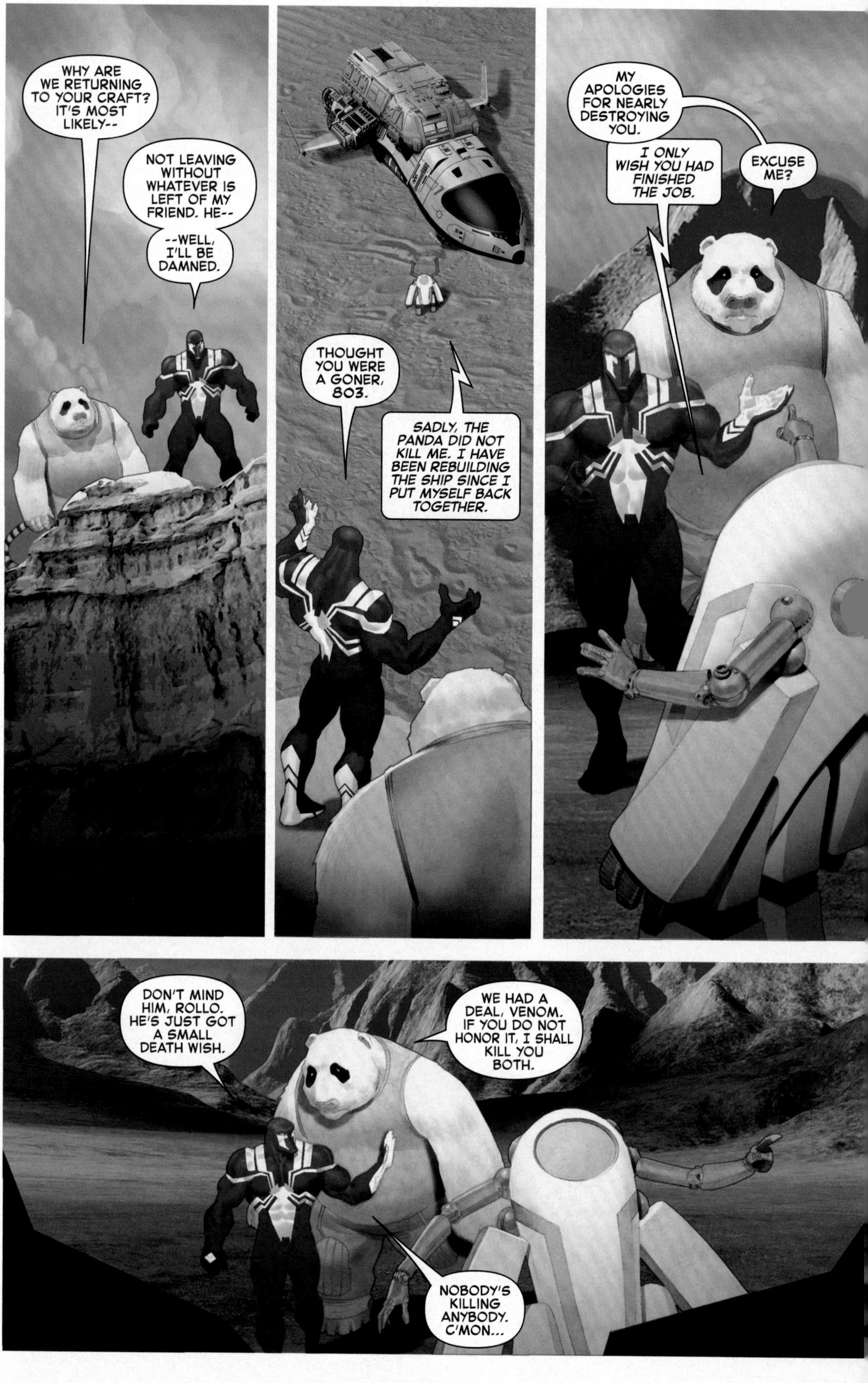
WHY ARE WE RETURNING TO YOUR CRAFT? IT'S MOST LIKELY--
NOT LEAVING WITHOUT WHATEVER IS LEFT OF MY FRIEND. HE--
--WELL, I'LL BE DAMNED.
THOUGHT YOU WERE A GONER, 803.
SADLY, THE PANDA DID NOT KILL ME. I HAVE BEEN REBUILDING THE SHIP SINCE I PUT MYSELF BACK TOGETHER.
MY APOLOGIES FOR NEARLY DESTROYING YOU.
I ONLY WISH YOU HAD FINISHED THE JOB.
EXCUSE ME?
DON'T MIND HIM, ROLLO. HE'S JUST GOT A SMALL DEATH WISH.
WE HAD A DEAL, VENOM. IF YOU DO NOT HONOR IT, I SHALL KILL YOU BOTH.
NOBODY'S KILLING ANYBODY. C'MON...

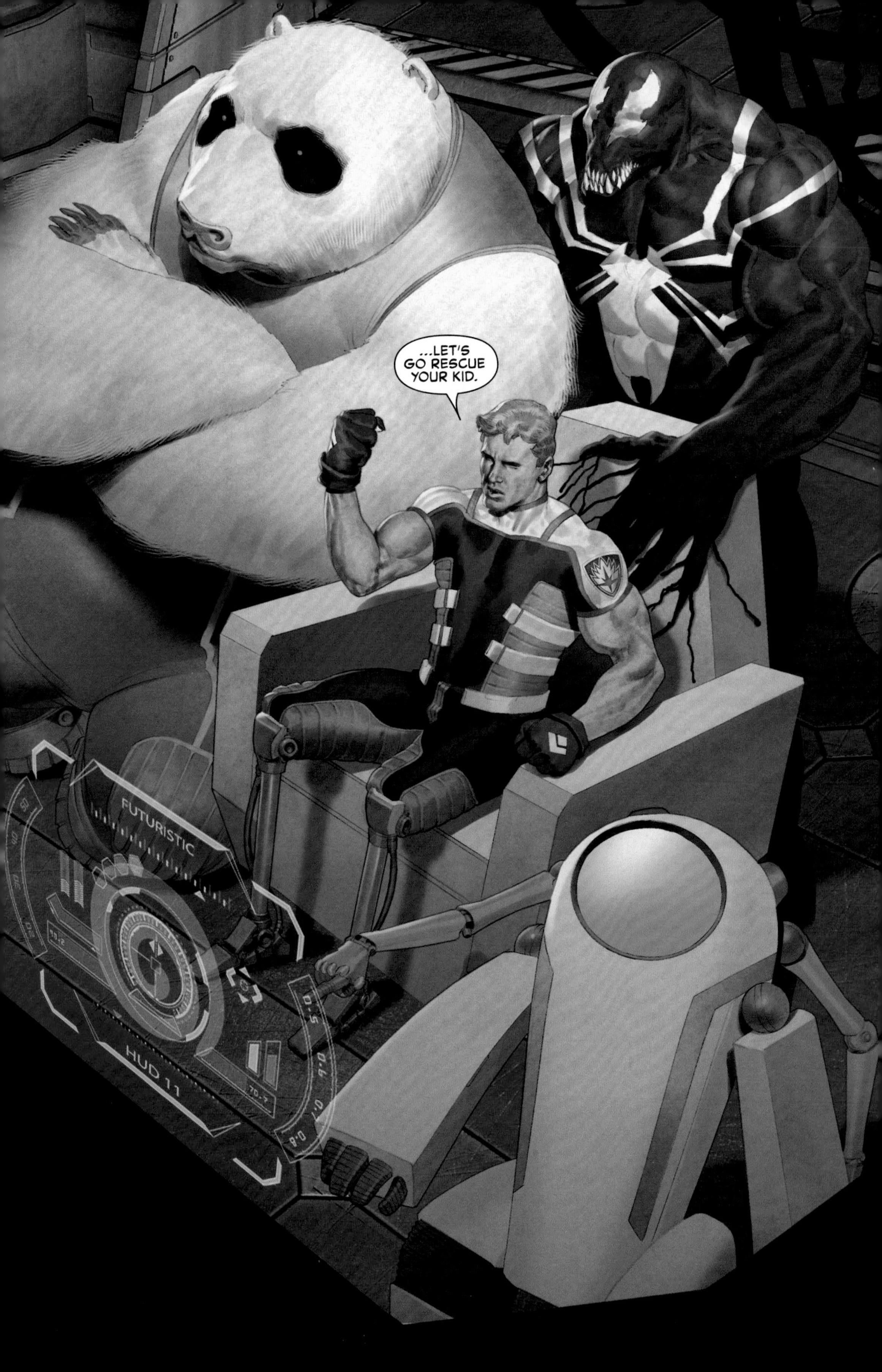
...LET'S GO RESCUE YOUR KID.
FUTURISTIC
HUD 11

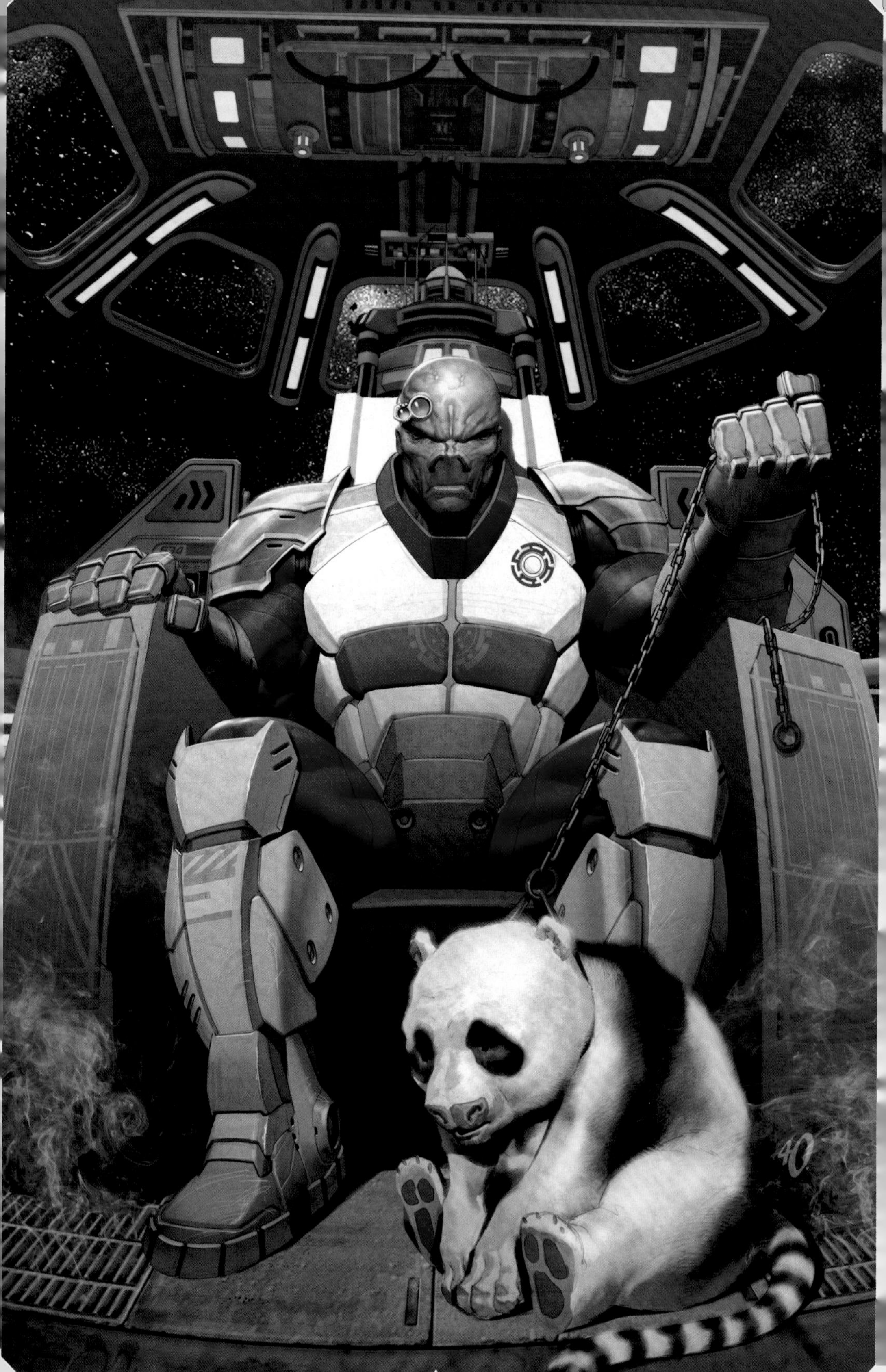

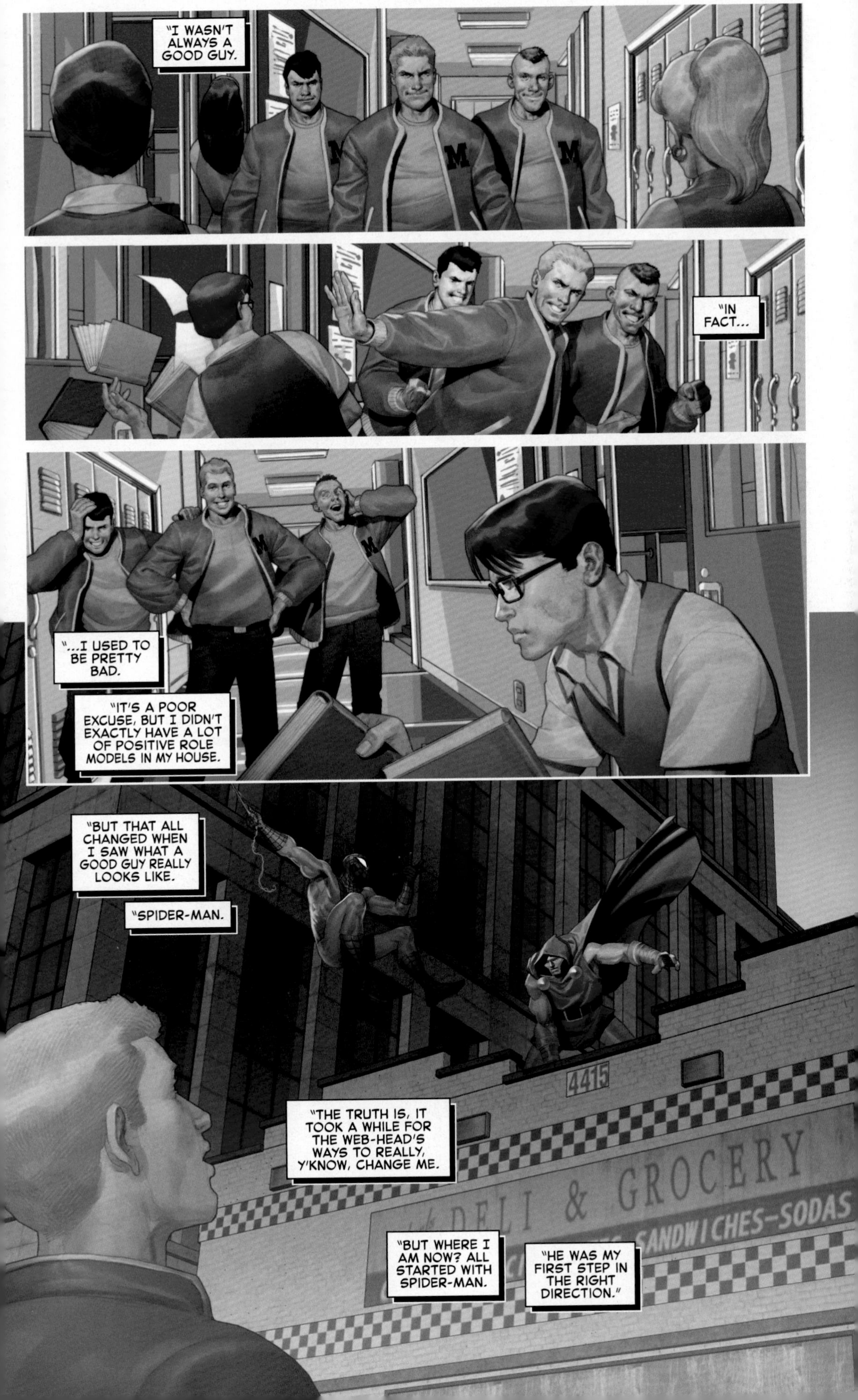
"I WASN'T ALWAYS A GOOD GUY.
"IN FACT...
"...I USED TO BE PRETTY BAD.
"IT'S A POOR EXCUSE, BUT I DIDN'T EXACTLY HAVE A LOT OF POSITIVE ROLE MODELS IN MY HOUSE.
"BUT THAT ALL CHANGED WHEN I SAW WHAT A GOOD GUY REALLY LOOKS LIKE.
"SPIDER-MAN.
4415
"THE TRUTH IS, IT TOOK A WHILE FOR THE WEB-HEAD'S WAYS TO REALLY, Y'KNOW, CHANGE ME.
DELI & GROCERY
SANDWICHES-SODAS
"BUT WHERE I AM NOW? ALL STARTED WITH SPIDER-MAN.
"HE WAS MY FIRST STEP IN THE RIGHT DIRECTION."

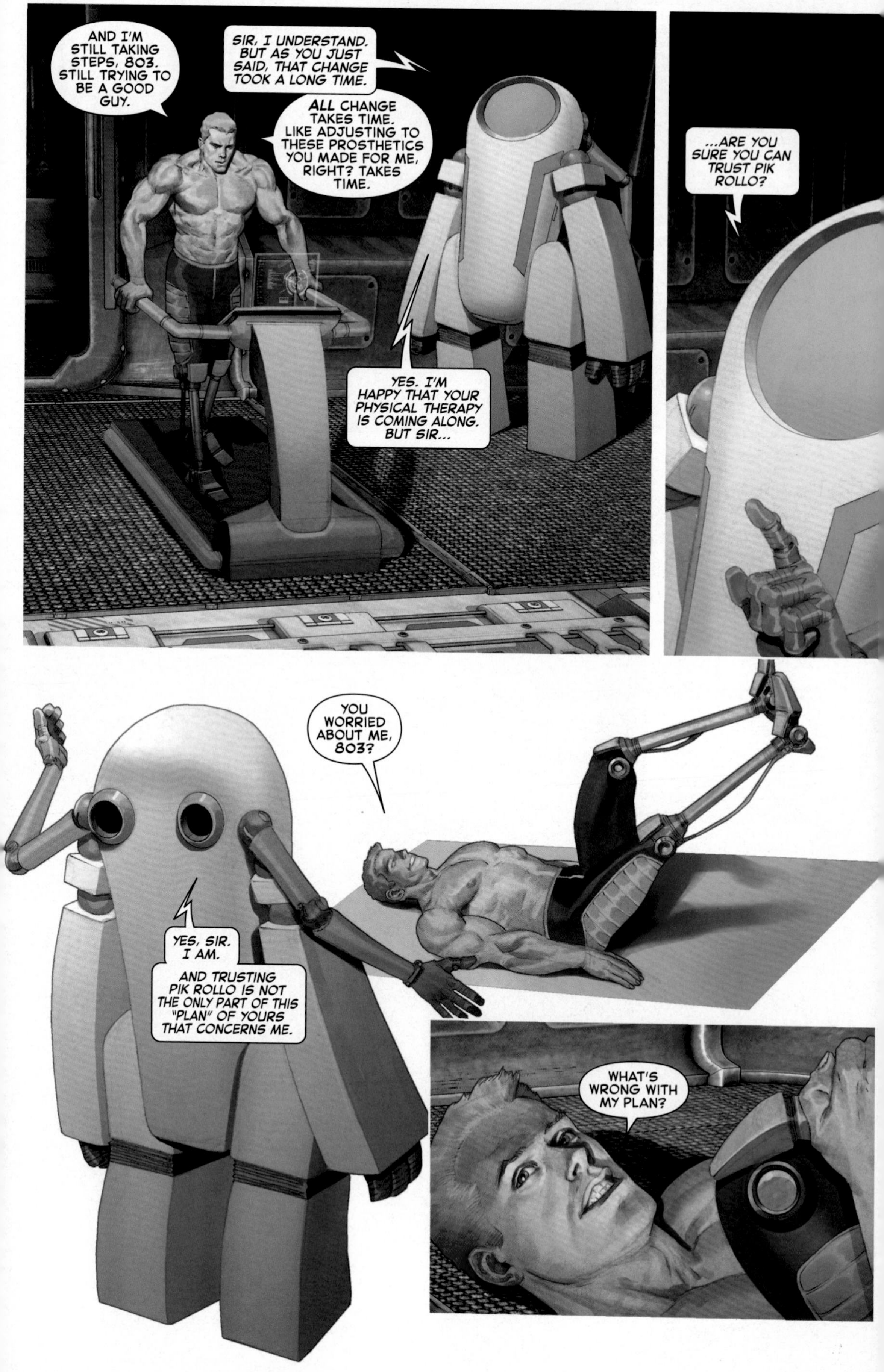
AND I'M STILL TAKING STEPS, 803. STILL TRYING TO BE A GOOD GUY.
SIR, I UNDERSTAND. BUT AS YOU JUST SAID, THAT CHANGE TOOK A LONG TIME.
ALL CHANGE TAKES TIME. LIKE ADJUSTING TO THESE PROSTHETICS YOU MADE FOR ME, RIGHT? TAKES TIME.
YES. I'M HAPPY THAT YOUR PHYSICAL THERAPY IS COMING ALONG. BUT SIR...
...ARE YOU SURE YOU CAN TRUST PIK ROLLO?
YOU WORRIED ABOUT ME, 803?
YES, SIR. I AM.
AND TRUSTING PIK ROLLO IS NOT THE ONLY PART OF THIS "PLAN" OF YOURS THAT CONCERNS ME.
WHAT'S WRONG WITH MY PLAN?

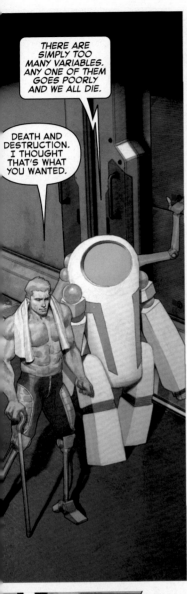

THERE ARE SIMPLY TOO MANY VARIABLES. ANY ONE OF THEM GOES POORLY AND WE ALL DIE.

DEATH AND DESTRUCTION. I THOUGHT THAT'S WHAT YOU WANTED.

MY DESTRUCTION, SIR. NOT YOURS.

YOUR CONCERN IS DULY NOTED. AND APPRECIATED, 803.

BUT DON'T FORGET: YOU HAVE ONE OF THE TOUGHEST PARTS IN THIS WHOLE THING.

SO, IT'S HIGHLY LIKELY YOU WON'T LIVE LONG ENOUGH TO SEE ME GET DOUBLE-CROSSED.

THIS IS MEANT TO COMFORT ME?

NOT REALLY, NO.

WE CAN TRUST PIK ROLLO. AND IF YOU CAN'T, THEN TRUST ME. OKAY?

ALL RIGHT, SIR.

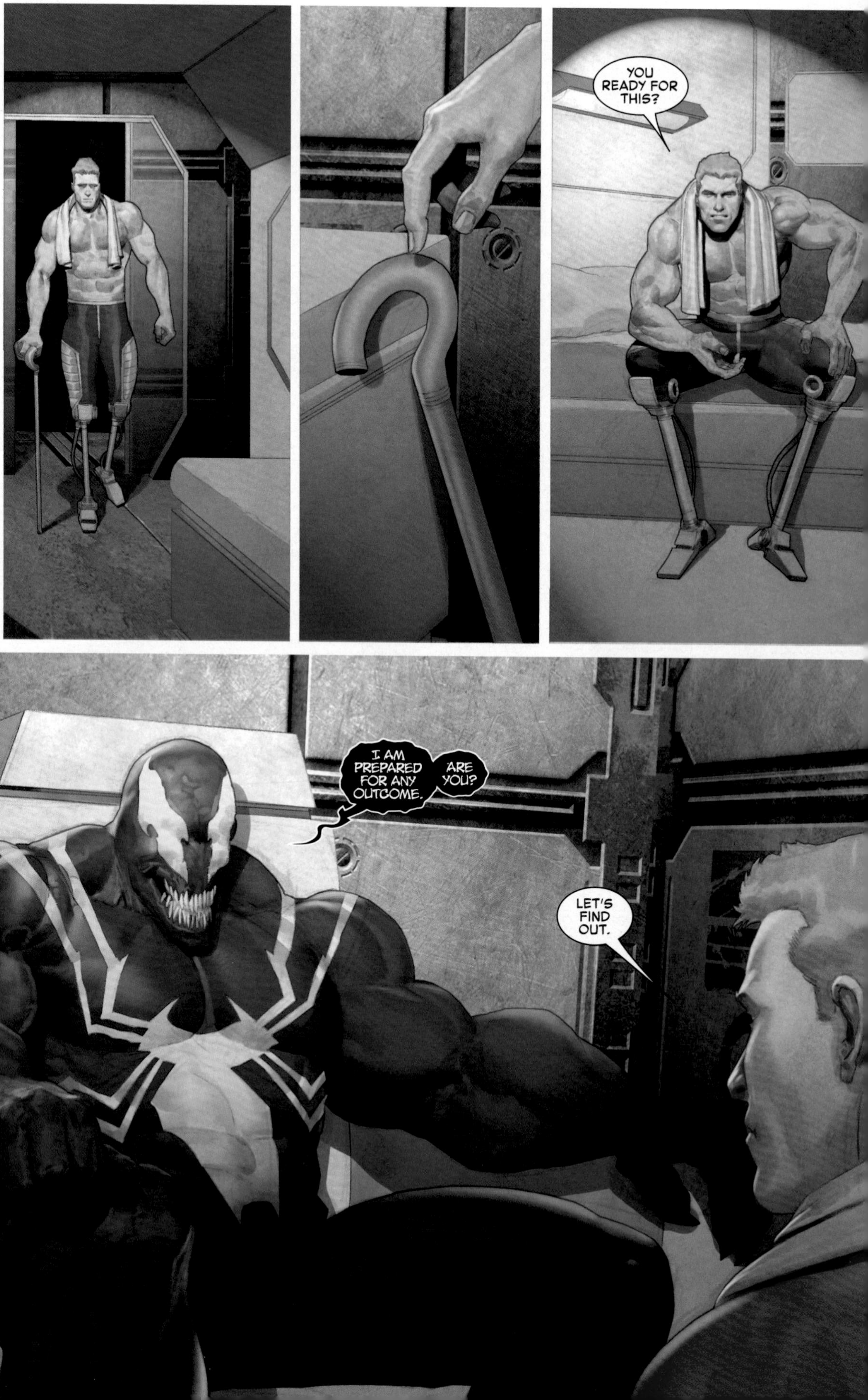
YOU READY FOR THIS?
I AM PREPARED FOR ANY OUTCOME.
ARE YOU?
LET'S FIND OUT.

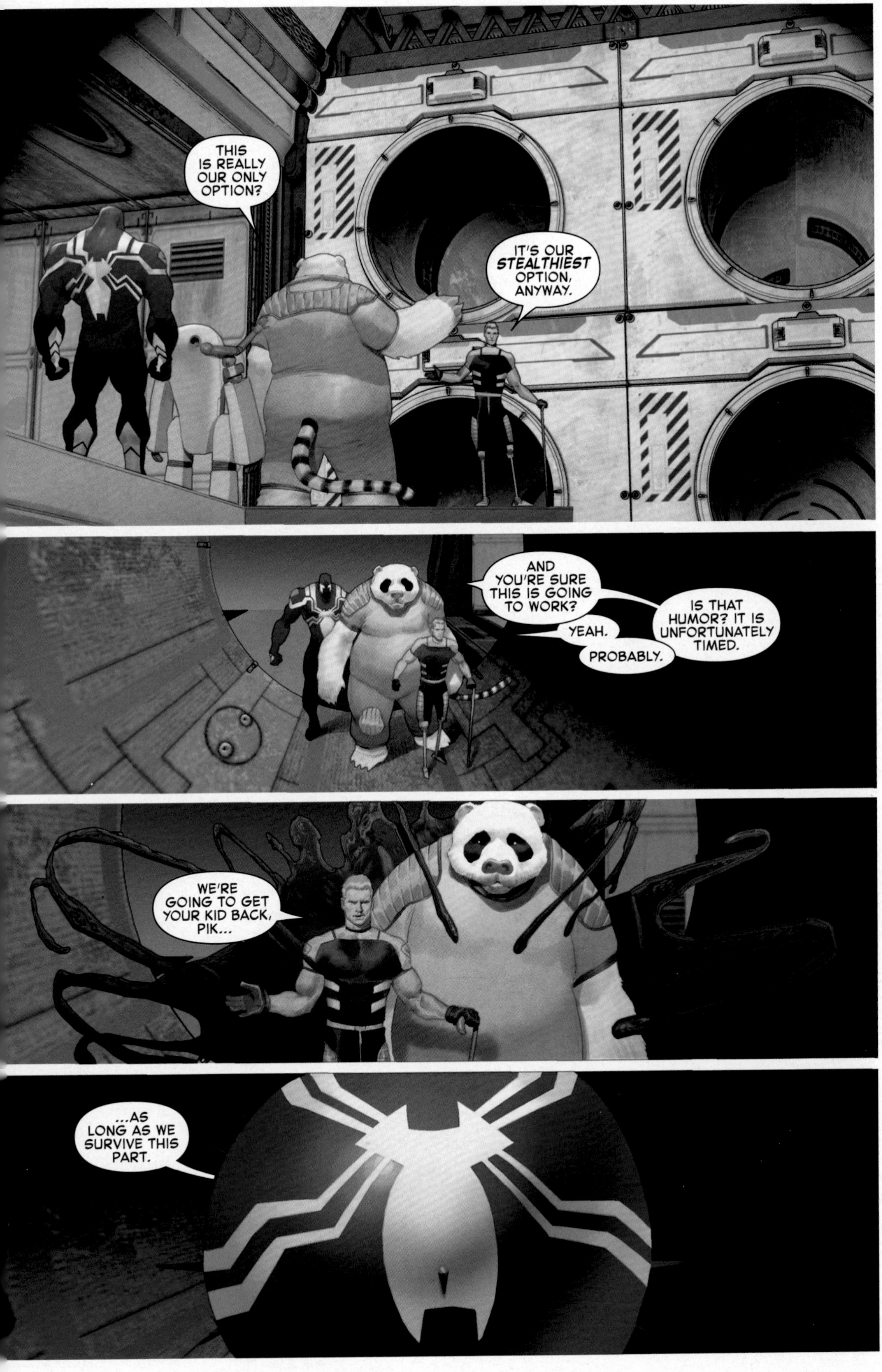
THIS IS REALLY OUR ONLY OPTION?
IT'S OUR STEALTHIEST OPTION, ANYWAY.
AND YOU'RE SURE THIS IS GOING TO WORK?
YEAH.
PROBABLY.
IS THAT HUMOR? IT IS UNFORTUNATELY TIMED.
WE'RE GOING TO GET YOUR KID BACK, PIK...
...AS LONG AS WE SURVIVE THIS PART.

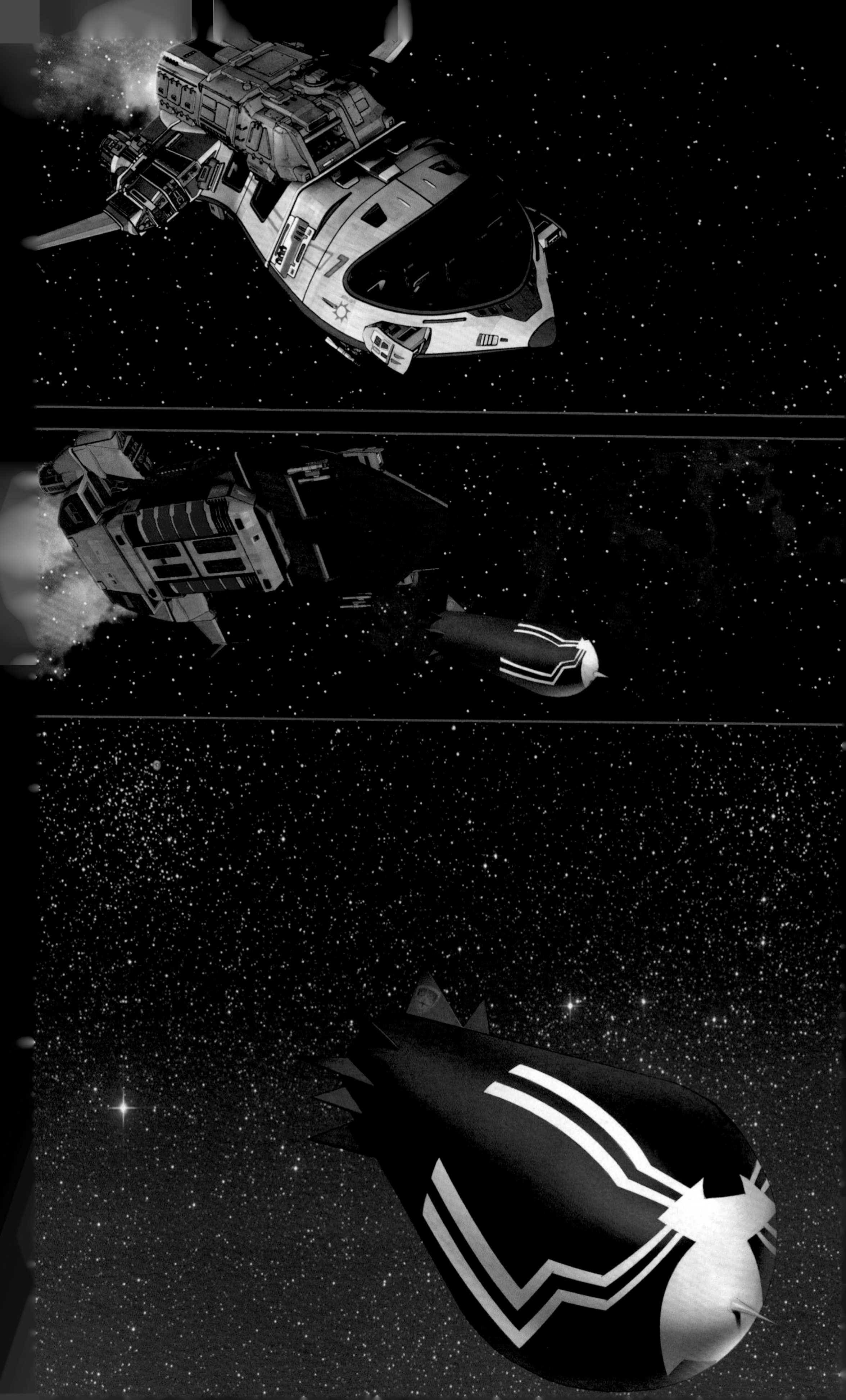

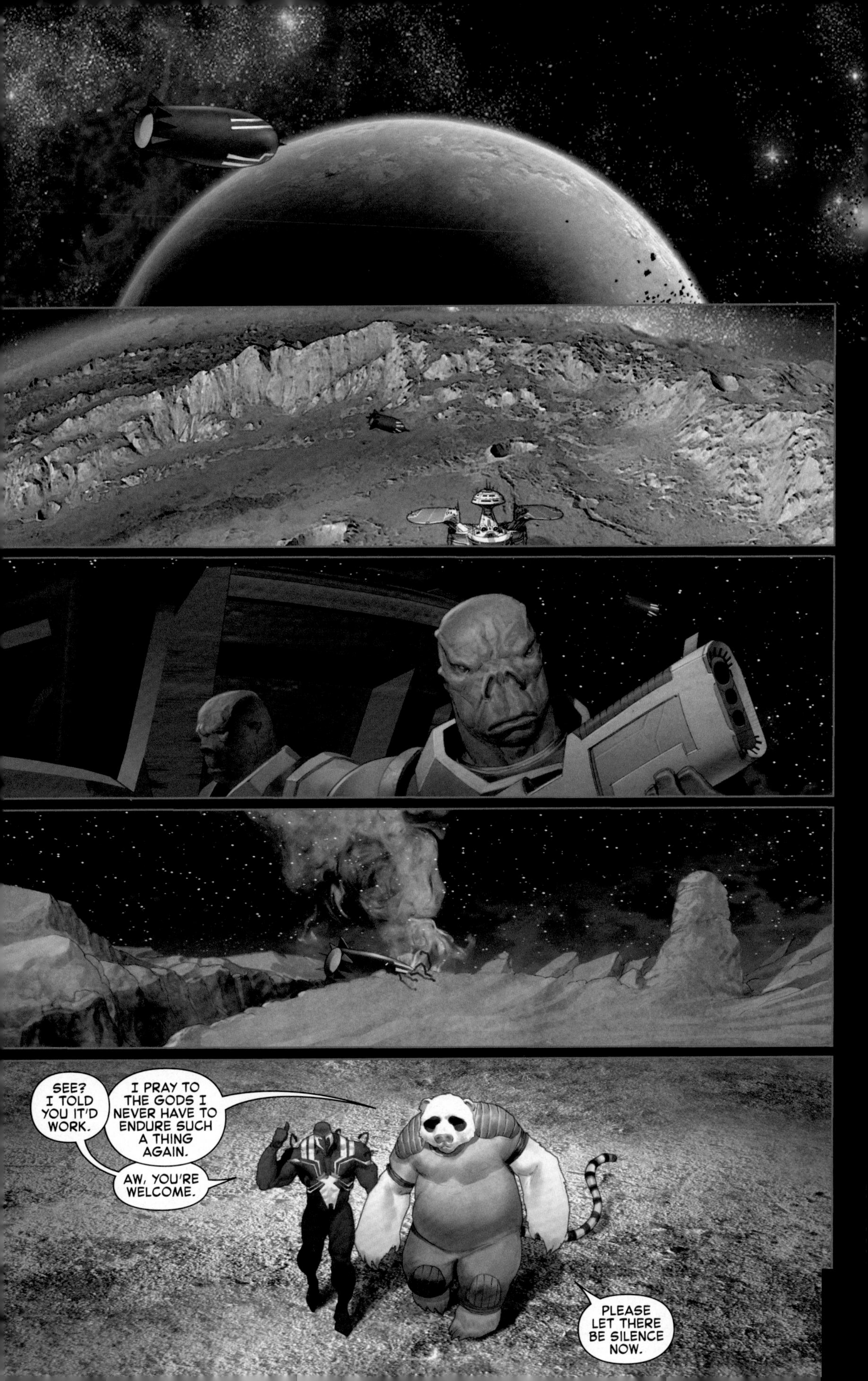
SEE? I TOLD YOU IT'D WORK.
I PRAY TO THE GODS I NEVER HAVE TO ENDURE SUCH A THING AGAIN.
AW, YOU'RE WELCOME.
PLEASE LET THERE BE SILENCE NOW.

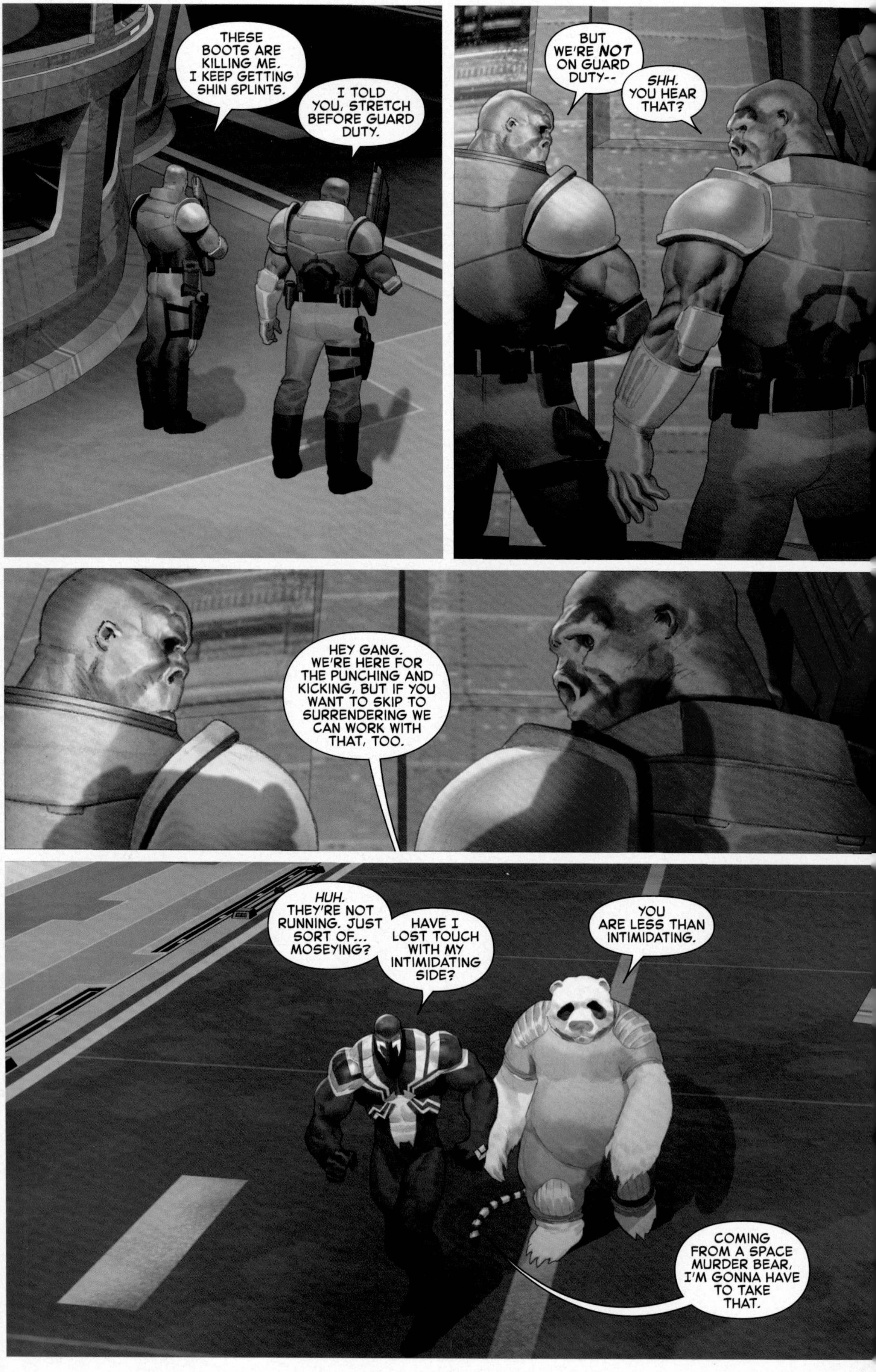
THESE BOOTS ARE KILLING ME. I KEEP GETTING SHIN SPLINTS.
I TOLD YOU, STRETCH BEFORE GUARD DUTY.
BUT WE'RE *NOT* ON GUARD DUTY--
SHH. YOU HEAR THAT?
HEY GANG. WE'RE HERE FOR THE PUNCHING AND KICKING, BUT IF YOU WANT TO SKIP TO SURRENDERING WE CAN WORK WITH THAT, TOO.
HUH. THEY'RE NOT RUNNING. JUST SORT OF... MOSEYING?
HAVE I LOST TOUCH WITH MY INTIMIDATING SIDE?
YOU ARE LESS THAN INTIMIDATING.
COMING FROM A SPACE MURDER BEAR, I'M GONNA HAVE TO TAKE THAT.

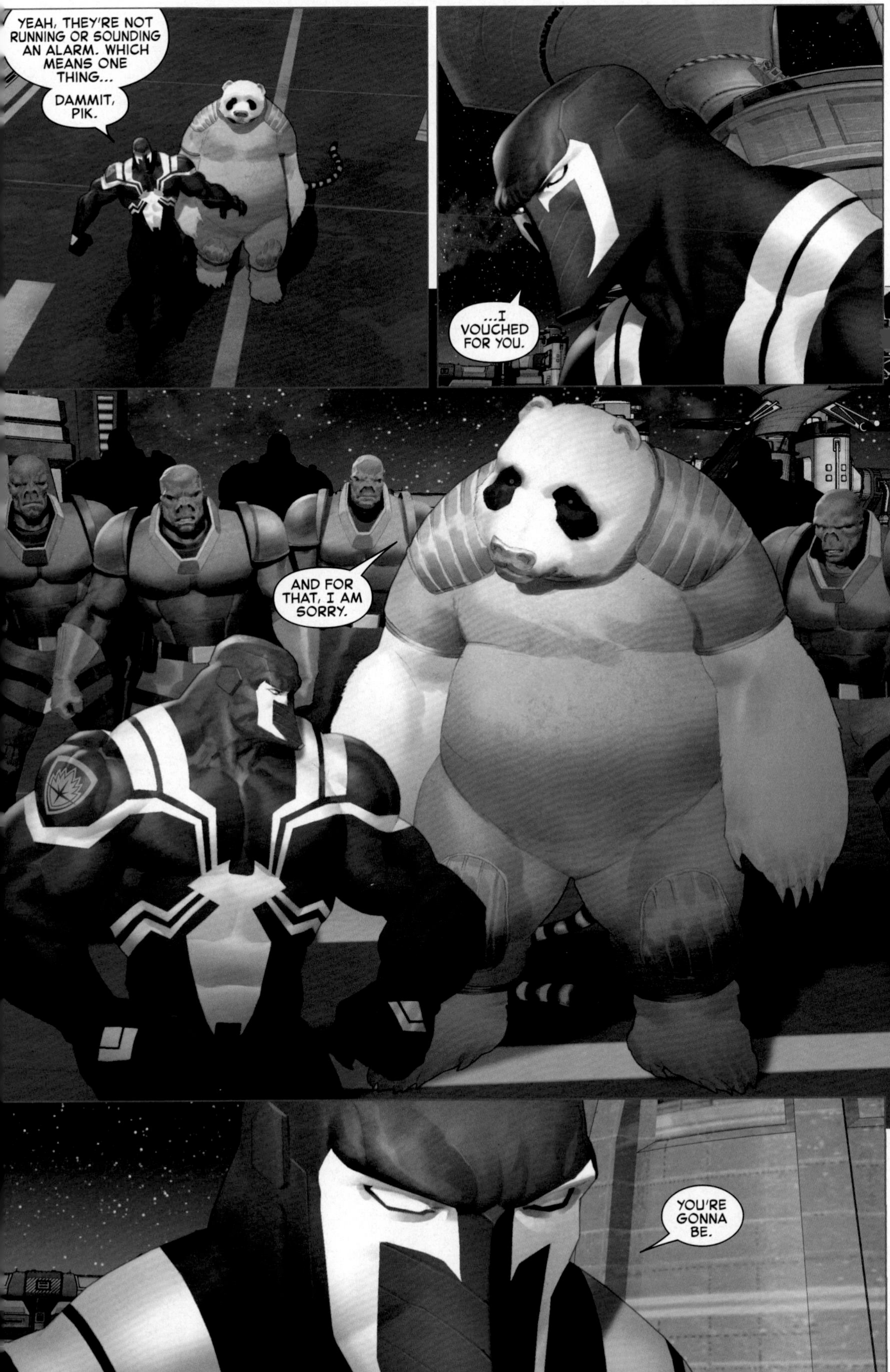
YEAH, THEY'RE NOT RUNNING OR SOUNDING AN ALARM. WHICH MEANS ONE THING...
DAMMIT, PIK.
...I VOUCHED FOR YOU.
AND FOR THAT, I AM SORRY.
YOU'RE GONNA BE.

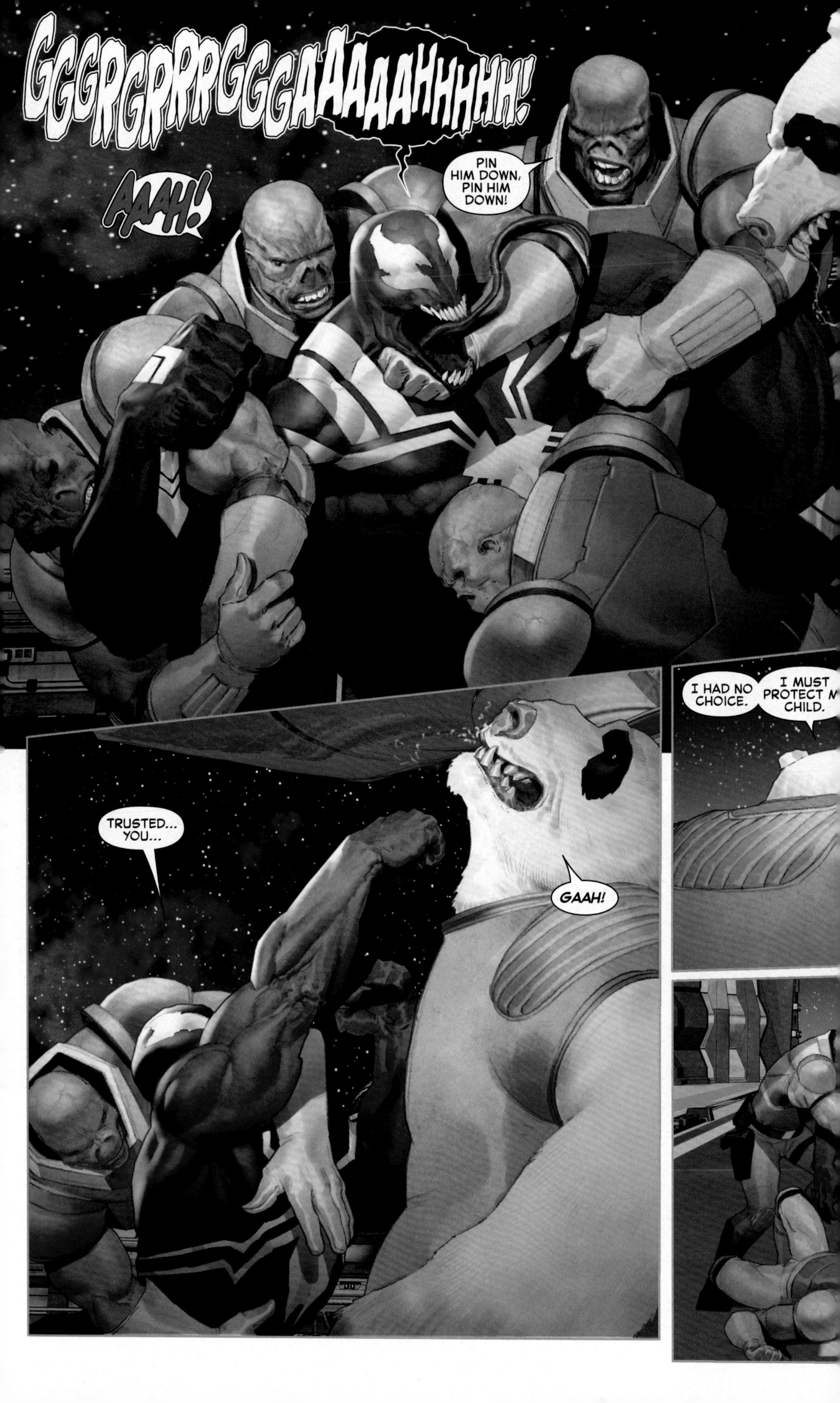
GGGRGRRRGGGAAAAAHHHHH!
AAAH!
PIN HIM DOWN, PIN HIM DOWN!
TRUSTED... YOU...
GAAH!
I HAD NO CHOICE.
I MUST PROTECT M
CHILD.

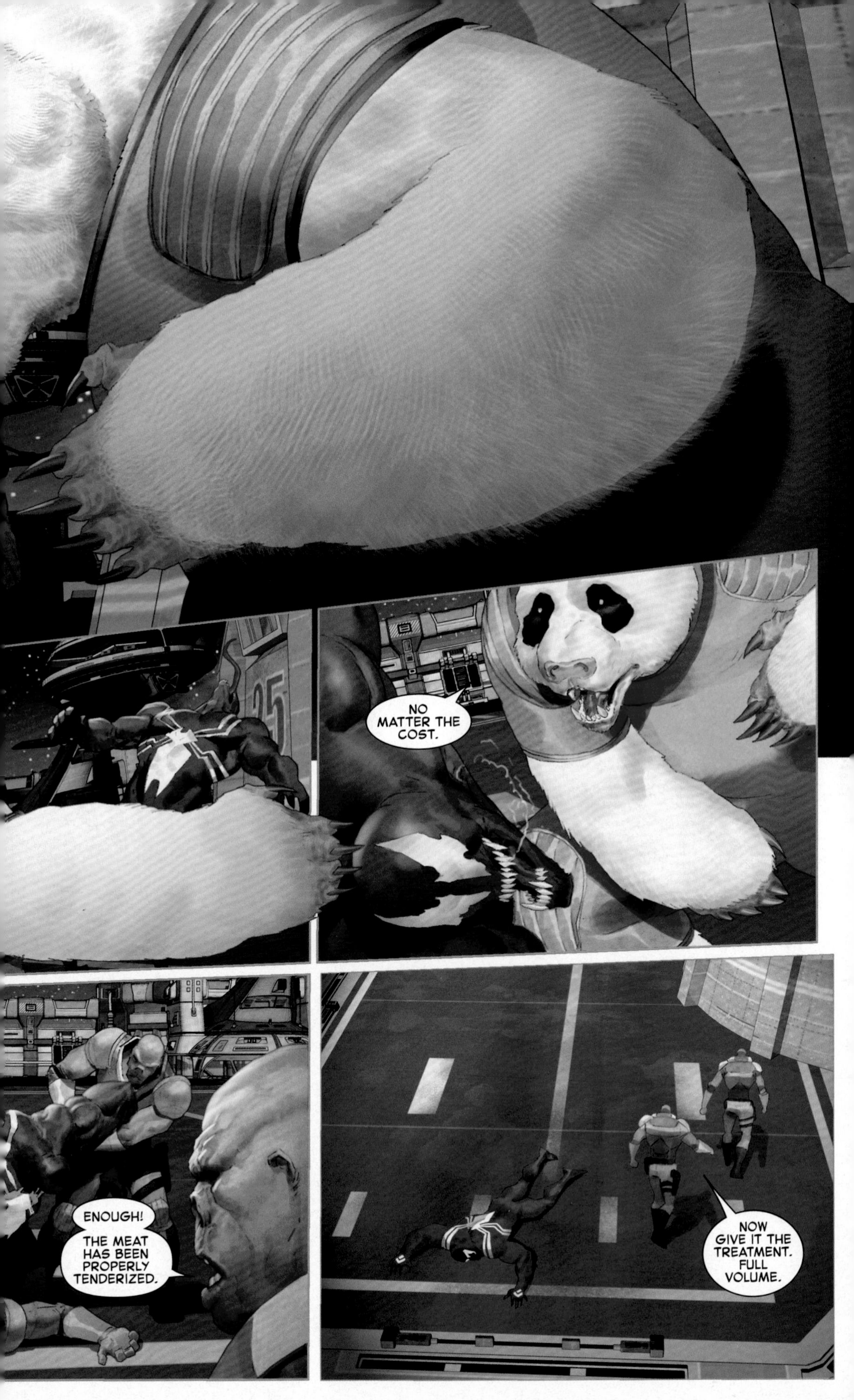
NO MATTER THE COST.
ENOUGH!
THE MEAT HAS BEEN PROPERLY TENDERIZED.
NOW GIVE IT THE TREATMENT. FULL VOLUME.

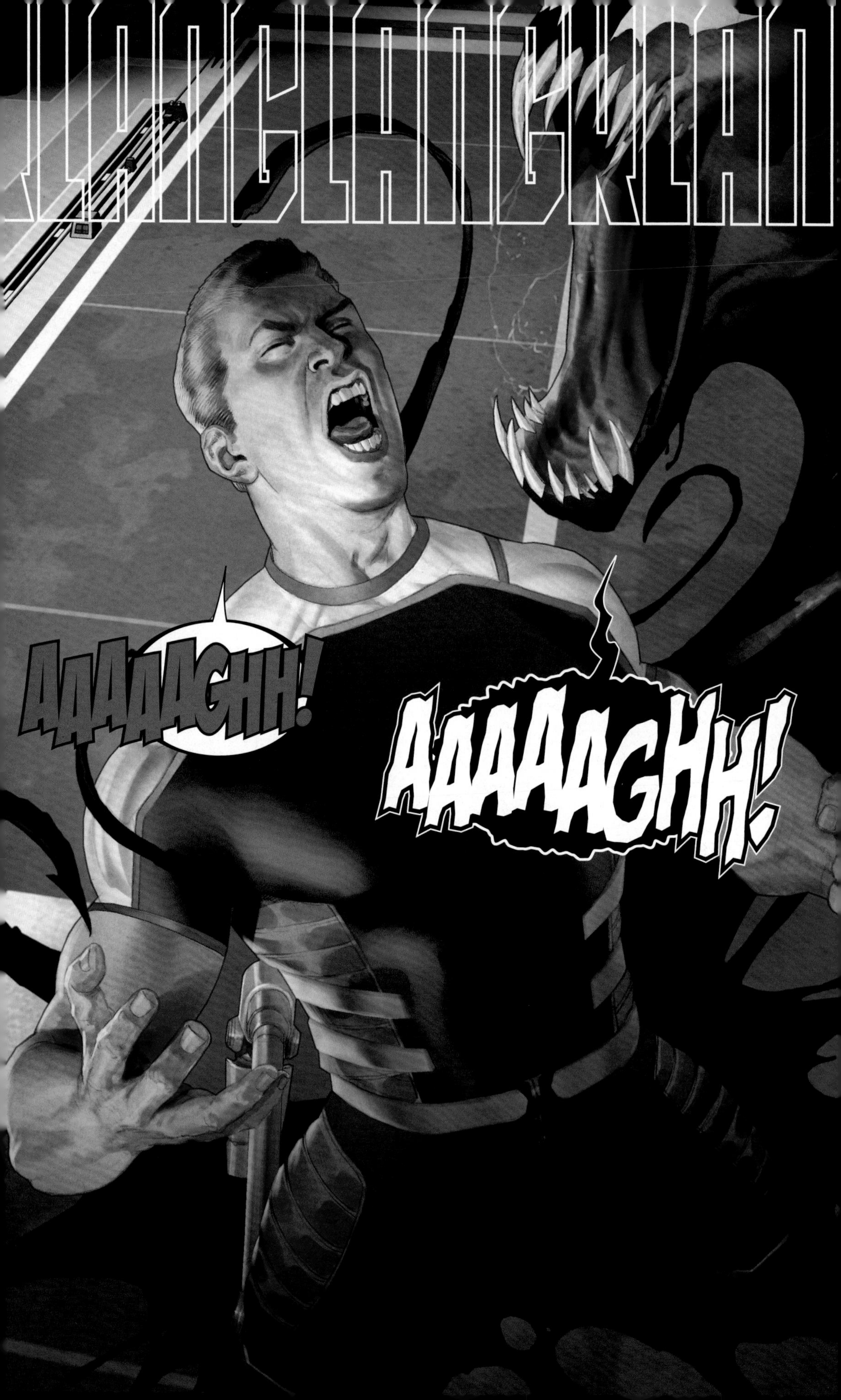
AAAAAGHH!
AAAAAGHH!

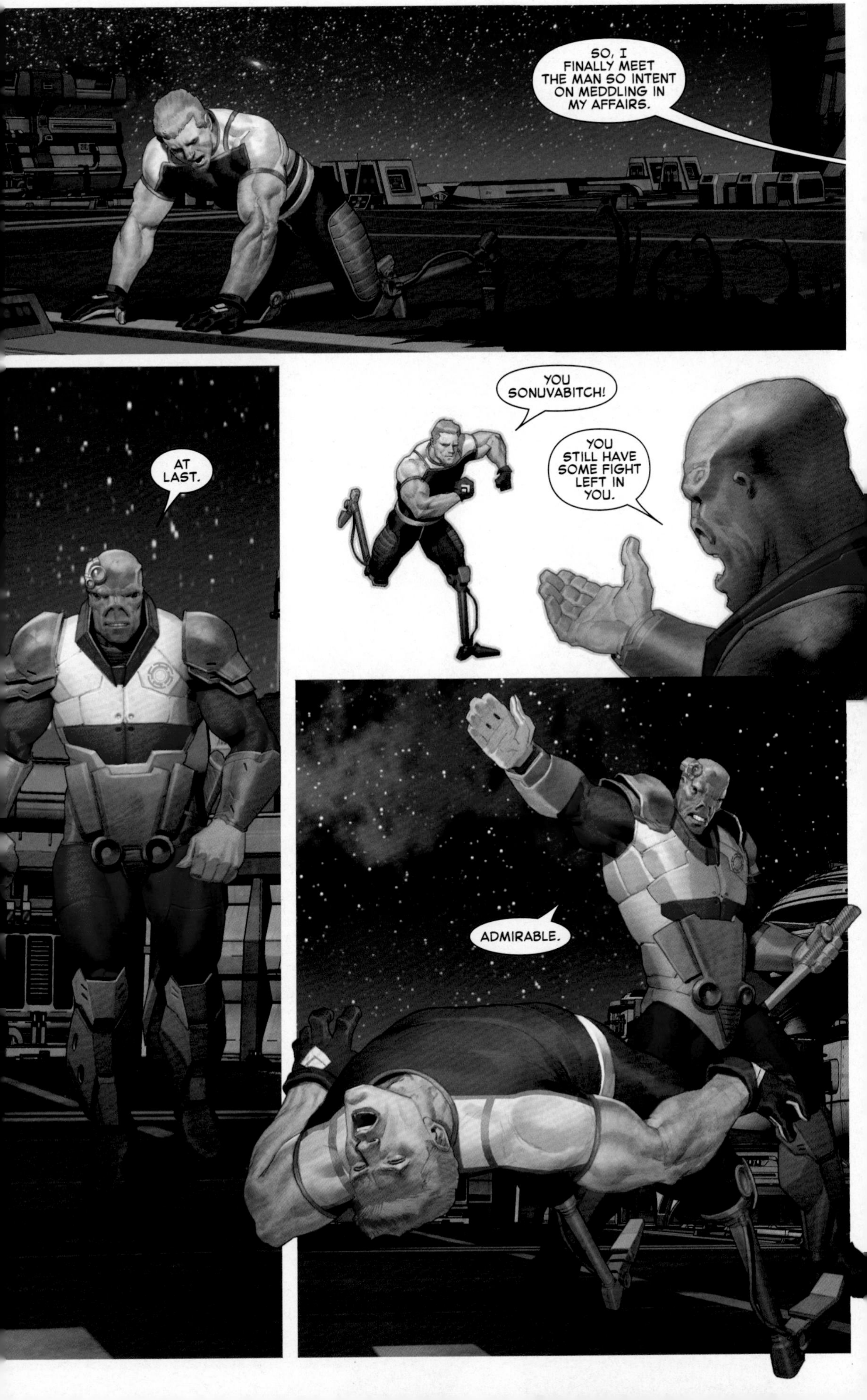
SO, I FINALLY MEET THE MAN SO INTENT ON MEDDLING IN MY AFFAIRS.
AT LAST.
YOU SONUVABITCH!
YOU STILL HAVE SOME FIGHT LEFT IN YOU.
ADMIRABLE.

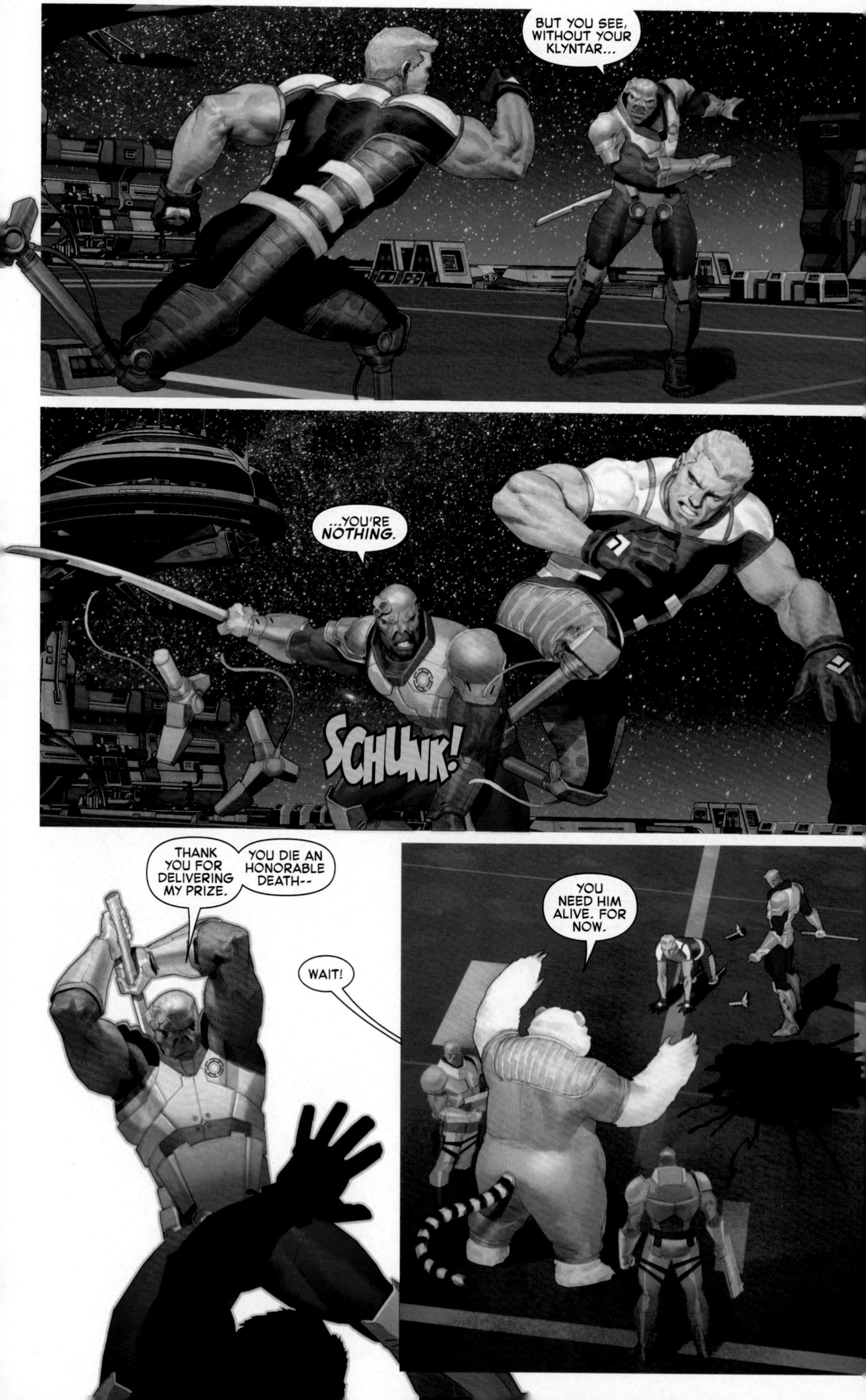
BUT YOU SEE, WITHOUT YOUR KLYNTAR...
...YOU'RE NOTHING.
SCHUNK!
THANK YOU FOR DELIVERING MY PRIZE.
YOU DIE AN HONORABLE DEATH--
WAIT!
YOU NEED HIM ALIVE. FOR NOW.

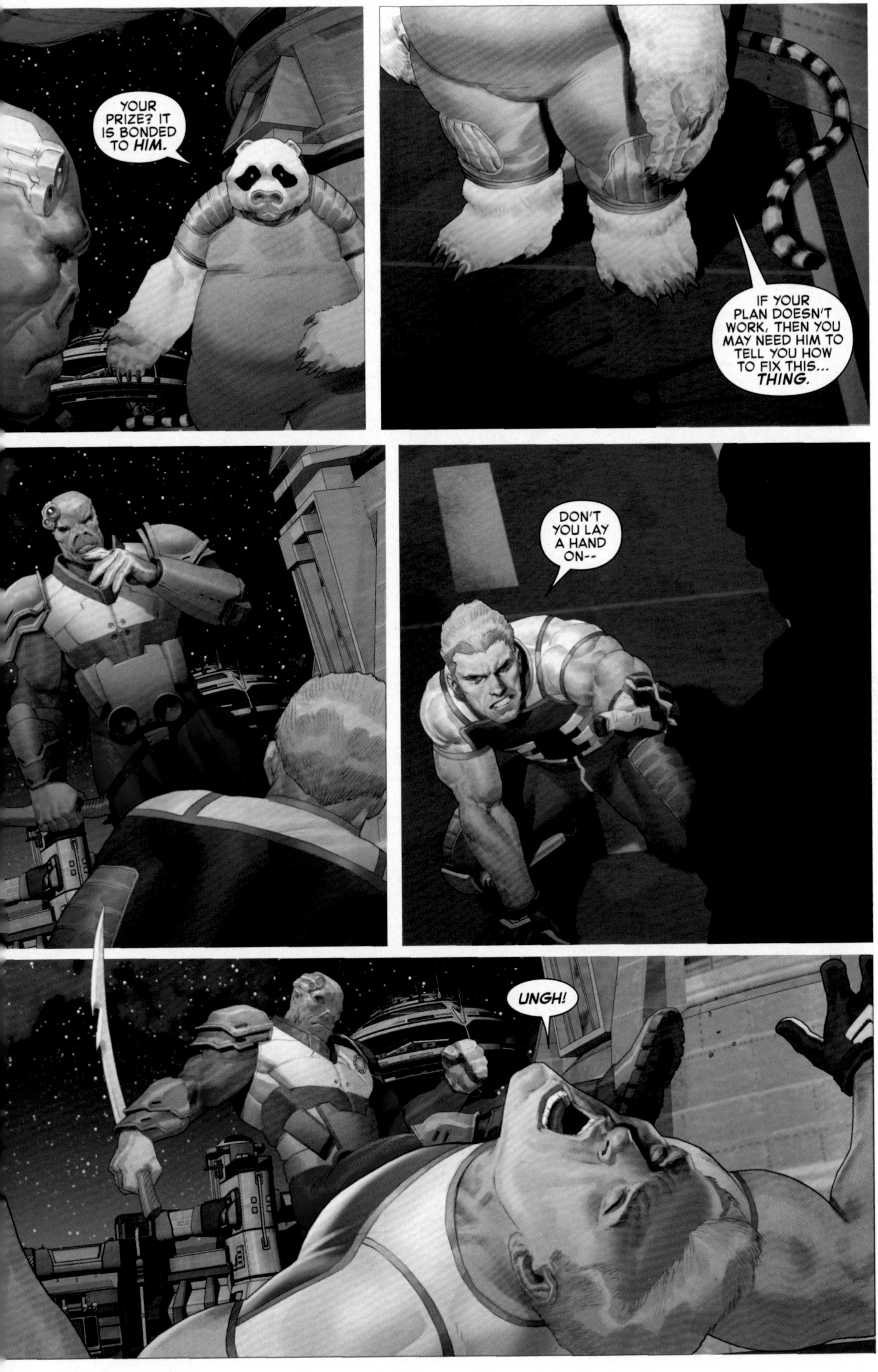

YOUR PRIZE? IT IS BONDED TO *HIM.*
IF YOUR PLAN DOESN'T WORK, THEN YOU MAY NEED HIM TO TELL YOU HOW TO FIX THIS... *THING.*
DON'T YOU LAY A HAND ON--
UNGH!

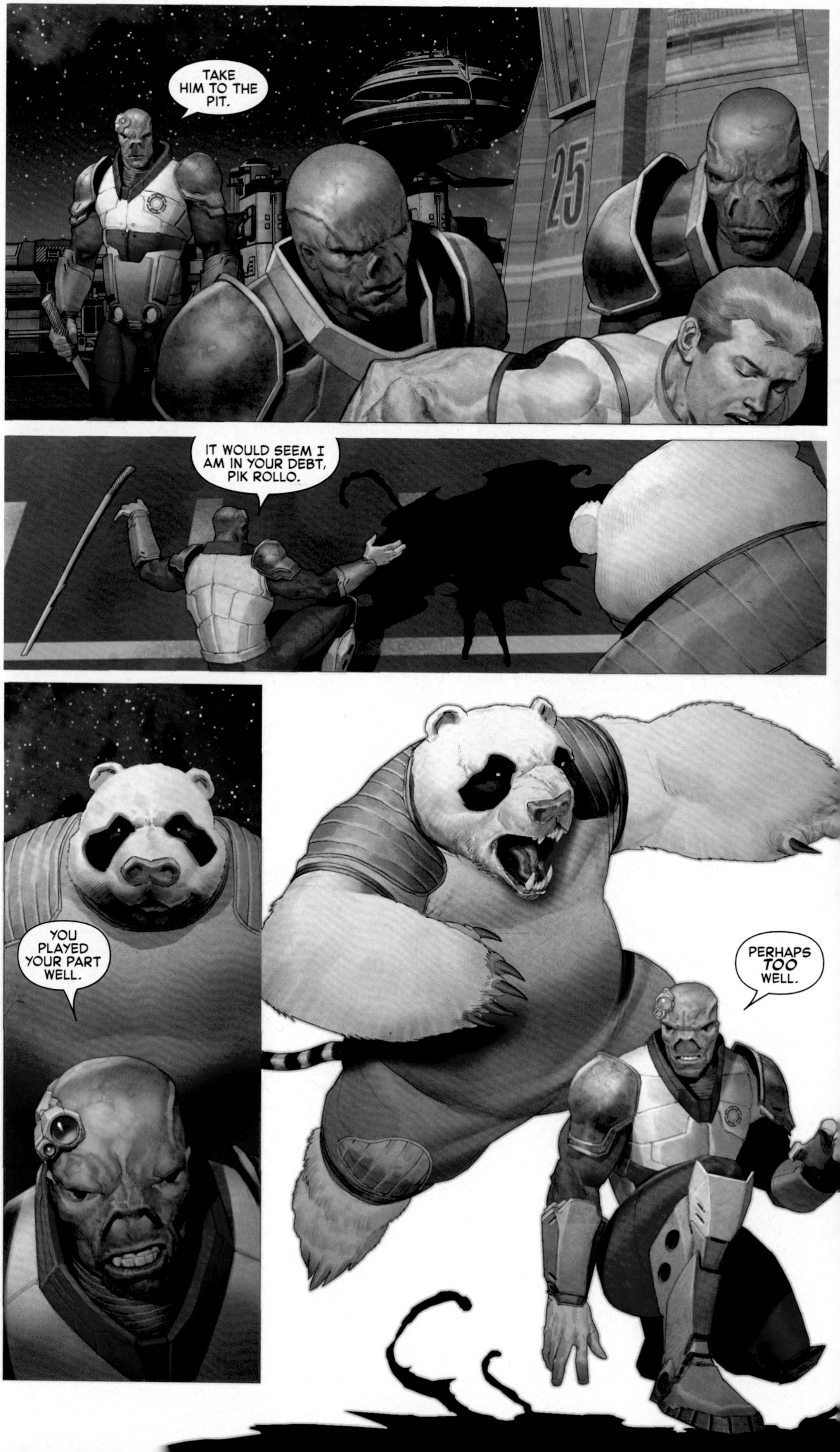
TAKE HIM TO THE PIT.
IT WOULD SEEM I AM IN YOUR DEBT, PIK ROLLO.
YOU PLAYED YOUR PART WELL.
PERHAPS *TOO* WELL.

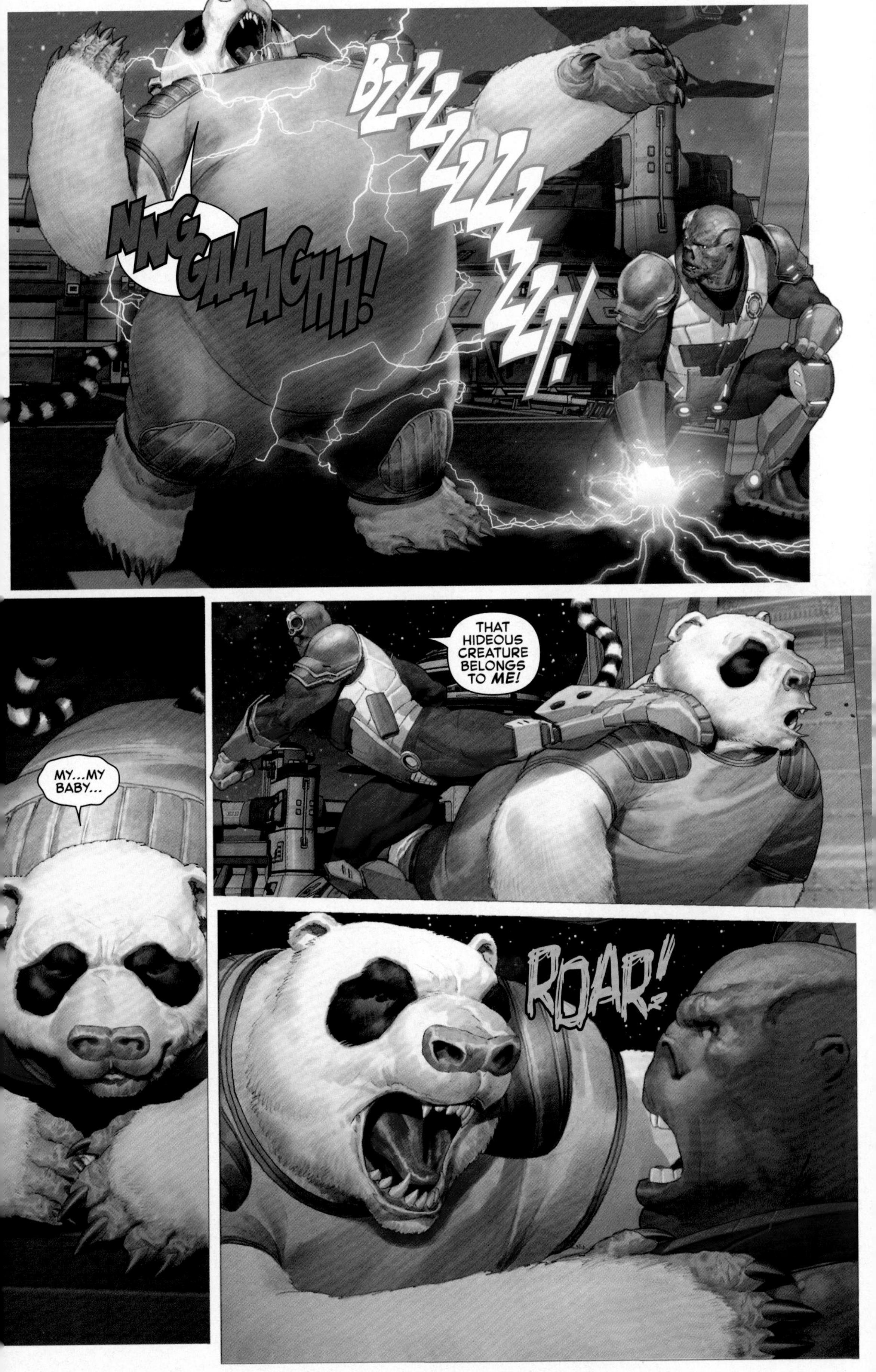
NNG GAAAGHH!
BZZZZZZZZZT!
MY...MY BABY...
THAT HIDEOUS CREATURE BELONGS TO ME!
ROAR!

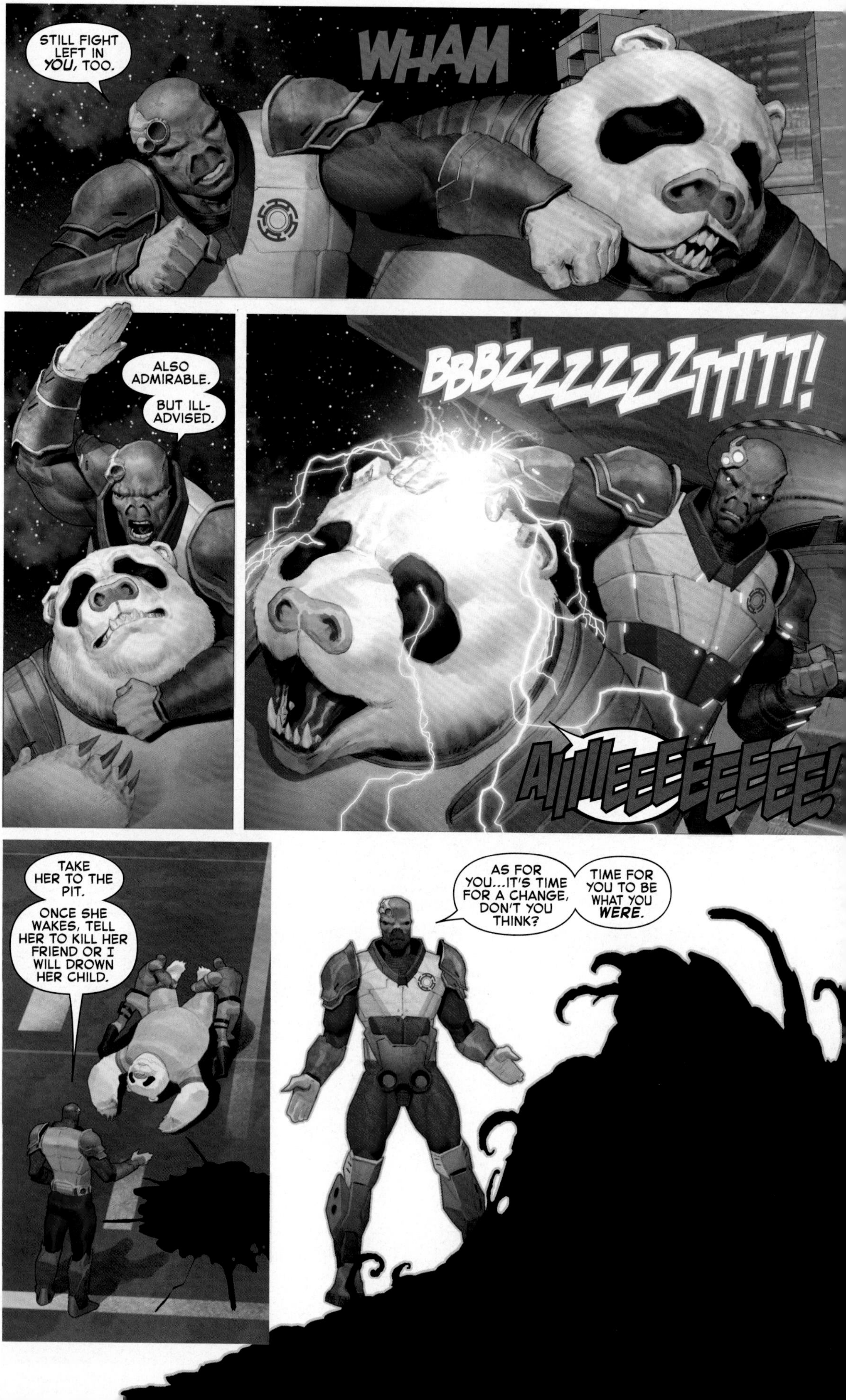

STILL FIGHT LEFT IN *YOU*, TOO.
WHAM
ALSO ADMIRABLE.
BUT ILL-ADVISED.
BBBZZZZZZZTTTTT!
AIIIIEEEEEEEEE!
TAKE HER TO THE PIT.
ONCE SHE WAKES, TELL HER TO KILL HER FRIEND OR I WILL DROWN HER CHILD.
AS FOR YOU...IT'S TIME FOR A CHANGE, DON'T YOU THINK?
TIME FOR YOU TO BE WHAT YOU *WERE*.

KKK-KLANG!

OOOF!

KKKK-CHUNG

...SEE...? TOLD YOU...IT'D... WORK...

...IF I WASN'T SO BROKEN...

...I WOULD BREAK YOU.

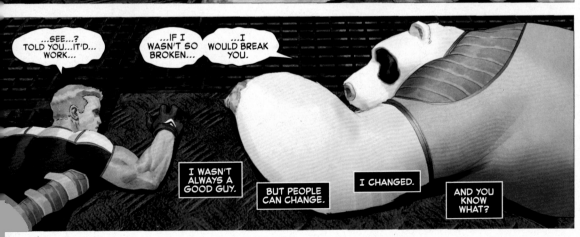

I WASN'T ALWAYS A GOOD GUY.

BUT PEOPLE CAN CHANGE.

I CHANGED.

AND YOU KNOW WHAT?

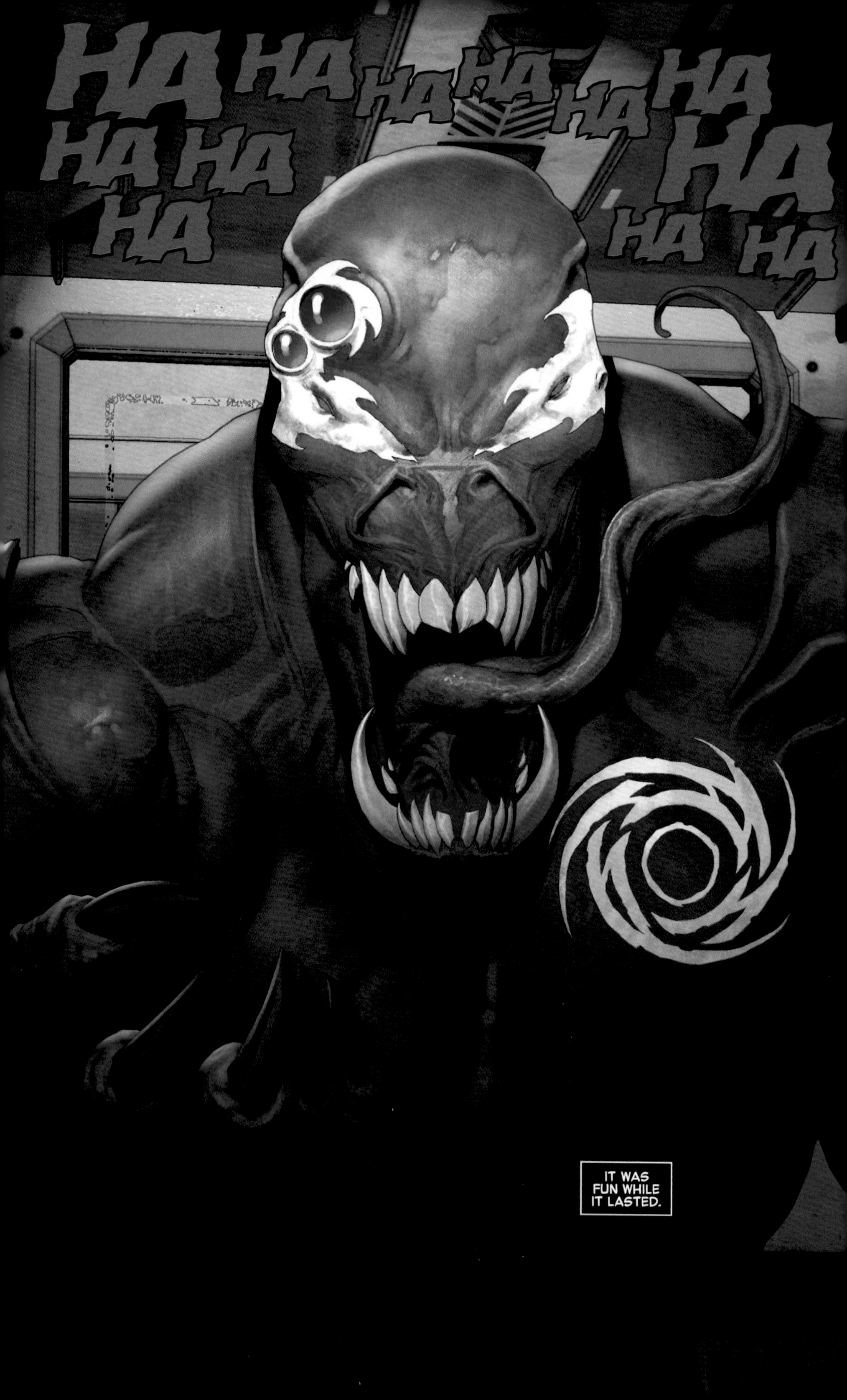
HA HA HA HA HA HA HA
HA HA HA HA
HA HA HA HA
IT WAS FUN WHILE IT LASTED.

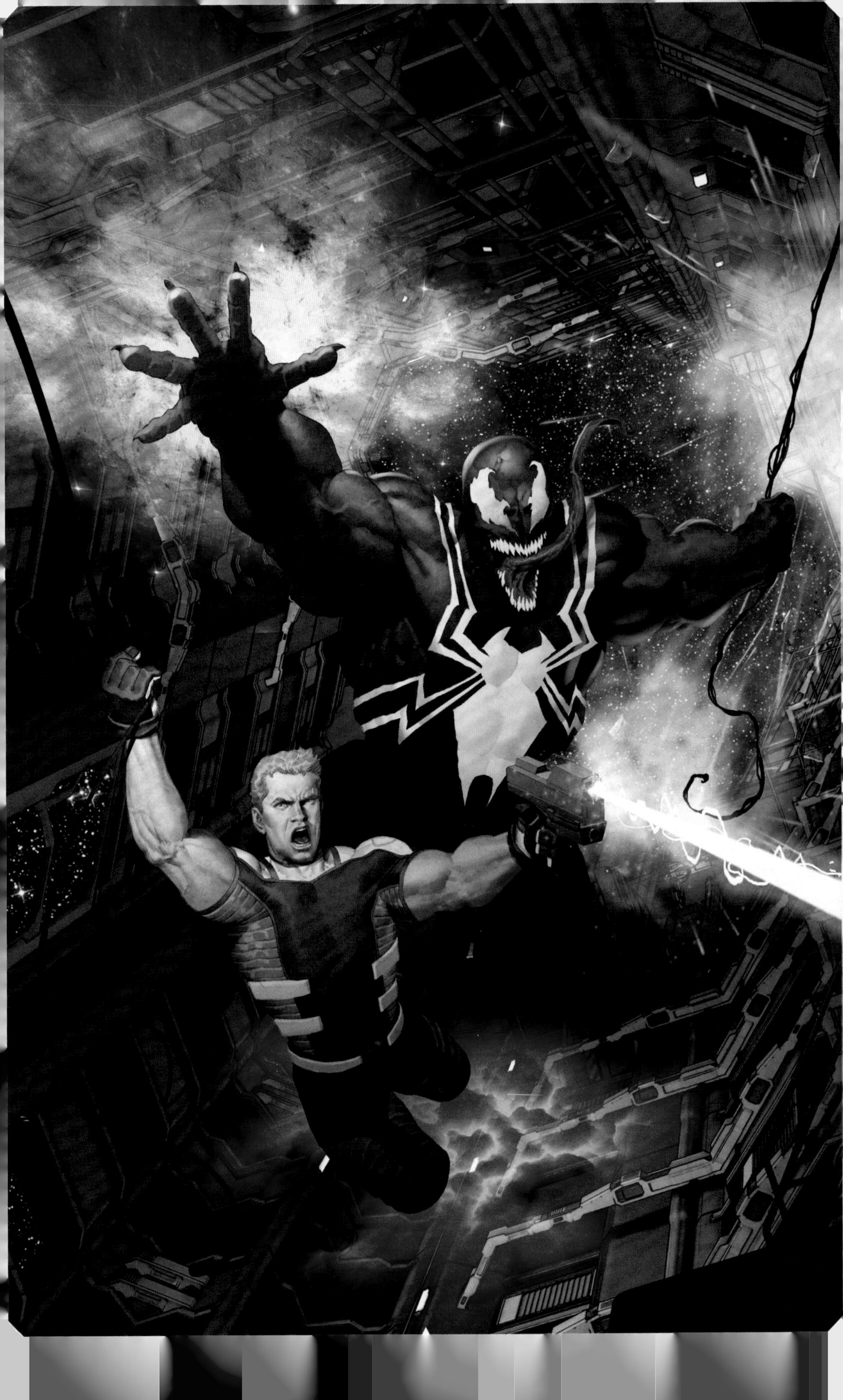

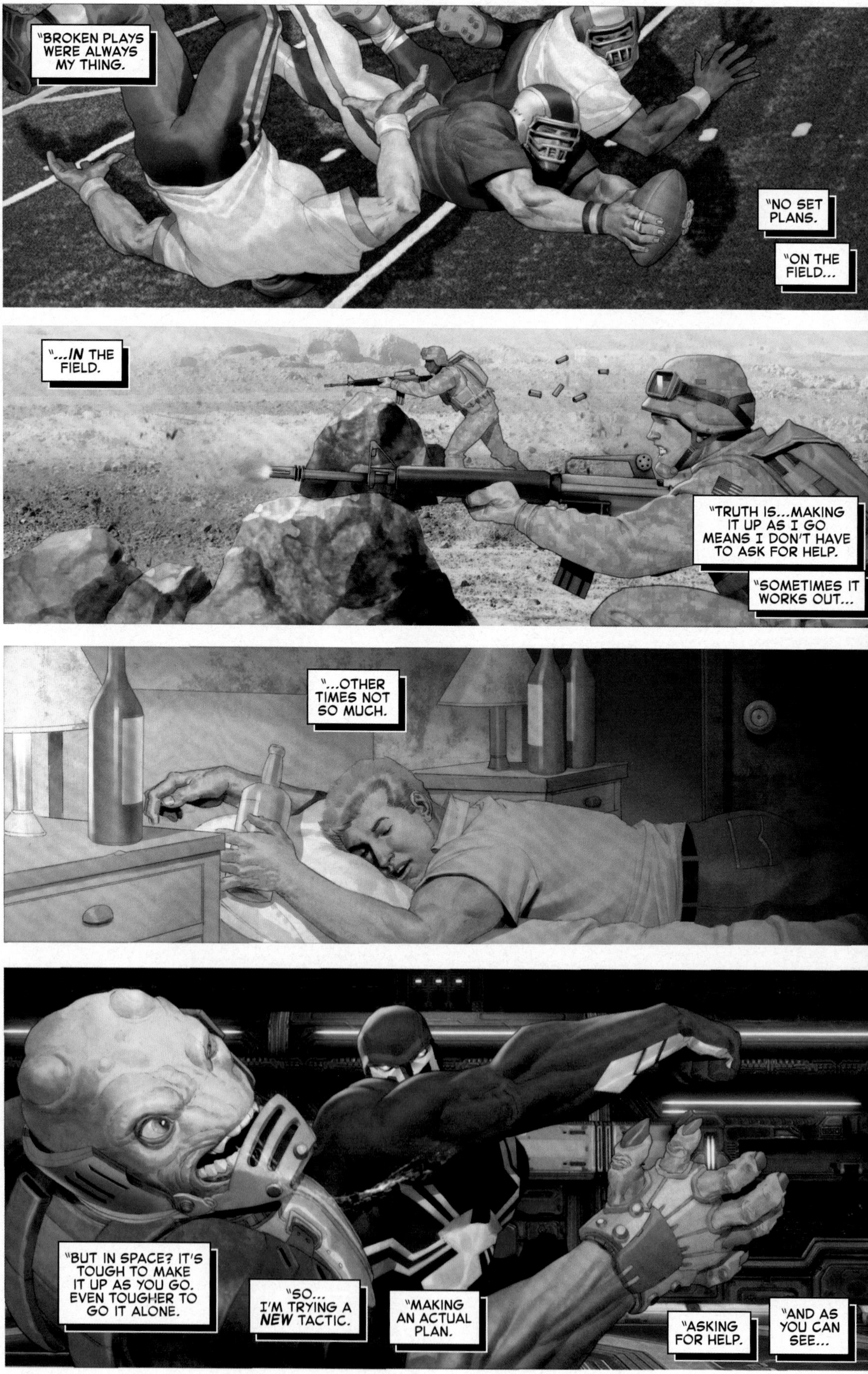
"BROKEN PLAYS WERE ALWAYS MY THING.
"NO SET PLANS.
"ON THE FIELD...
"...IN THE FIELD.
"TRUTH IS...MAKING IT UP AS I GO MEANS I DON'T HAVE TO ASK FOR HELP.
"SOMETIMES IT WORKS OUT...
"...OTHER TIMES NOT SO MUCH.
"BUT IN SPACE? IT'S TOUGH TO MAKE IT UP AS YOU GO. EVEN TOUGHER TO GO IT ALONE.
"SO... I'M TRYING A NEW TACTIC.
"MAKING AN ACTUAL PLAN.
"ASKING FOR HELP.
"AND AS YOU CAN SEE...

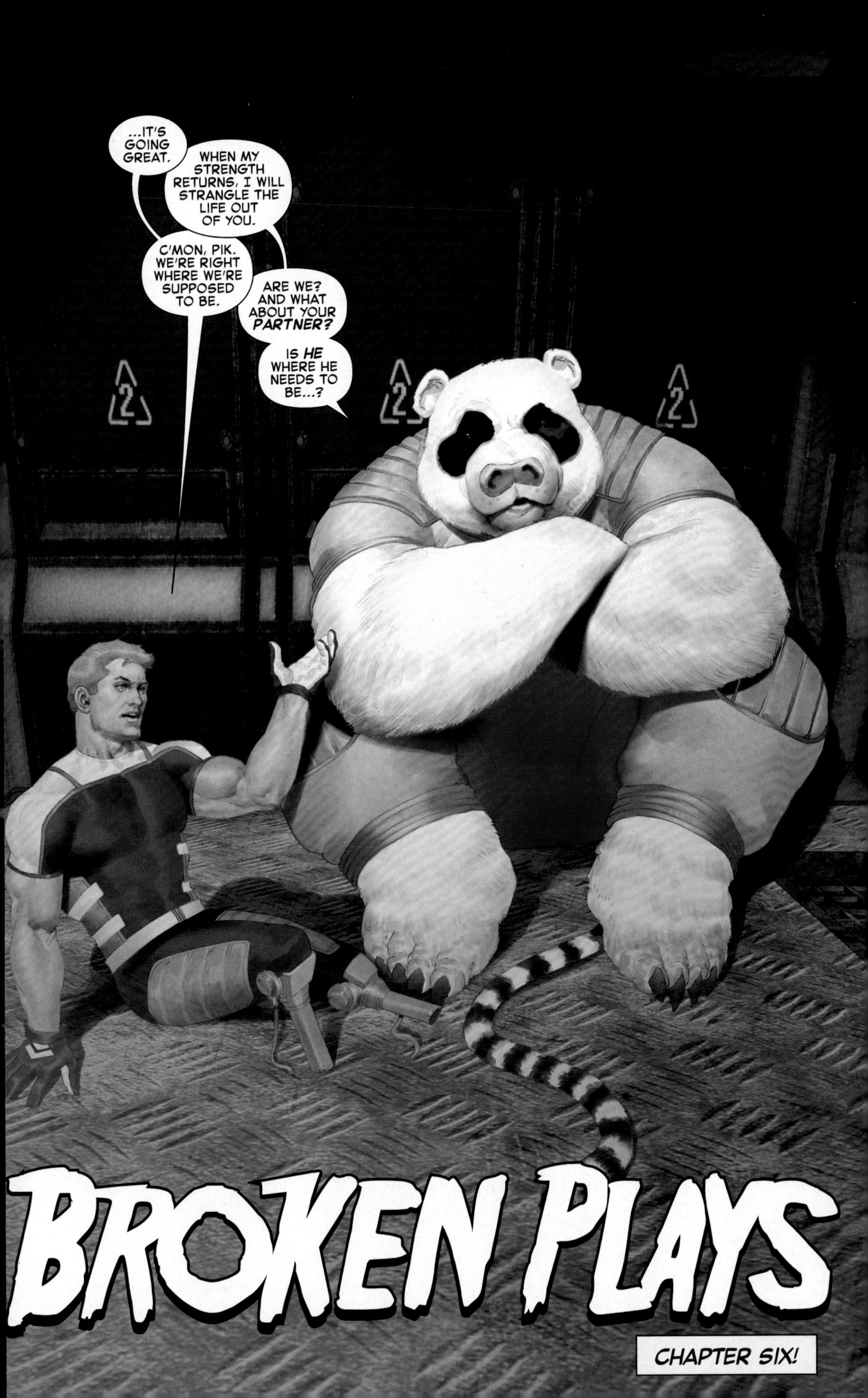
...IT'S GOING GREAT.
WHEN MY STRENGTH RETURNS, I WILL STRANGLE THE LIFE OUT OF YOU.
C'MON, PIK. WE'RE RIGHT WHERE WE'RE SUPPOSED TO BE.
ARE WE? AND WHAT ABOUT YOUR PARTNER?
IS HE WHERE HE NEEDS TO BE...?
BROKEN PLAYS
CHAPTER SIX!

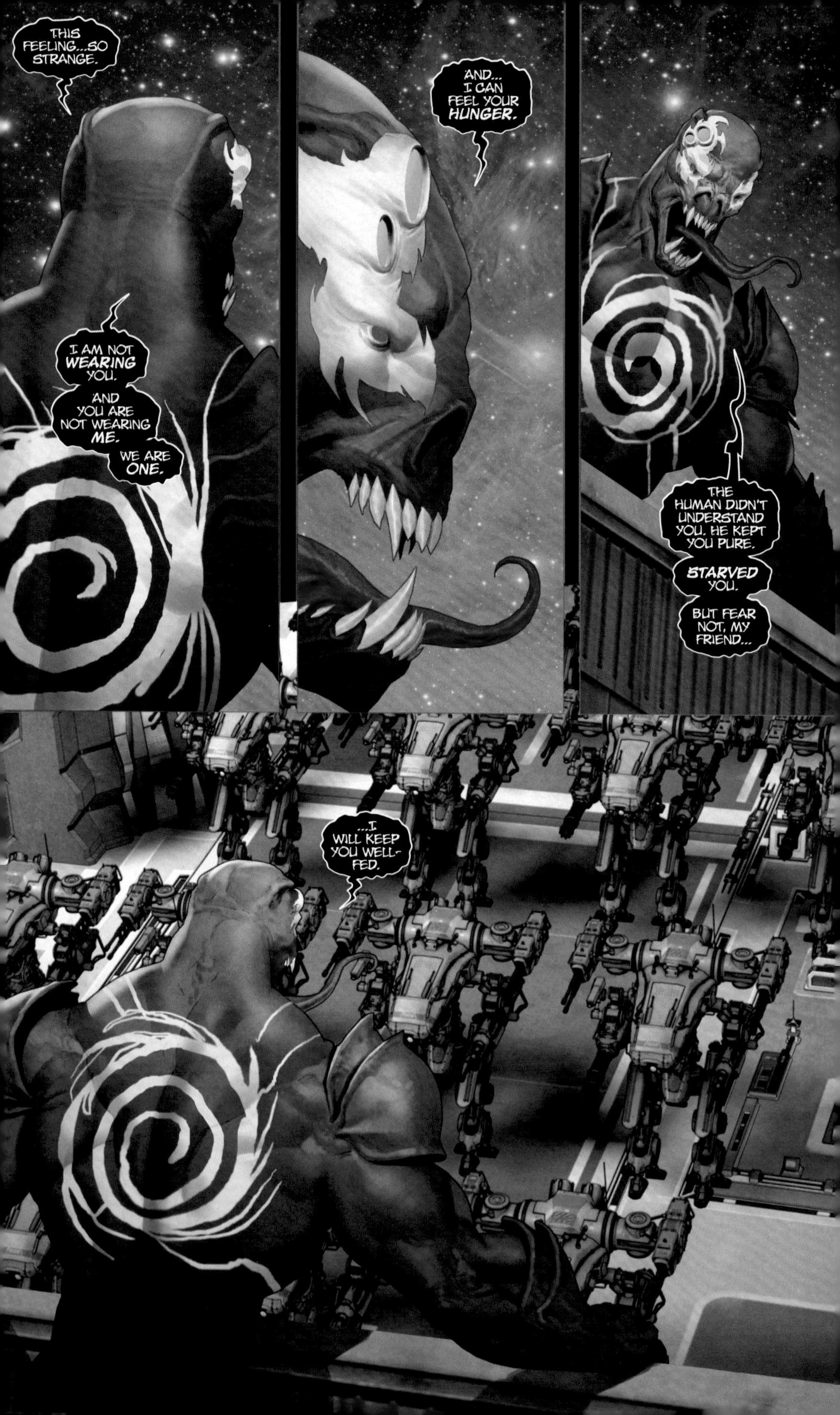
THIS FEELING...SO STRANGE.
I AM NOT WEARING YOU.
AND YOU ARE NOT WEARING ME.
WE ARE ONE.
AND... I CAN FEEL YOUR HUNGER.
THE HUMAN DIDN'T UNDERSTAND YOU. HE KEPT YOU PURE.
STARVED YOU.
BUT FEAR NOT, MY FRIEND...
...I WILL KEEP YOU WELL-FED.

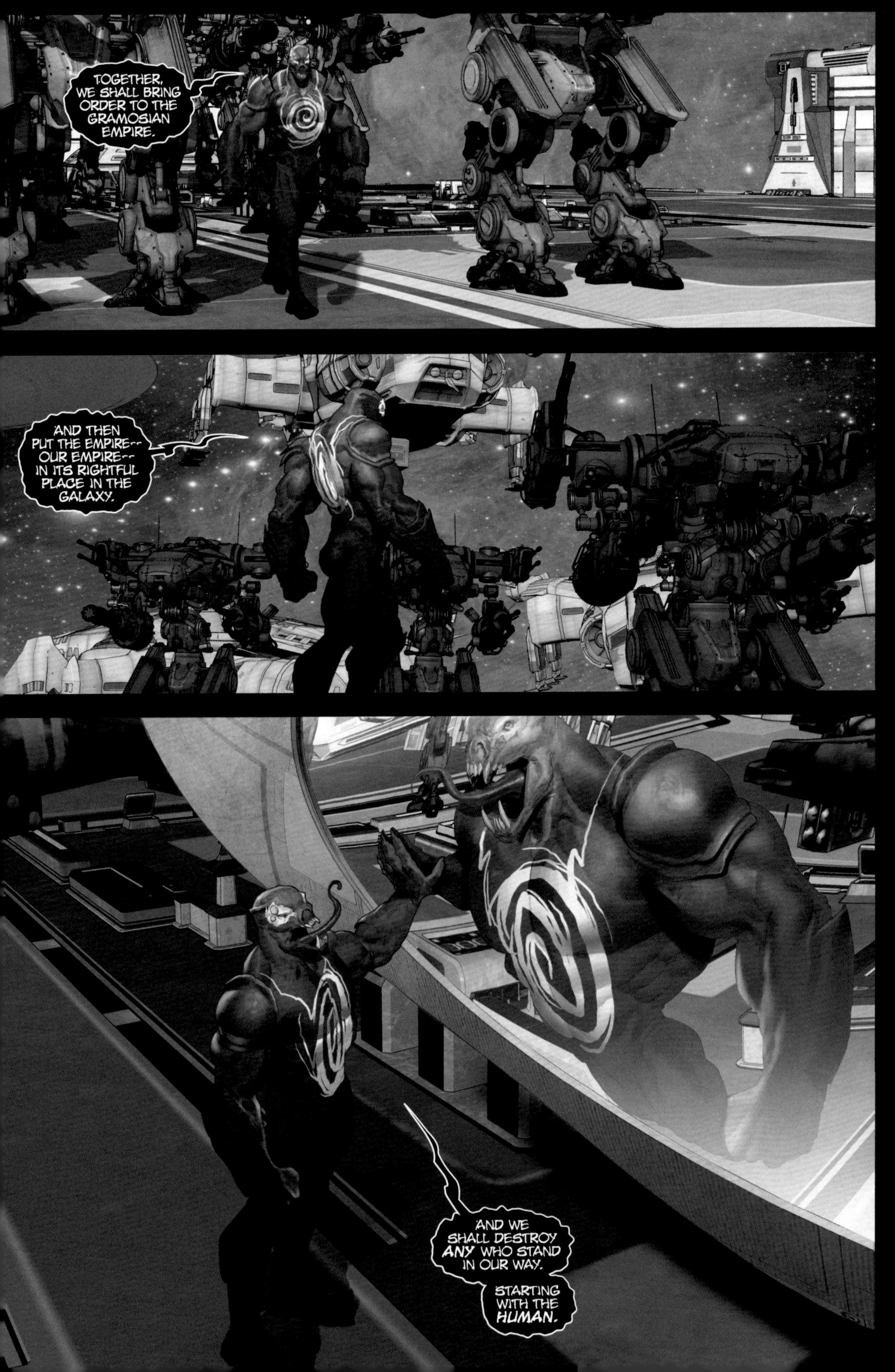
TOGETHER, WE SHALL BRING ORDER TO THE GRAMOSIAN EMPIRE.
AND THEN PUT THE EMPIRE-- OUR EMPIRE-- IN ITS RIGHTFUL PLACE IN THE GALAXY.
AND WE SHALL DESTROY ANY WHO STAND IN OUR WAY.
STARTING WITH THE HUMAN.

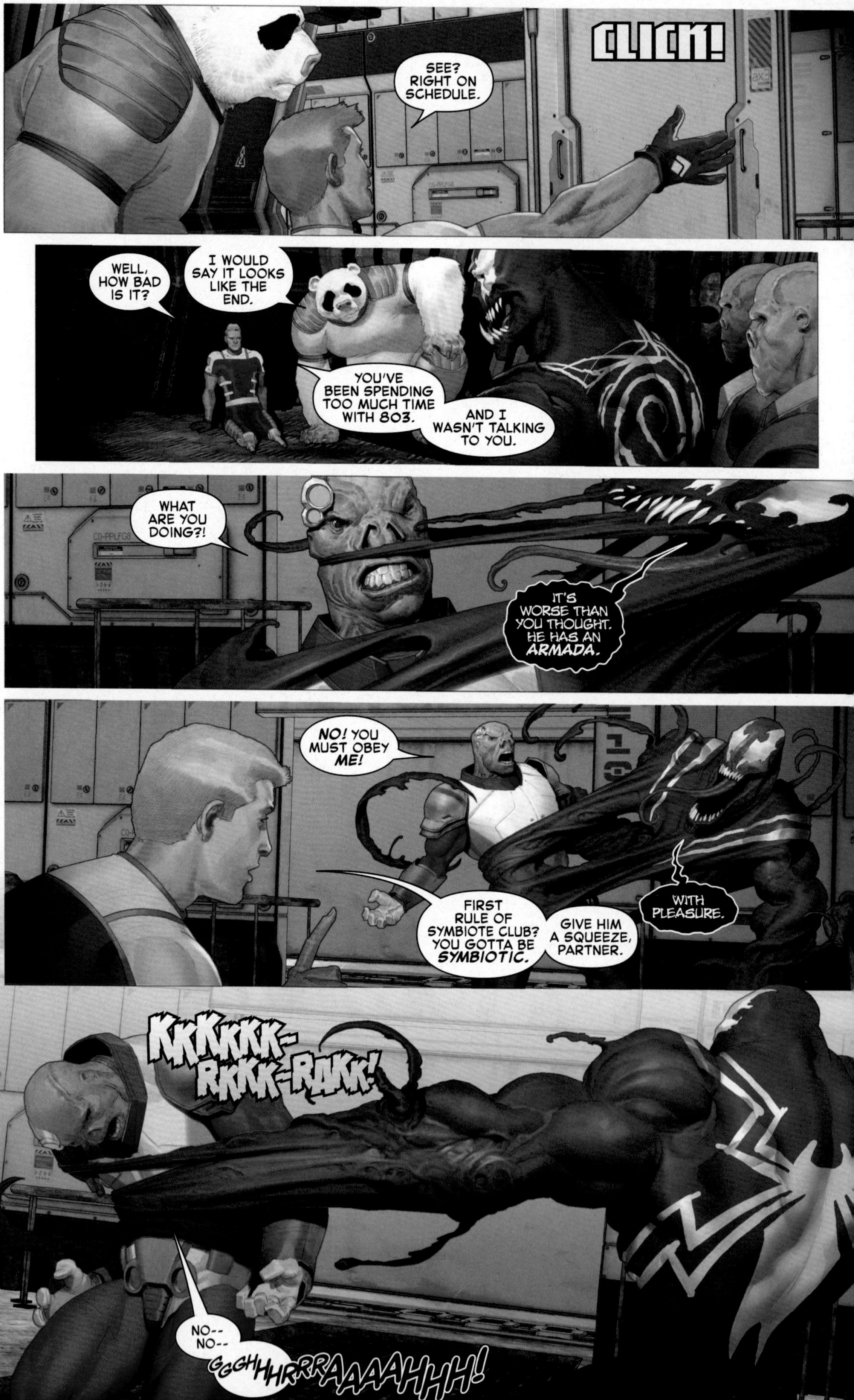
CLICK!
SEE? RIGHT ON SCHEDULE.
WELL, HOW BAD IS IT?
I WOULD SAY IT LOOKS LIKE THE END.
YOU'VE BEEN SPENDING TOO MUCH TIME WITH 803.
AND I WASN'T TALKING TO YOU.
WHAT ARE YOU DOING?!
IT'S WORSE THAN YOU THOUGHT. HE HAS AN ARMADA.
NO! YOU MUST OBEY ME!
FIRST RULE OF SYMBIOTE CLUB? YOU GOTTA BE SYMBIOTIC.
GIVE HIM A SQUEEZE, PARTNER.
WITH PLEASURE.
KKKKKK-RKKK-RAKK!
NO-- NO-- GGGHHHRRRRAAAAHHH!

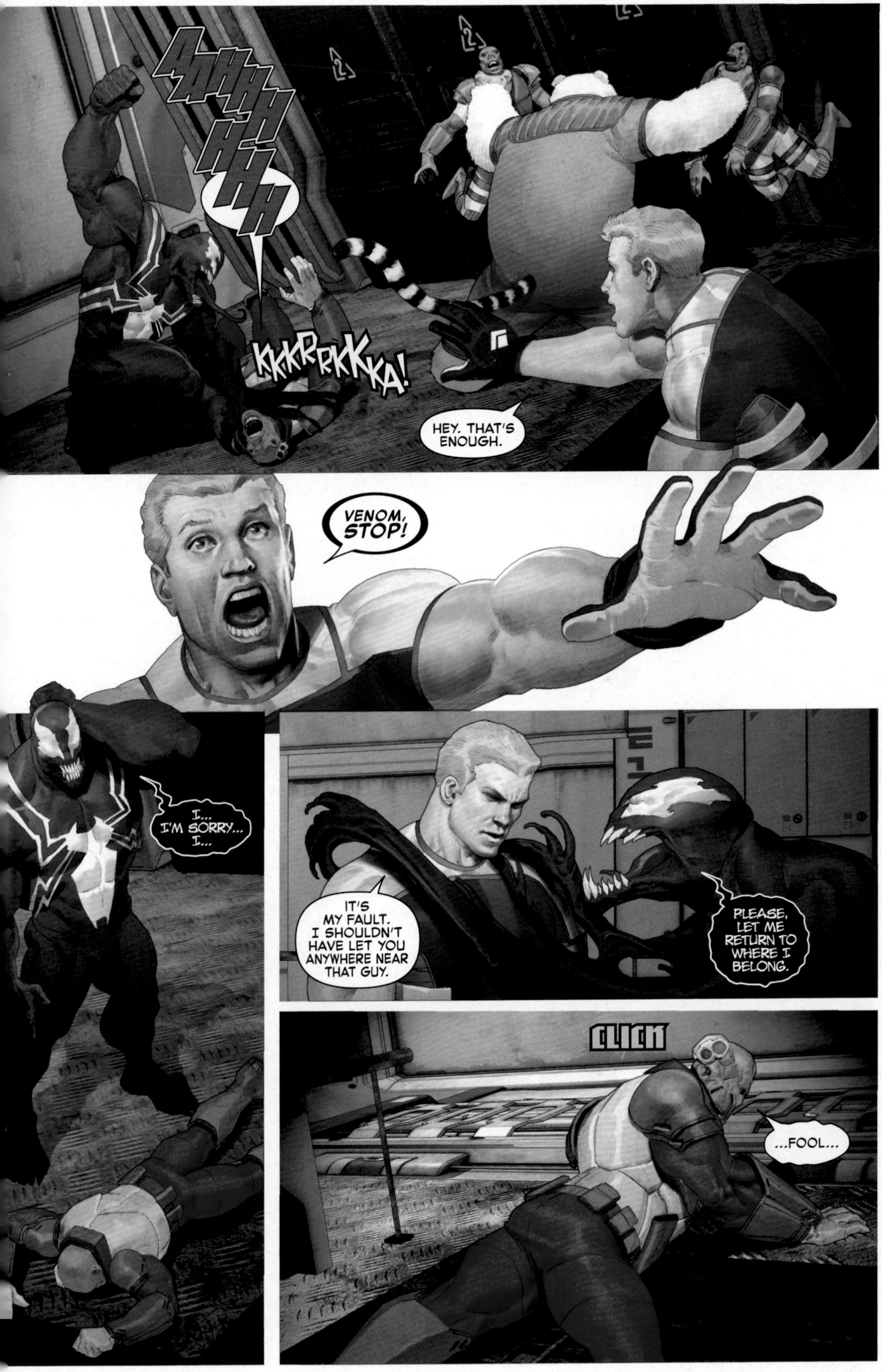
AAHHHHHHHHH
KKKRRKKKA!
HEY. THAT'S ENOUGH.
VENOM, STOP!
I... I'M SORRY... I...
IT'S MY FAULT. I SHOULDN'T HAVE LET YOU ANYWHERE NEAR THAT GUY.
PLEASE, LET ME RETURN TO WHERE I BELONG.
CLICK
...FOOL...

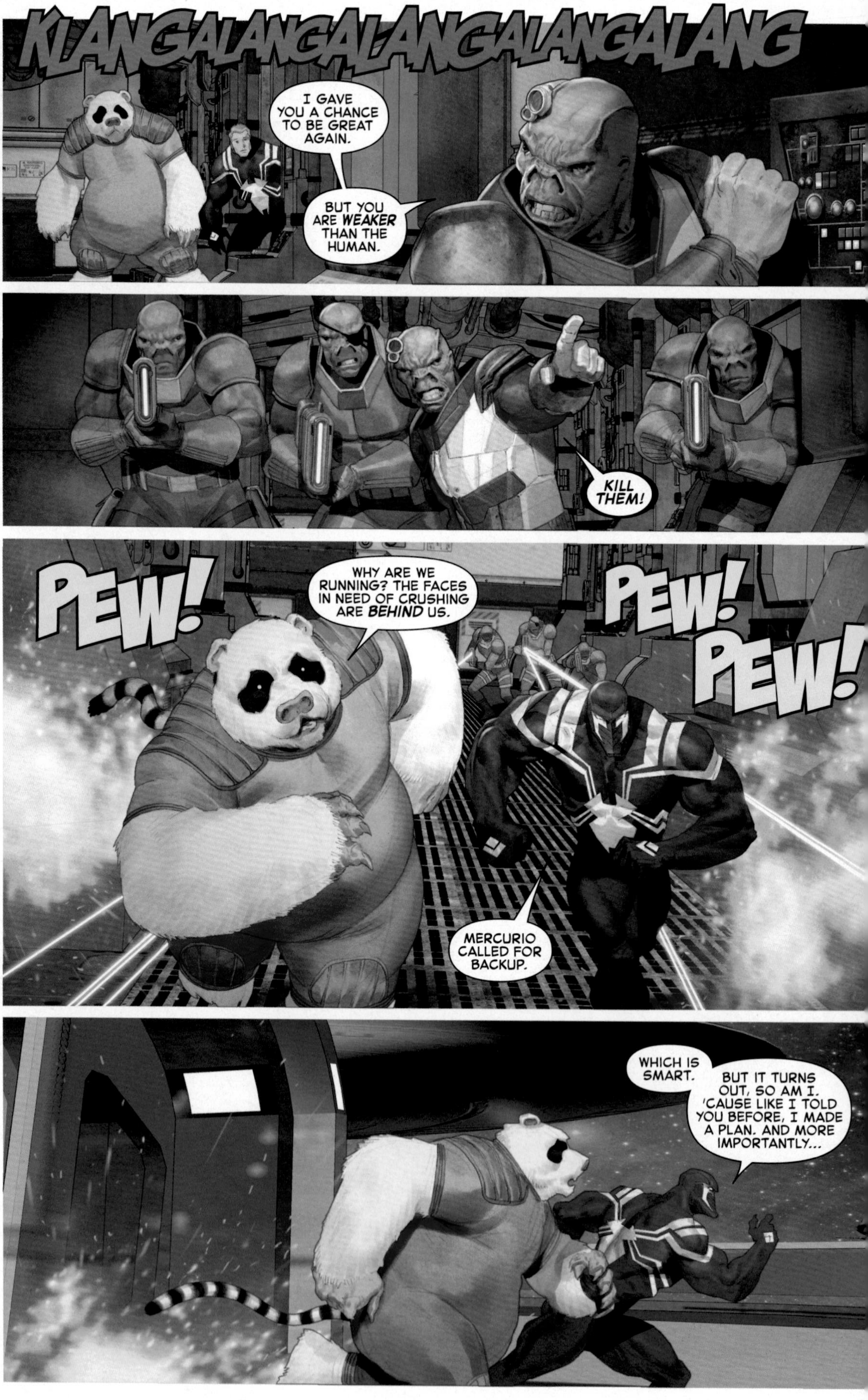
KLANGALANGALANGALANGALANG
I GAVE YOU A CHANCE TO BE GREAT AGAIN.
BUT YOU ARE *WEAKER* THAN THE HUMAN.
KILL THEM!
PEW!
WHY ARE WE RUNNING? THE FACES IN NEED OF CRUSHING ARE *BEHIND* US.
PEW! PEW!
MERCURIO CALLED FOR BACKUP.
WHICH IS SMART.
BUT IT TURNS OUT, SO AM I. 'CAUSE LIKE I TOLD YOU BEFORE, I MADE A PLAN. AND MORE IMPORTANTLY...

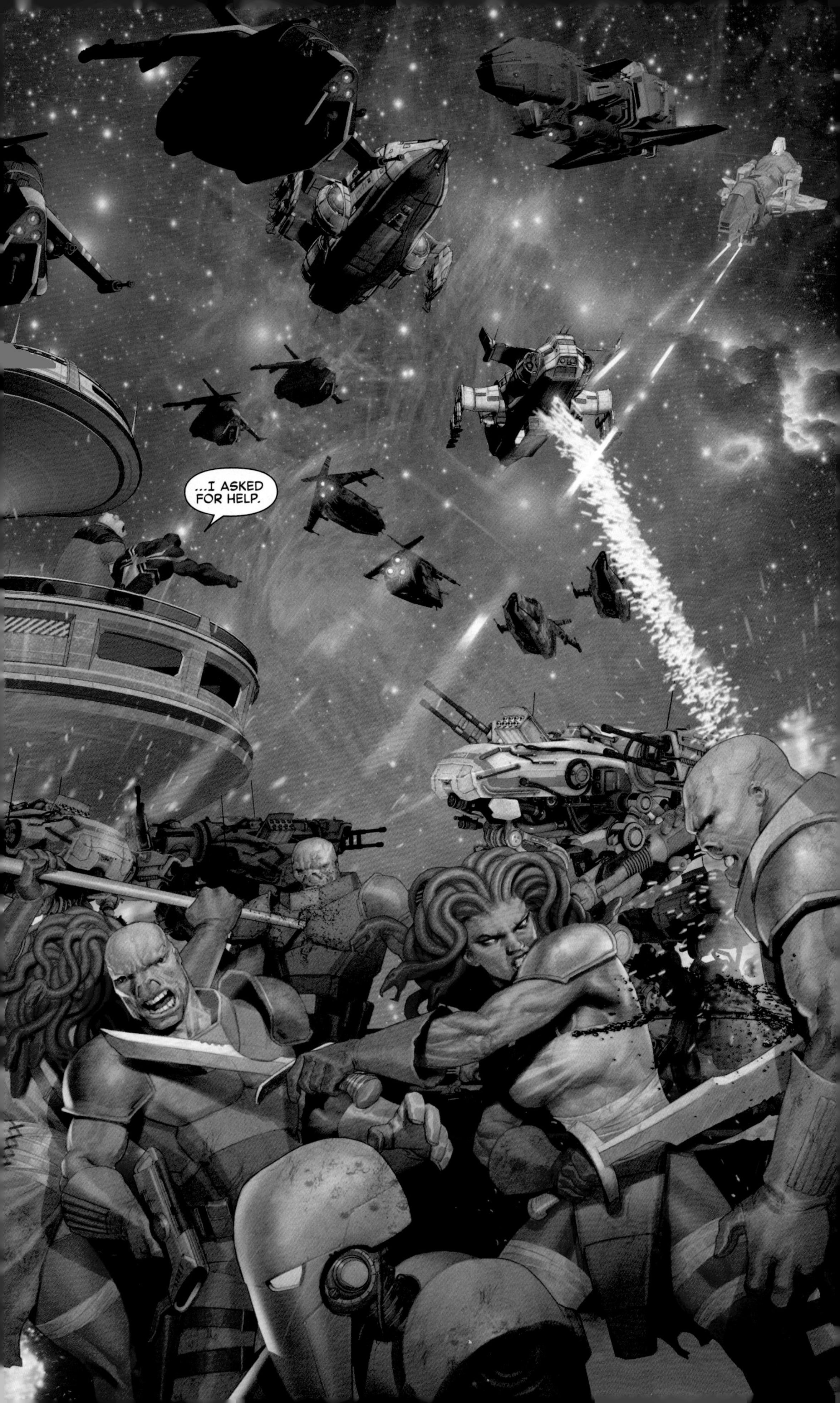
...I ASKED FOR HELP.

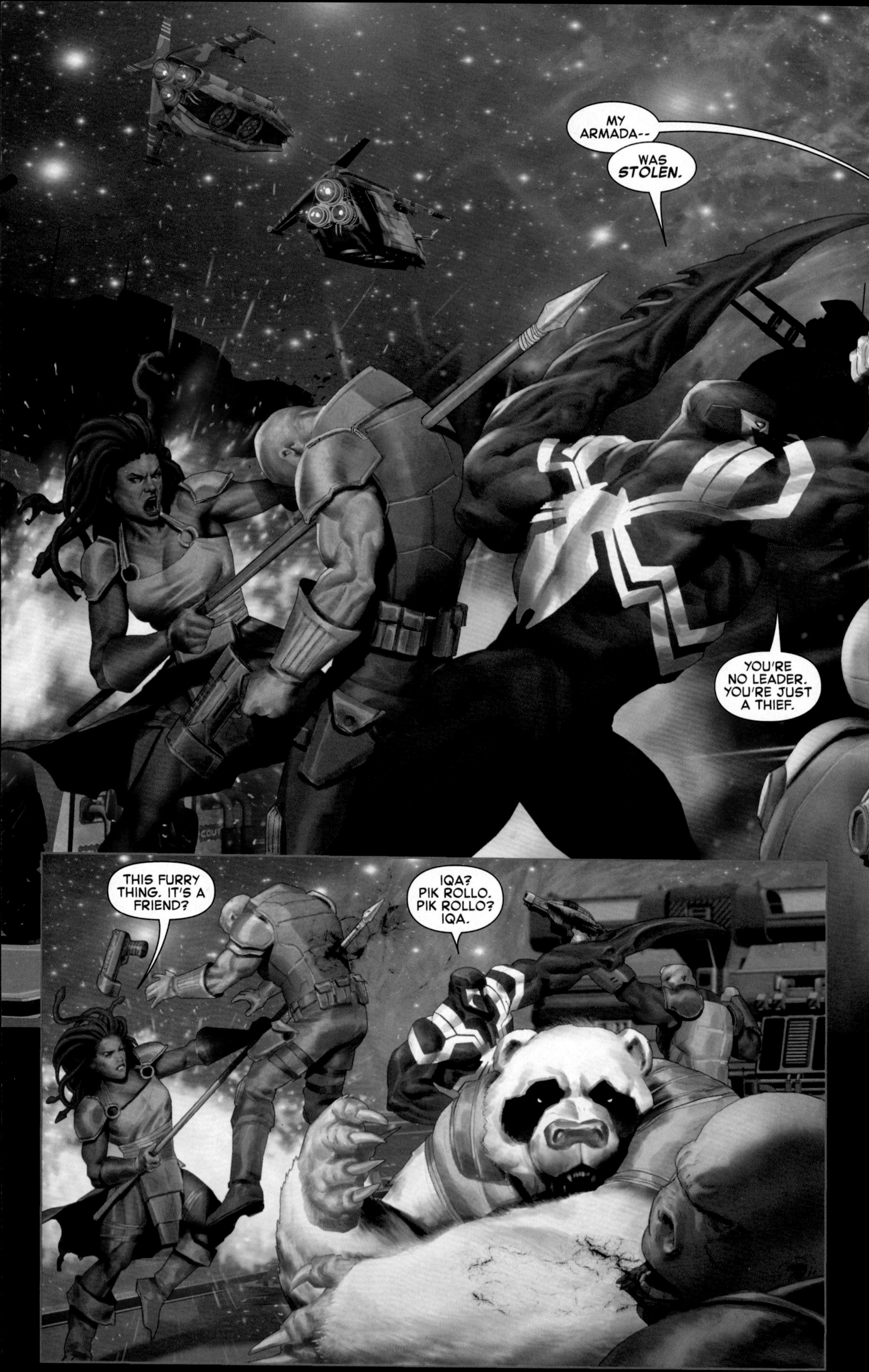
MY ARMADA--
WAS STOLEN.
YOU'RE NO LEADER. YOU'RE JUST A THIEF.
THIS FURRY THING. IT'S A FRIEND?
IQA? PIK ROLLO. PIK ROLLO? IQA.

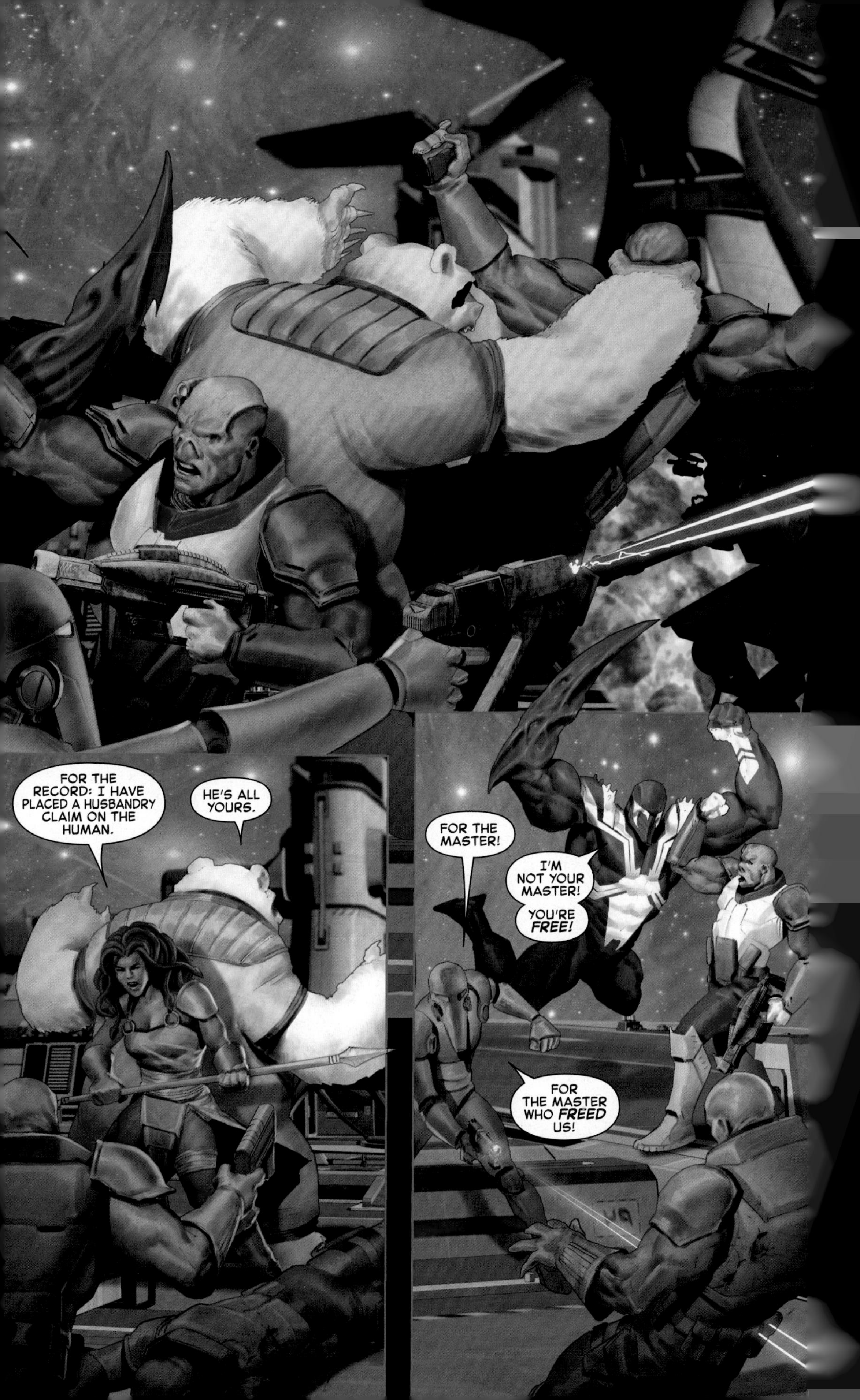
FOR THE RECORD: I HAVE PLACED A HUSBANDRY CLAIM ON THE HUMAN.
HE'S ALL YOURS.
FOR THE MASTER!
I'M NOT YOUR MASTER!
YOU'RE FREE!
FOR THE MASTER WHO FREED US!

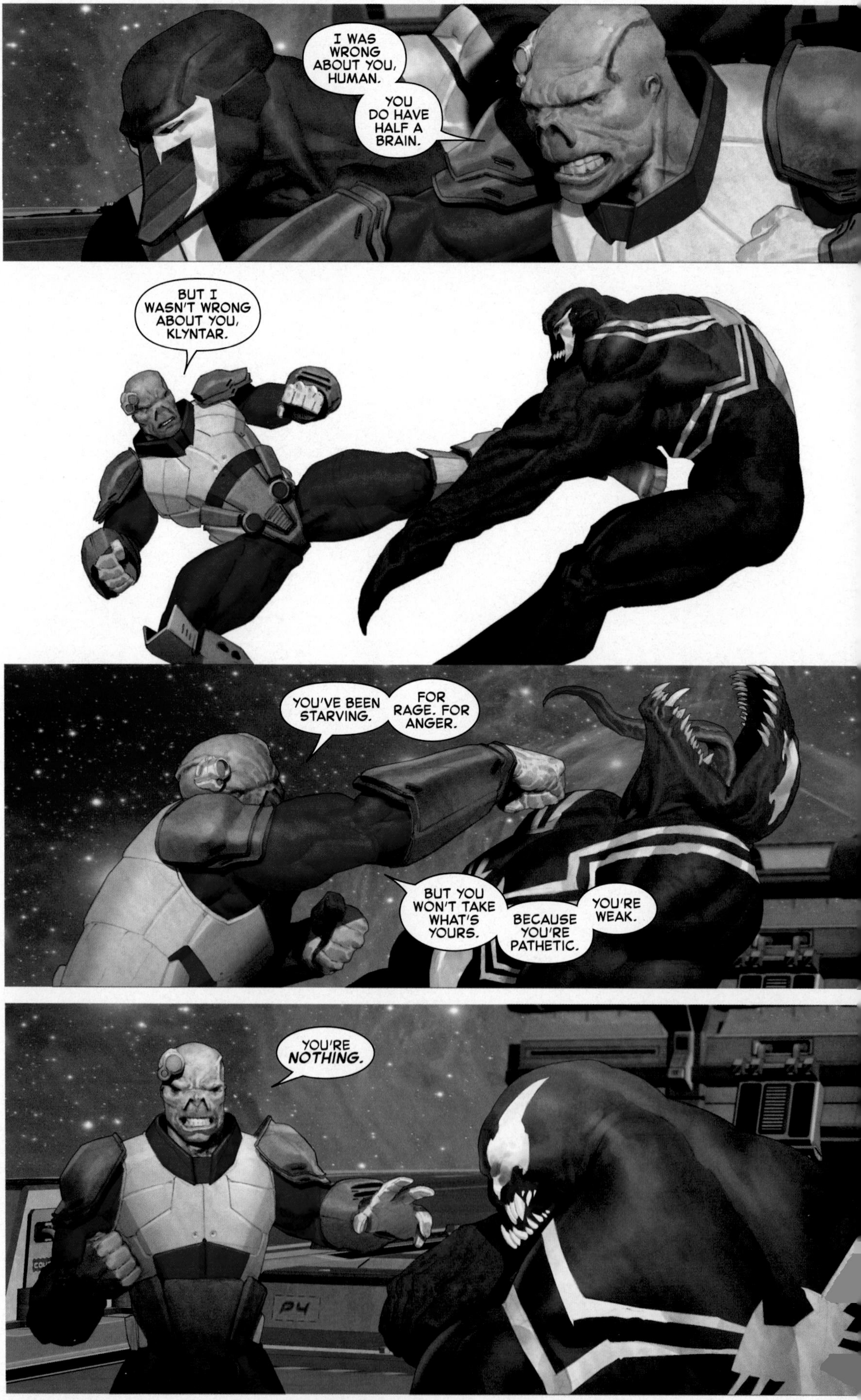
I WAS WRONG ABOUT YOU, HUMAN.
YOU DO HAVE HALF A BRAIN.
BUT I WASN'T WRONG ABOUT YOU, KLYNTAR.
YOU'VE BEEN STARVING.
FOR RAGE. FOR ANGER.
BUT YOU WON'T TAKE WHAT'S YOURS.
BECAUSE YOU'RE PATHETIC.
YOU'RE WEAK.
YOU'RE *NOTHING.*

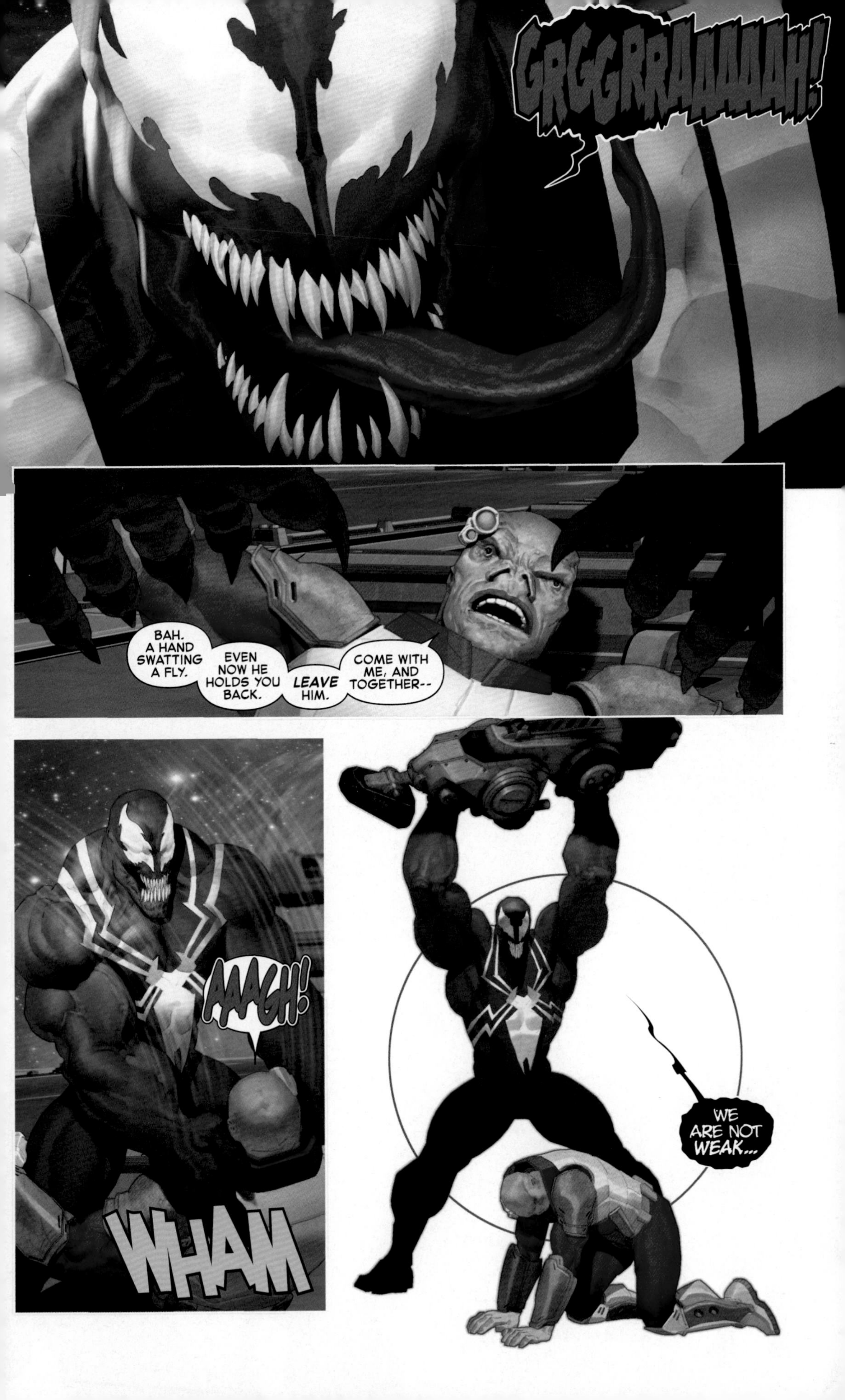
GRGGRRAAAAAH!
BAH. A HAND SWATTING A FLY.
EVEN NOW HE HOLDS YOU BACK.
LEAVE HIM.
COME WITH ME, AND TOGETHER--
AAAGH!
WHAM
WE ARE NOT WEAK...

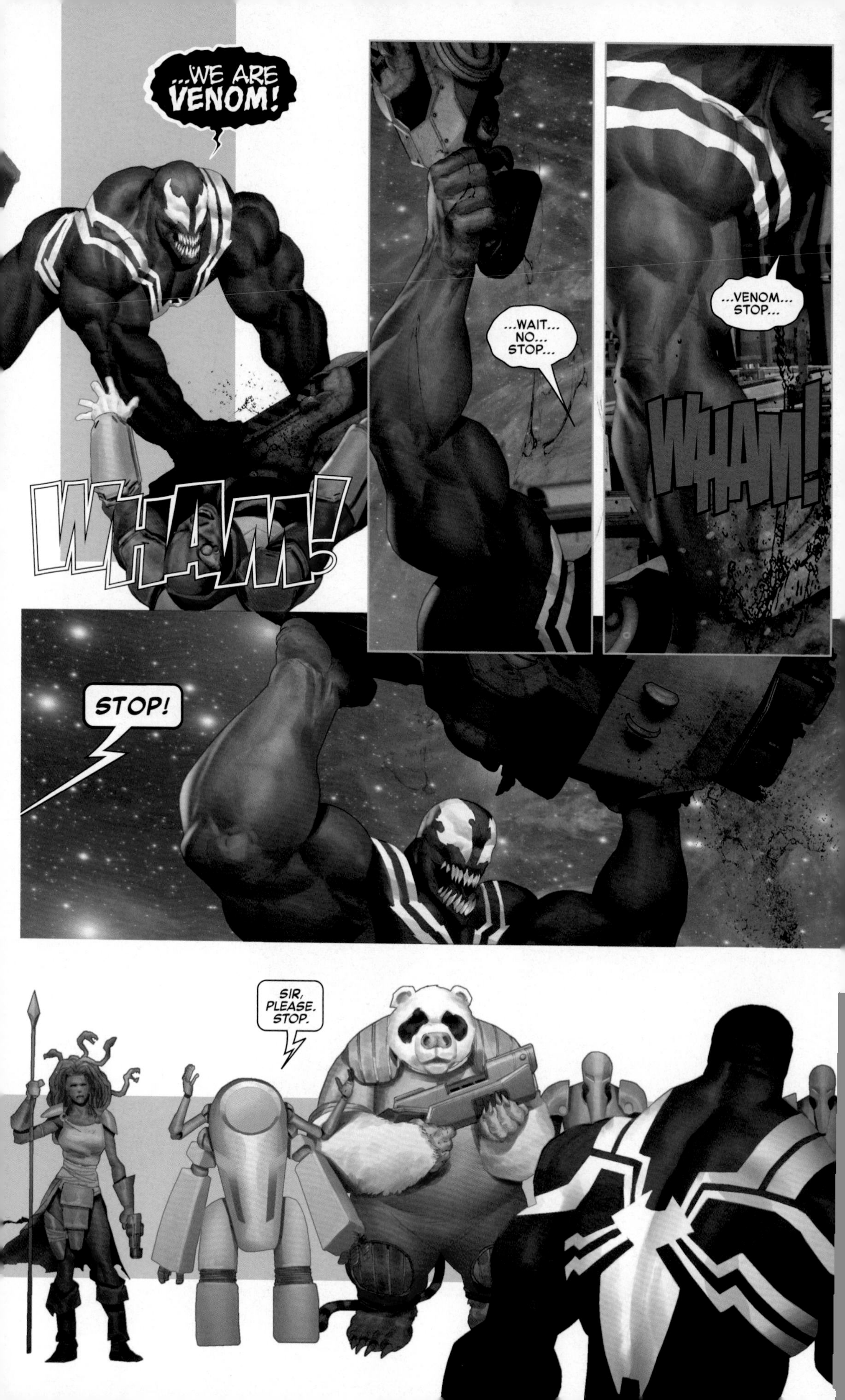

...WE ARE VENOM!
WHAM!
...WAIT... NO... STOP...
...VENOM... STOP...
WHAM!
STOP!
SIR, PLEASE. STOP.

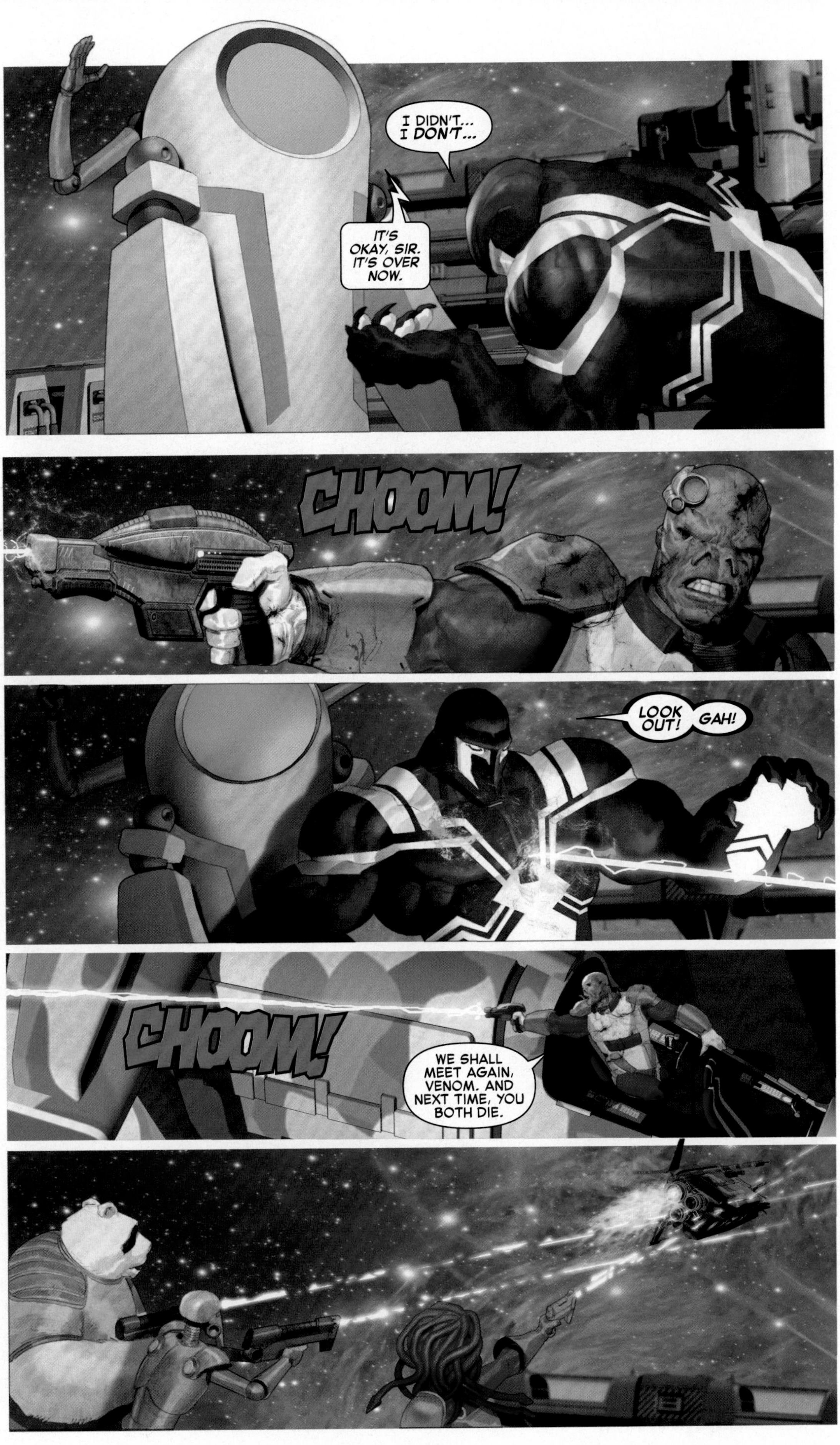

I DIDN'T... I DON'T...
IT'S OKAY, SIR. IT'S OVER NOW.
CHOOM!
LOOK OUT!
GAH!
CHOOM!
WE SHALL MEET AGAIN, VENOM. AND NEXT TIME, YOU BOTH DIE.

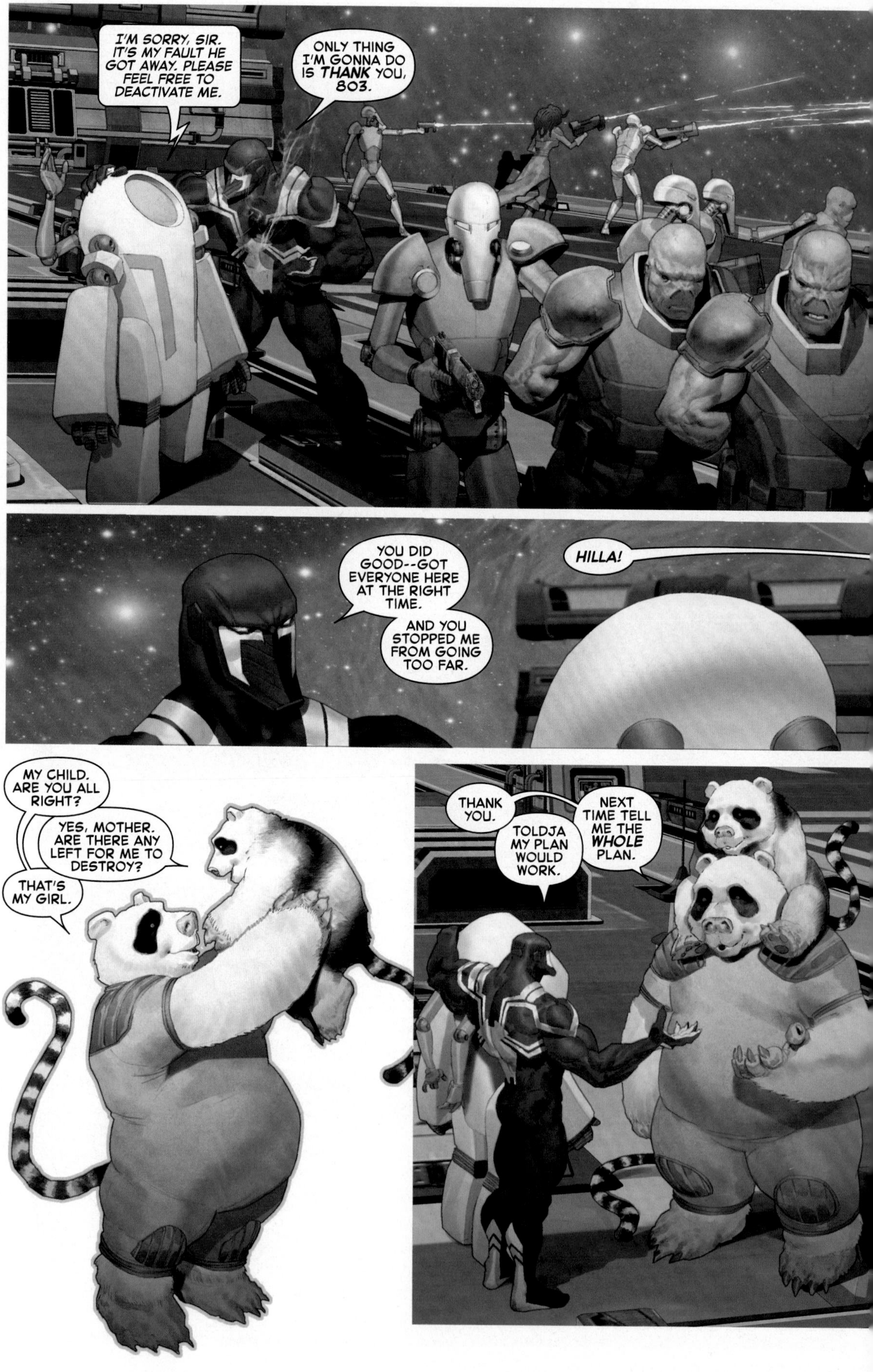

I'M SORRY, SIR. IT'S MY FAULT HE GOT AWAY. PLEASE FEEL FREE TO DEACTIVATE ME.
ONLY THING I'M GONNA DO IS THANK YOU, 803.
YOU DID GOOD--GOT EVERYONE HERE AT THE RIGHT TIME.
AND YOU STOPPED ME FROM GOING TOO FAR.
HILLA!
MY CHILD. ARE YOU ALL RIGHT?
YES, MOTHER. ARE THERE ANY LEFT FOR ME TO DESTROY?
THAT'S MY GIRL.
THANK YOU.
TOLDJA MY PLAN WOULD WORK.
NEXT TIME TELL ME THE WHOLE PLAN.

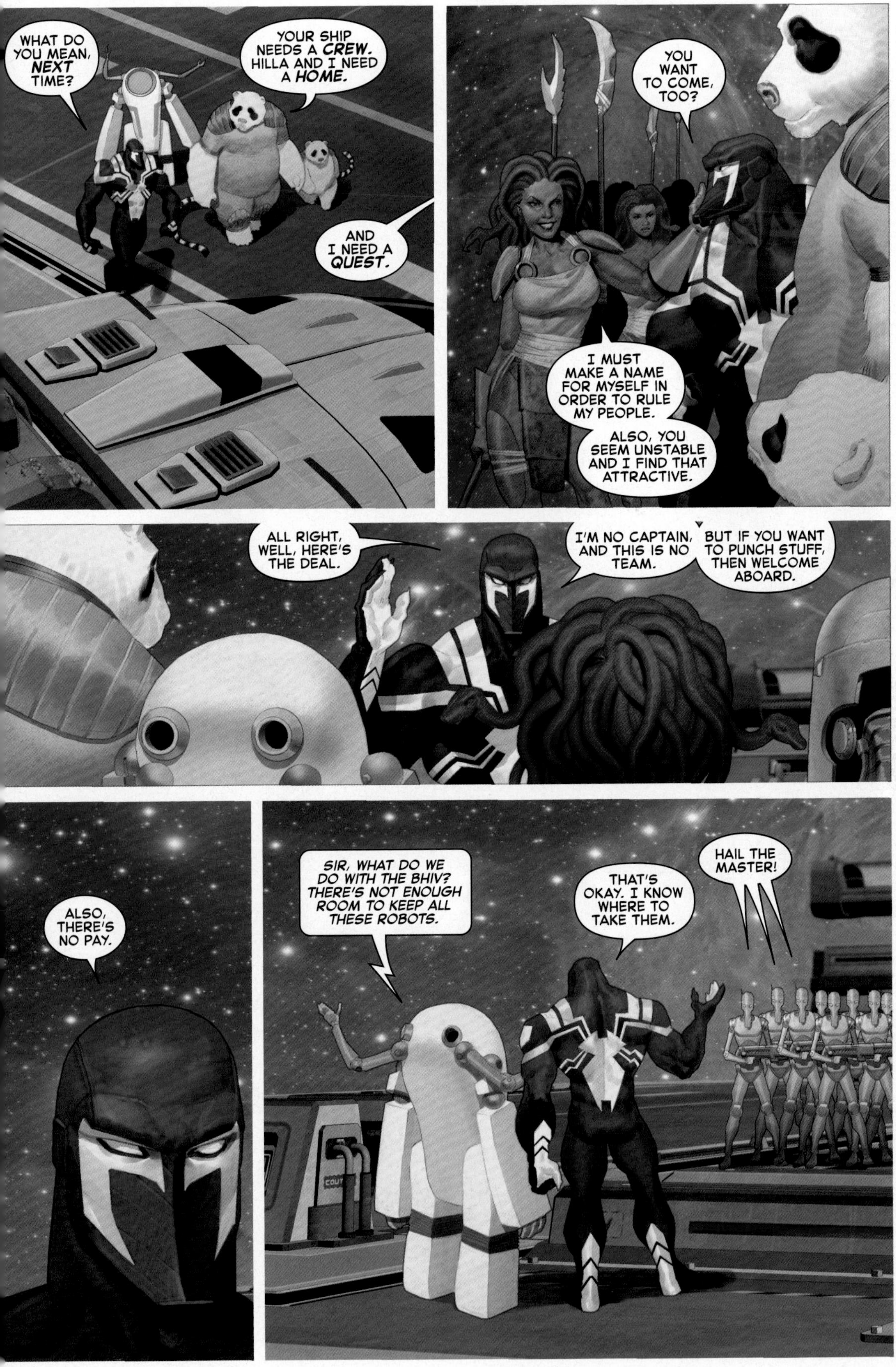
WHAT DO YOU MEAN, NEXT TIME?
YOUR SHIP NEEDS A CREW. HILLA AND I NEED A HOME.
AND I NEED A QUEST.
YOU WANT TO COME, TOO?
I MUST MAKE A NAME FOR MYSELF IN ORDER TO RULE MY PEOPLE.
ALSO, YOU SEEM UNSTABLE AND I FIND THAT ATTRACTIVE.
ALL RIGHT, WELL, HERE'S THE DEAL.
I'M NO CAPTAIN, AND THIS IS NO TEAM.
BUT IF YOU WANT TO PUNCH STUFF, THEN WELCOME ABOARD.
ALSO, THERE'S NO PAY.
SIR, WHAT DO WE DO WITH THE BHIV? THERE'S NOT ENOUGH ROOM TO KEEP ALL THESE ROBOTS.
THAT'S OKAY. I KNOW WHERE TO TAKE THEM.
HAIL THE MASTER!

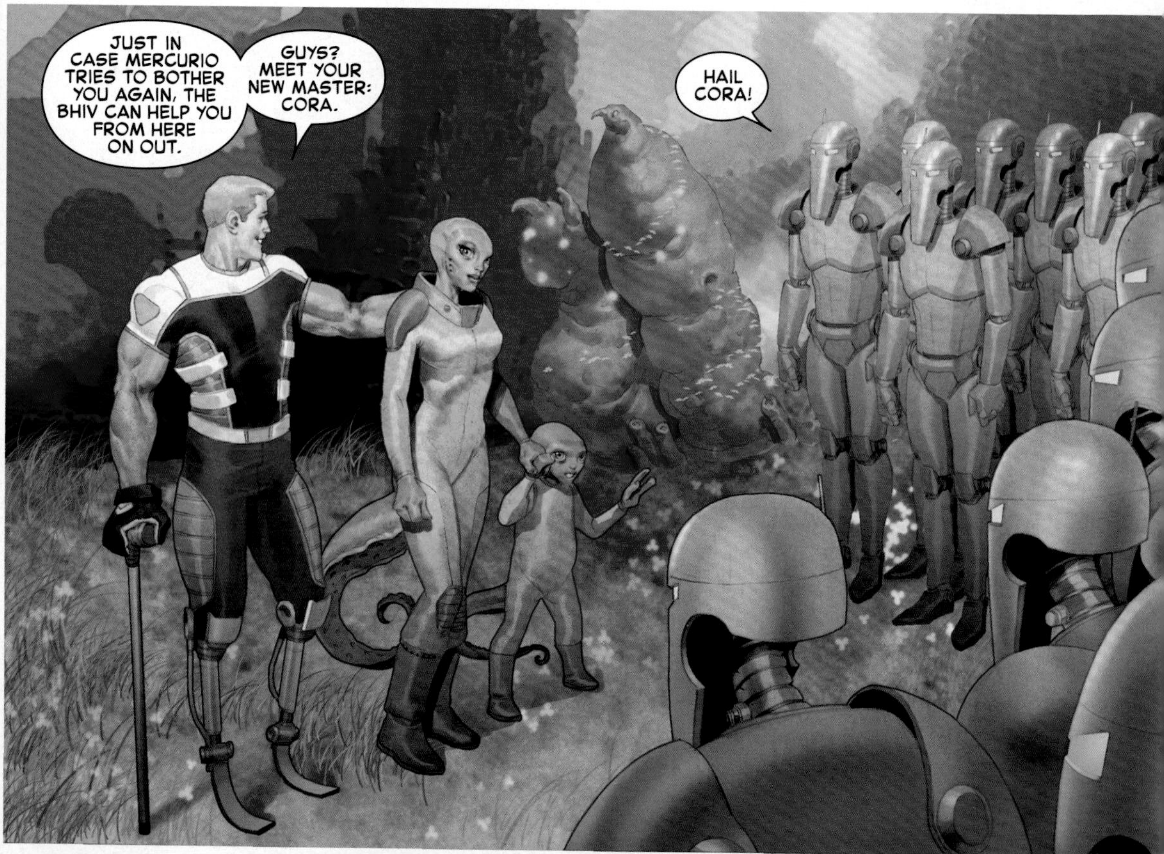
JUST IN CASE MERCURIO TRIES TO BOTHER YOU AGAIN, THE BHIV CAN HELP YOU FROM HERE ON OUT.
GUYS? MEET YOUR NEW MASTER: CORA.
HAIL CORA!

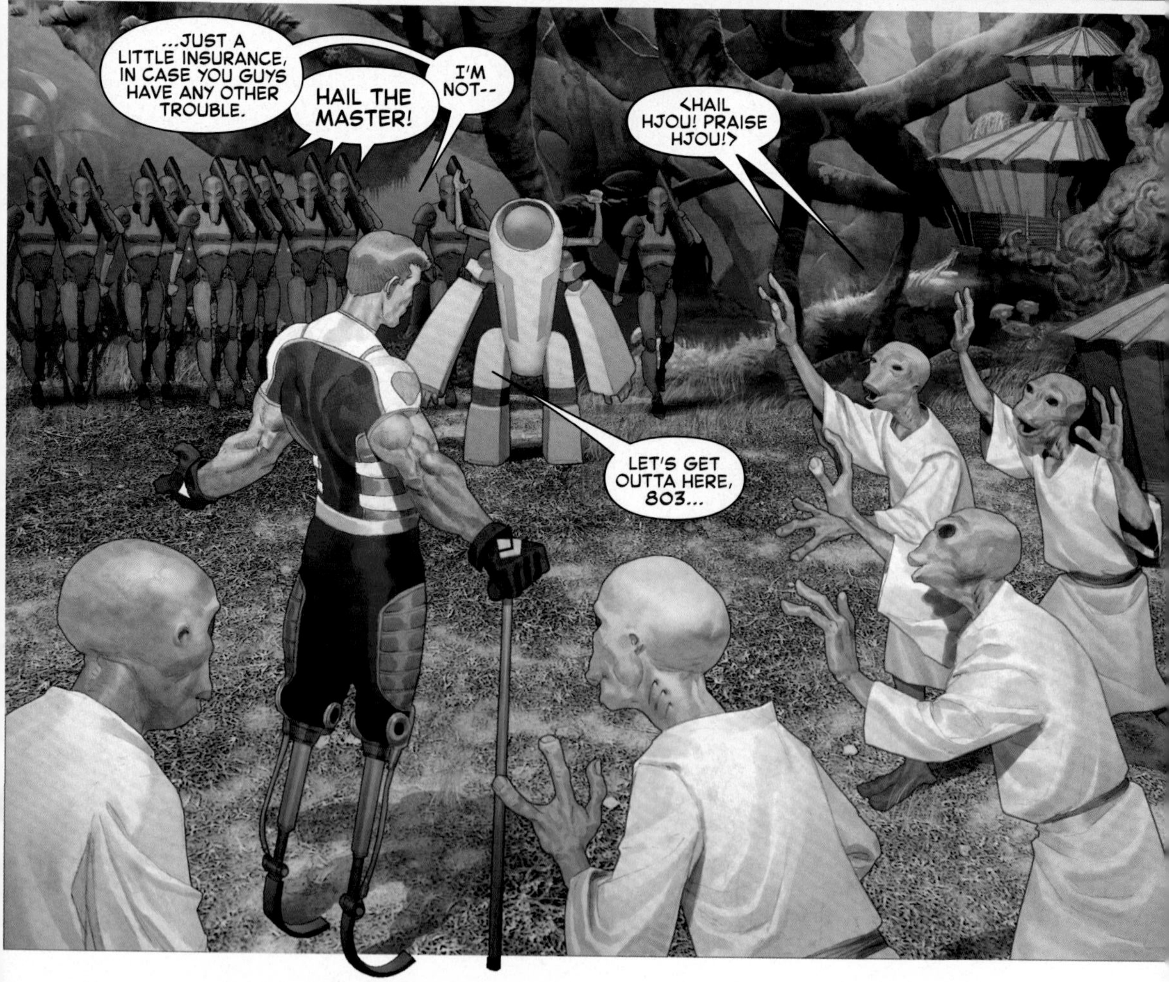
...JUST A LITTLE INSURANCE, IN CASE YOU GUYS HAVE ANY OTHER TROUBLE.
HAIL THE MASTER!
I'M NOT--
<HAIL HJOU! PRAISE HJOU!>
LET'S GET OUTTA HERE, 803...

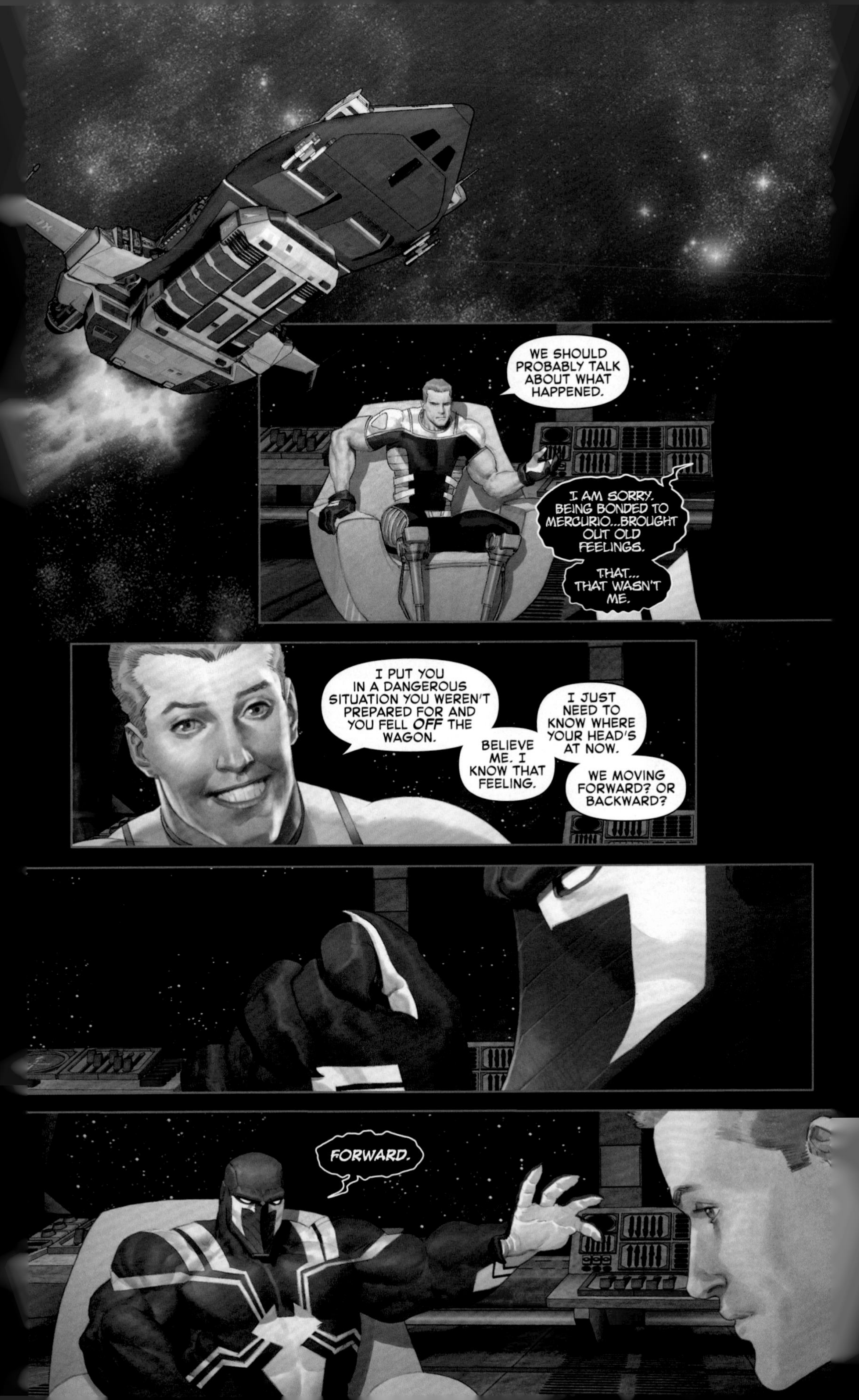
WE SHOULD PROBABLY TALK ABOUT WHAT HAPPENED.
I AM SORRY. BEING BONDED TO MERCURIO...BROUGHT OUT OLD FEELINGS.
THAT... THAT WASN'T ME.
I PUT YOU IN A DANGEROUS SITUATION YOU WEREN'T PREPARED FOR AND YOU FELL *OFF* THE WAGON.
BELIEVE ME. I KNOW THAT FEELING.
I JUST NEED TO KNOW WHERE YOUR HEAD'S AT NOW.
WE MOVING FORWARD? OR BACKWARD?
FORWARD.

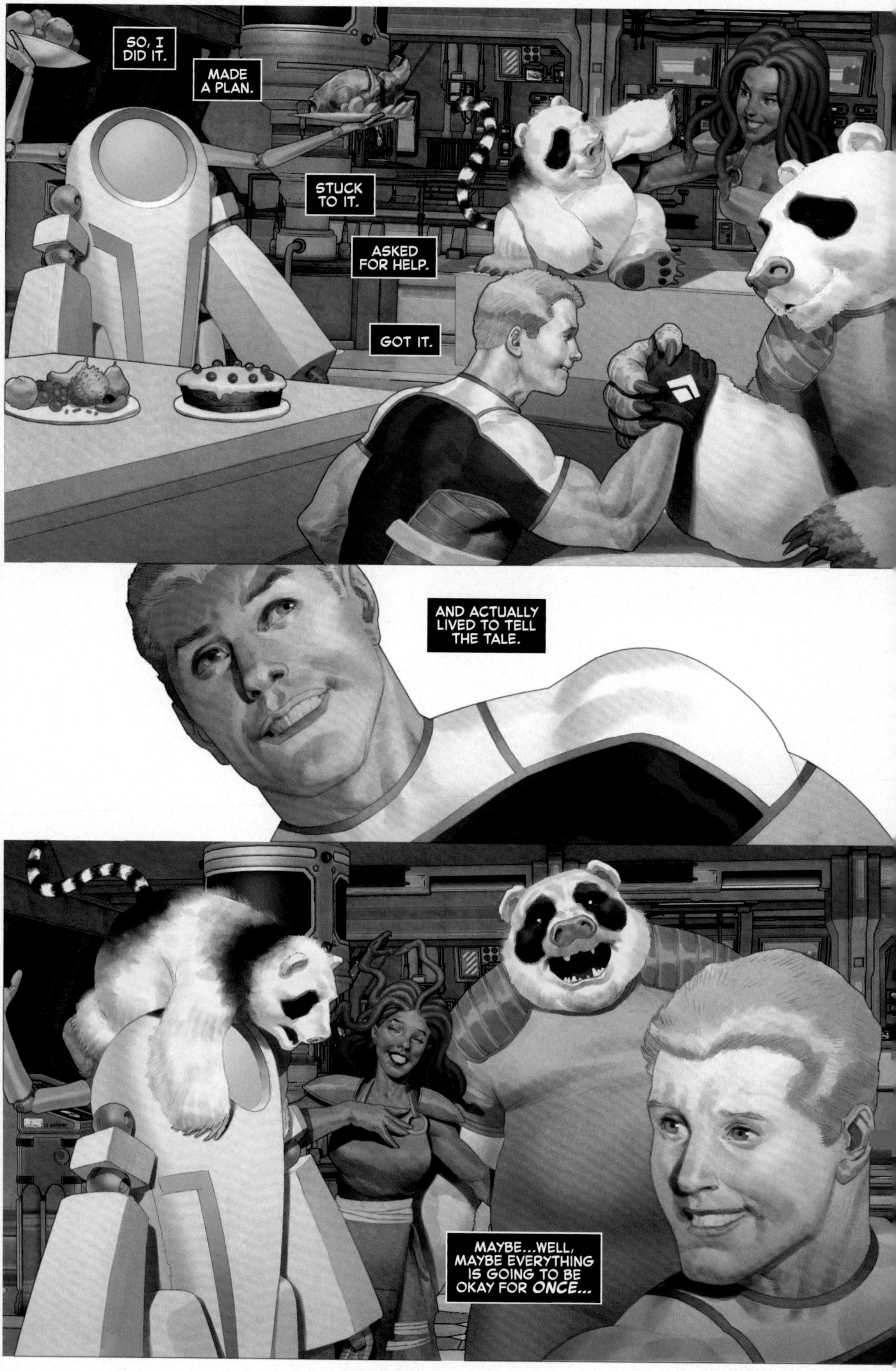

SO, I DID IT.
MADE A PLAN.
STUCK TO IT.
ASKED FOR HELP.
GOT IT.
AND ACTUALLY LIVED TO TELL THE TALE.
MAYBE...WELL, MAYBE EVERYTHING IS GOING TO BE OKAY FOR *ONCE*...

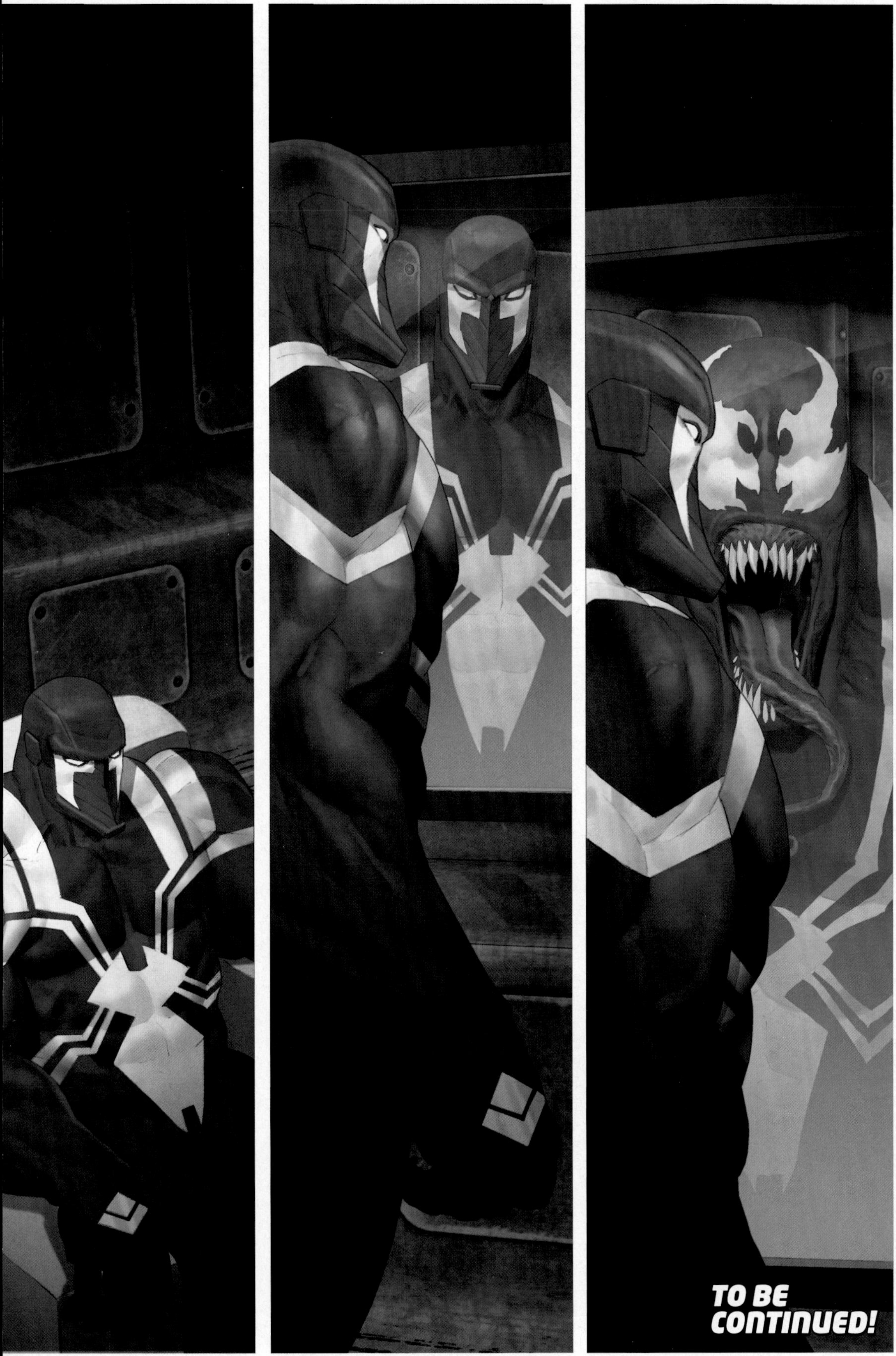
TO BE
CONTINUED!

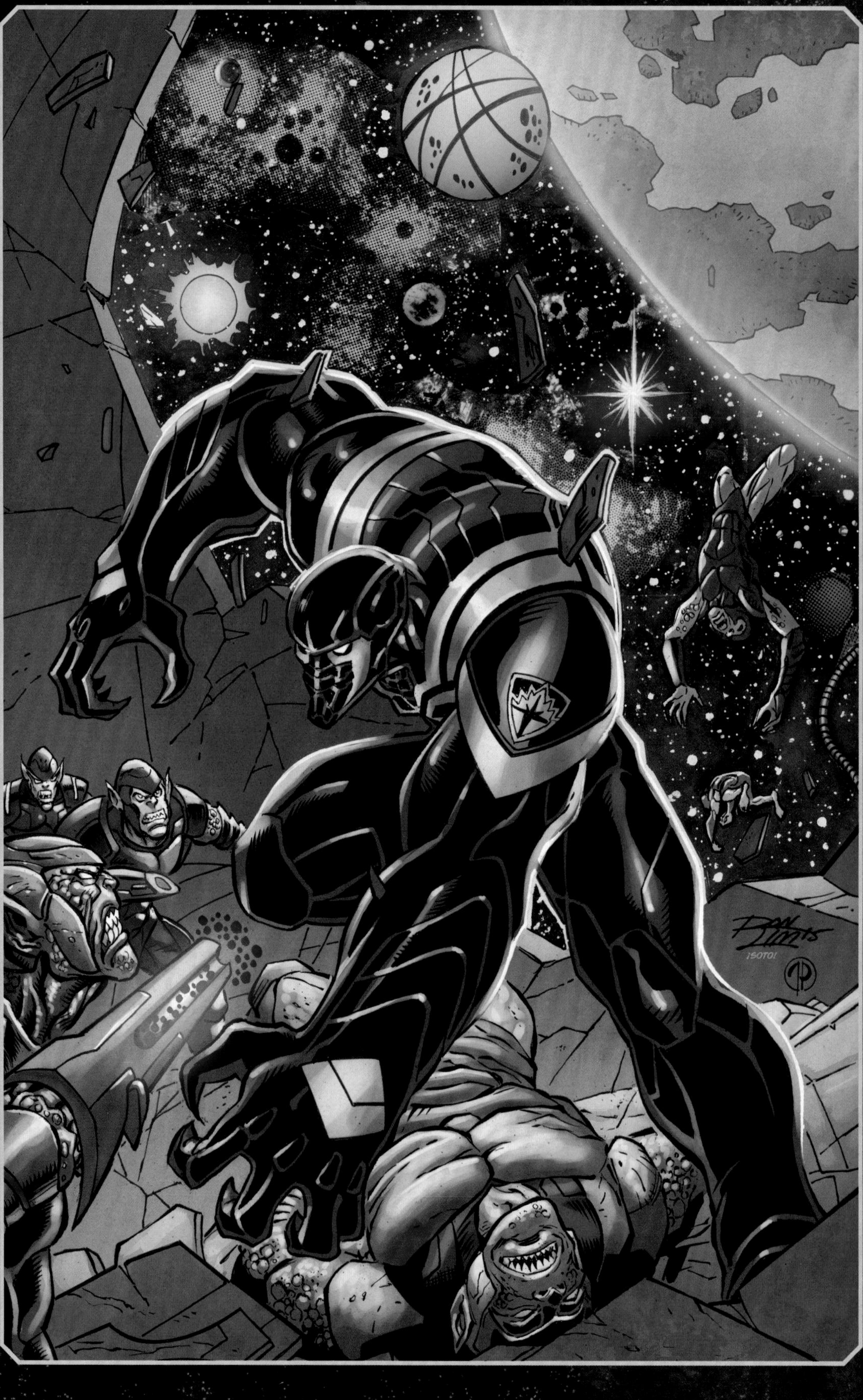

#1 variant by **RON LIM, TOM PALMER & DAVE McCAIG**

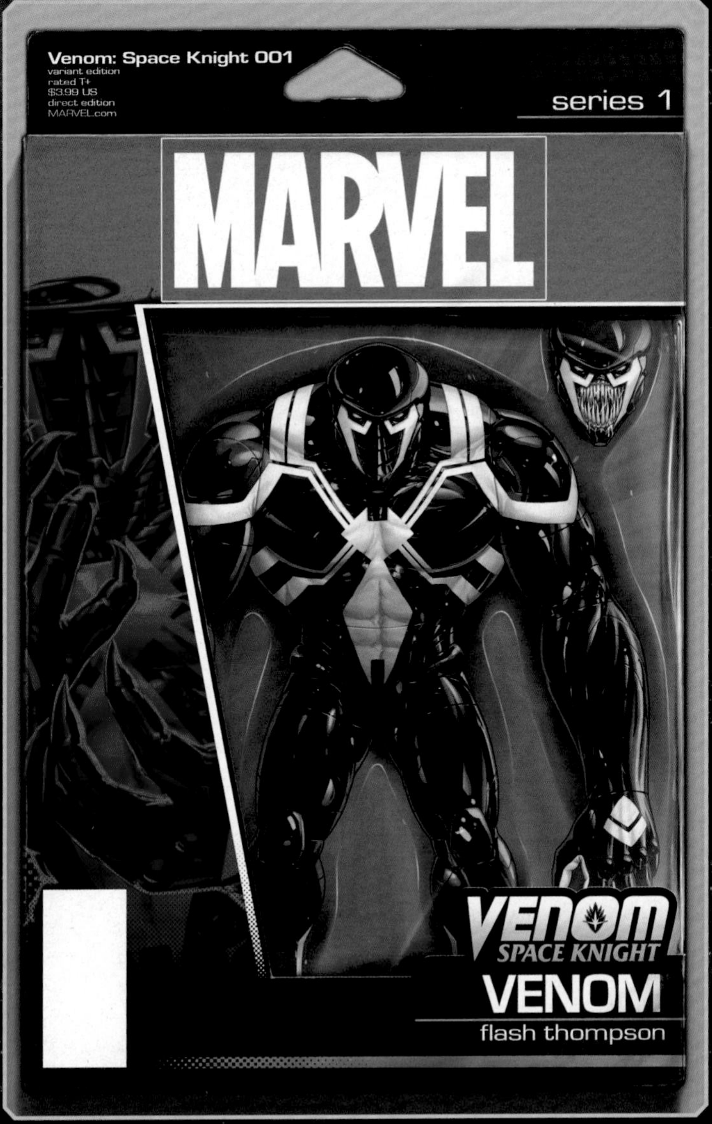
Venom: Space Knight 001
variant edition
rated T+
$3.99 US
direct edition
MARVEL.com
series 1
MARVEL
VENOM
SPACE KNIGHT
VENOM
flash thompson

#1 Action Figure variant by
JOHN TYLER CHRISTOPHER

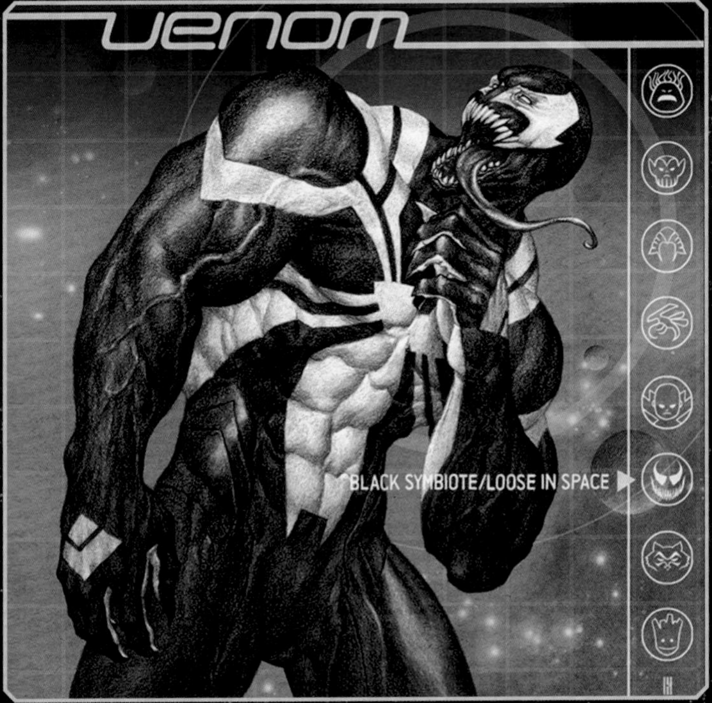
venom
BLACK SYMBIOTE/LOOSE IN SPACE

#1 Hip-Hop variant by
MIKE CHOI

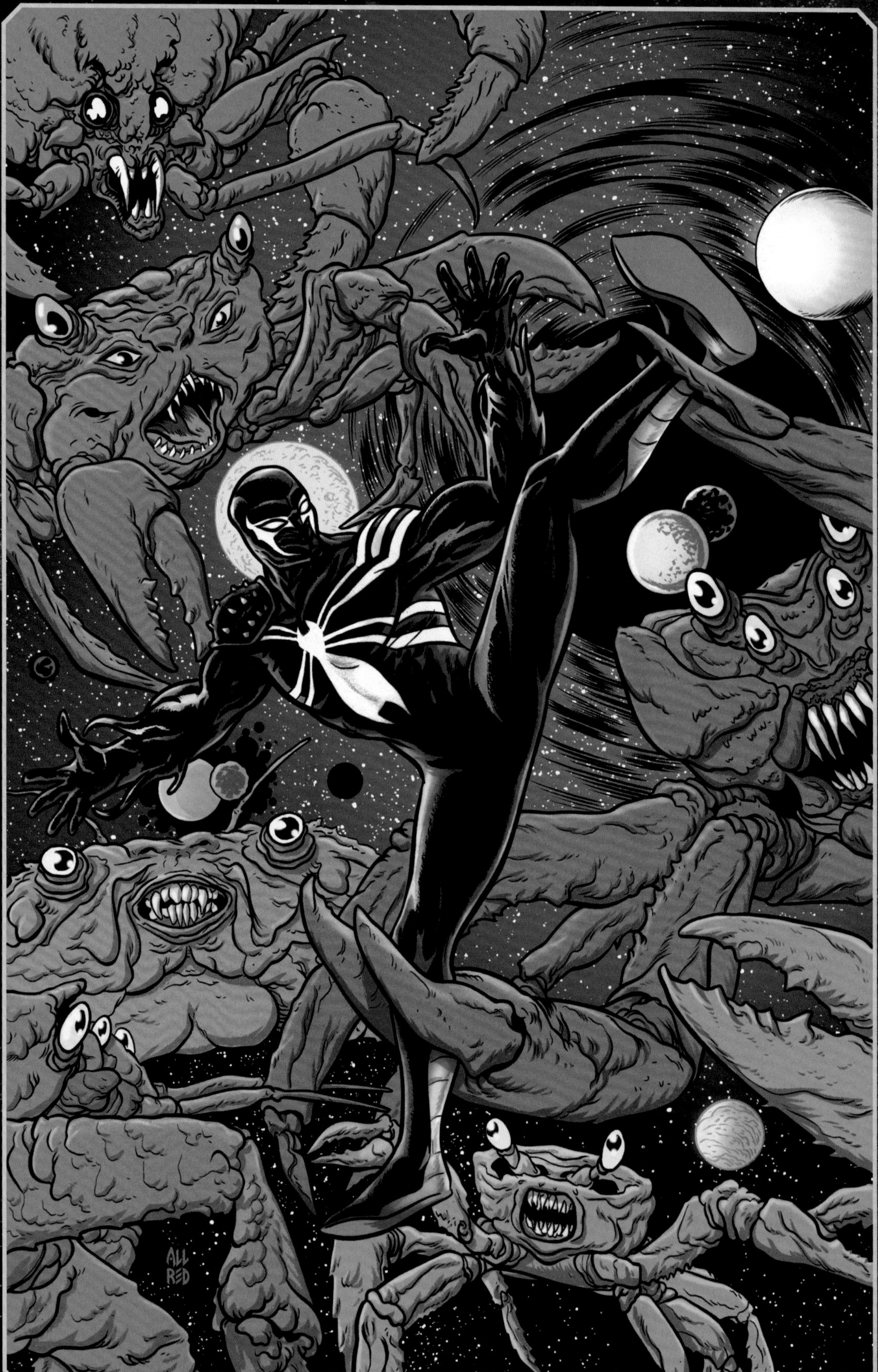
ALL
RED

#2 variant by **MIKE ALLRED** & **LAURA ALLRED**

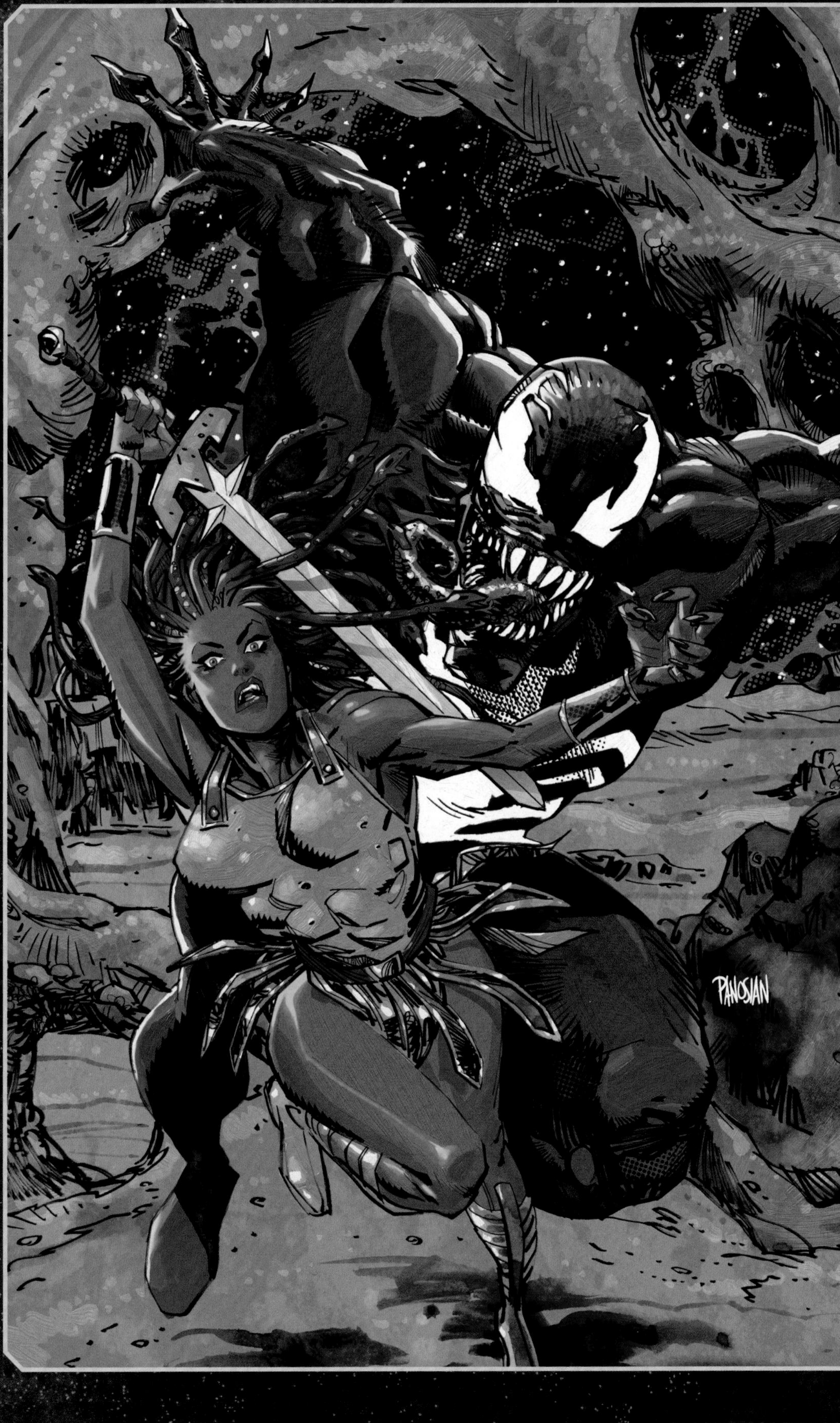
PANOSIAN

#3 variant by **DAN PANOSIAN**

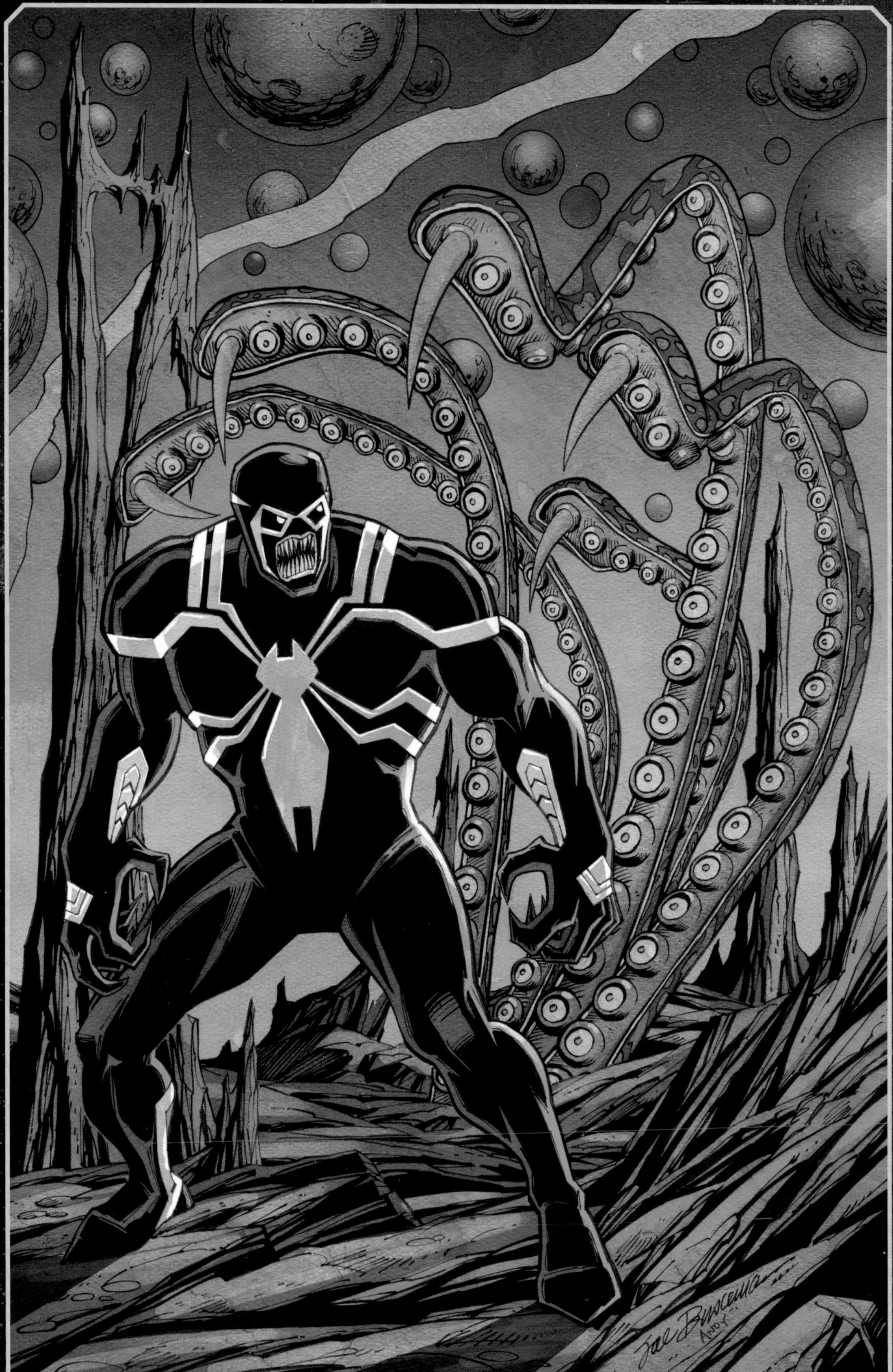

#4 variant by **SAL BUSCEMA** & **ANDY TROY**